Researching
Your Family
History Online

FOR

DUMMIES®

2ND EDITION

Researching Your Family History Online

FOR DUMMIES®

2ND EDITION

by Dr Nick Barratt, Sarah-Jane Newbery,
Jenny Thomas, Matthew L. Helm
and April Leigh Helm

A John Wiley and Sons, Ltd, Publication

Researching Your Family History Online For Dummies®, 2nd Edition

Published by
John Wiley & Sons, Ltd
The Atrium
Southern Gate
Chichester
West Sussex
PO19 8SQ
England

E-mail (for orders and customer service enquires): cs-books@wiley.co.uk

Visit our Home Page on www.wiley.com

Copyright © 2009 John Wiley & Sons, Ltd, Chichester, West Sussex, England

Published by John Wiley & Sons, Ltd, Chichester, West Sussex

For general information on our other products and services, please contact our Customer Care Department within the U.S. at 800-762-2974, outside the U.S. at 317-572-3993, or fax 317-572-4002.

For technical support, please visit www.wiley.com/techsupport.

Wiley also publishes its books in a variety of electronic format. Some content that appears in print may not be available in electronic books.

British Library Cataloguing in Publication Data: A catalogue re[cord for this book is available from the] British Library

ISBN: 978-0-470-74535-9

Printed and bound in Great Britain by Bell & Bain Ltd, Glasgow

10 9 8 7 6 5 4 3 2 1

WILEY

About the Authors

Dr Nick Barratt is the consultant editor for this book. Nick has run Sticks Research Agency, which undertakes genealogical, legal and academic research, since 2000, and has presented a variety of television programmes including the award-winning series *Who Do You Think You Are?*, as well as *History Mysteries, Hidden House History, So You Think You're Royal?, Secrets from the Attic* and *Live the Dream: As Seen on Screen*. He also makes regular appearances as a genealogical expert on *This Morning* and *BBC Breakfast*. Nick acted as the specialist consultant for the first four series of *Who Do You Think You Are?*, overseeing all the genealogical research. He has authored several books including *Tracing The History of Your House* and *The Who Do You Think You Are Encyclopaedia of Family History*. Nick has a PhD in medieval history. You can visit his website at www.stick.org.uk.

Sarah-Jane Newbery has worked for Sticks Research Agency for three years, overseeing historical and genealogical research for a variety of television and radio projects as well as coordinating research for private clients. Prior to joining SRA, Sarah worked as a reader advisor at the National Archives, and has since contributed to many genealogical articles for magazines, websites and production companies. Sarah has a degree in Early Modern History from St Mary's College (University of Surrey).

Jenny Thomas was the co-author of the first UK edition of this book. In 2002, she graduated from Oxford in Ancient and Modern History. Jenny has worked on seven series of the BBC television programme *Who Do You Think You Are?* and now runs the genealogical and archive research for the series. She has also worked on Channel 4's *Not Forgotten* and other historical documentaries. Jenny contributes to genealogical and historical debate and education on television and radio, and in magazines and newspapers. She also works as an independent researcher and lecturer.

Matthew L. Helm is the Executive Vice President and Chief Technology Officer for FamilyToolbox.net, Inc. He's the creator and maintainer of the award-winning Helm's Genealogy Toolbox, Helm/Helms Family Research Page and a variety of other websites. Matthew speaks at national genealogical conventions, lectures to genealogical and historical societies and is a director of the Federation of Genealogical Societies. Matthew holds an A.B. in History and an M.S. in Library and Information Science from the University of Illinois at Urbana-Champaign.

April Leigh Helm is the President of FamilyToolbox.net, Inc. April lectures on genealogy and other topics for various conferences and groups. She holds a B.S. in Journalism and an Ed.M. in Higher Education Administration from the University of Illinois at Urbana-Champaign.

Together, the Helms have co-authored *Family Tree Maker For Dummies, Your Official America Online Guide to Genealogy Online* and *Get Your Degree Online*.

Publisher's Acknowledgements

We're proud of this book; please send us your comments through our Dummies online registration form located at www.dummies.com/register/.

Some of the people who helped bring this book to market include the following:

Commissioning, Editorial, and Media Development

Development Editor: Steve Edwards
(Previous Edition: Amie Tibble, Daniel Mersey and Rachael Chilvers)

Content Editor: Jo Theedom

Commissioning Editor: Nicole Hermitage

Publishing Assistant: Jennifer Prytherch

Technical Editor: Sue Stafford

Proofreader: Helen Heyes

Production Manager: Daniel Mersey

Cover Photos: © Patrick Casey/Alamy

Cartoons: Ed McLachlan

Composition Services

Project Coordinator: Lynsey Stanford

Layout and Graphics: SDJumper

Proofreaders: Melissa Cossell, Jessica Kramer

Indexer: Ty Koontz

Contents at a Glance

Table of Contents

Introduction

- -

Genealogy, as you've probably noticed, is all the rage. Everyone's talking about it. People of all ages are catching the genealogy bug: teenagers are researching alongside their grandparents, and children are researching with their parents. Fathers, sons, mothers, daughters, uncles, aunts, grand-parents, great-grandparents – and even the in-laws – are beginning to take a curious interest in earlier generations of your family.

Perhaps members of your own family are chiding you for how little you know about your immediate ancestors. Perhaps you feel out of things at family reunions, where you don't like to ask 'So who *is* Great-great-uncle Bernard, anyway?' You may even feel embarrassed and nervous because you aren't sure how to begin your own research.

Beneath the embarrassment at how little you know, you may have discov-ered a more profound and deeply rooted desire to research your family tree. Perhaps you want to find out about the part your ancestors played in his-tory. No doubt you remember the occasional humorous family story, and wish you had asked more at the time. Or perhaps you have an increasing desire to find out about the stock from which you're built. Maybe you have distinctive looks, talents or characteristics and want to discover where they came from. Perhaps you've visited castles, museums, country houses, old tin mines or cotton mills and wondered how any of them relate to you. You may feel there's more to genealogy than having fun, solving interesting puzzles and compiling data, photos and memories to display at your family reunion. Perhaps as you begin your research you discover that genealogy's your route both into the past and into yourself.

You may think this is all rather dramatic – and perhaps you're right. But genealogy can be as much or as little as you want it to be. Genealogy can be an enjoyable hobby to wile away rainy afternoons or keep your brain ticking over. It can be a way of meeting interesting people and learning new things. It provides an excuse for a good day out to visit places significant to your ancestors. It brings families closer together as they become aware of their shared heritage. And it may spark your imagination as you start to under-stand how your great-great-grandma lived as a little girl. And it can become a healthy obsession!

Twenty years ago, genealogical research was very different. As a genealogist, you had to carry notebooks to archives all over the county, trawl through microfilmed copies of censuses and spend long and often unrewarding hours ploughing through records for which no indexes had been compiled. Each clue in those days was a hard-won achievement. And so only a few hard-core genealogists had the time, energy and money to do any serious research.

With the advent of the computer and the constant expansion of genealogical resources on the Internet, the genealogy landscape has changed beyond recognition. You can now lay a solid foundation and pursue a good deal of your research without leaving the comfort of your home. Genealogy online is both the present and the future.

Indeed, things have changed even since we published the first edition of this book! Since then, various organisations have made more and more records available online, the most significant of which are the 1911 census returns. Also, more genealogy websites than ever are now out there, many of which enable you to load your family tree directly to their site. The best news of all is that more help than ever before is now available, both from organisations and from other genealogists, and all at the touch of a button!

But before you get started, we should give you a couple of warnings. First, genealogy is very addictive. You may find yourself staying up into the wee hours on the trail of an elusive ancestor. So don't blame us if your boss complains about you falling asleep at work because you've been up all night with Great-great-uncle Stanley. Second, and more seriously, bear in mind that online research is one of many tools for finding info about your ancestors. If you want to research your genealogy thoroughly, you'll have to use a whole range of these tools – many of which we discuss in this book.

Now the health warnings are out of the way, we can turn our minds to the task in hand. So put the kids to bed, let the cat out and shut yourself away with your computer. Your ancestors are calling you and waiting to be found!

About This Book

Researching your family history online can be like digging up a chest of buried treasure. So many amazing things catch your eye that you may not know what to look at first. You quickly learn that all that glistens isn't necessarily gold. Before long you may need a little guidance – and that's where this book comes in. We help you become a discriminating treasure-hunter by showing you the location of useful genealogy websites and how to use them to their full potential to meet your research goals.

Having said that, you're probably asking how this book differs from the other genealogy books you see in the bookshops. We believe this book has three crucial differences. First, many genealogy books are out-of-date: They discuss only the traditional methods of genealogical research and get you travelling hundreds of miles to visit archives, graveyards and ancestral homes and then using a good old typewriter to summarise your results. These books neglect the growing wealth of online resources that save you a great deal of time, money and trouble, whereas this book brings you bang up to date. Second, other books that *do* cover online genealogy tend to group resources by how genealogists access them – for example, listing all websites, chat rooms and so on together. This approach is fine, but it doesn't show you how to integrate the many Internet resources to achieve your genealogical goals and to build up a rounded picture of the identities, lives and times of your ancestors. As genealogists, we understand that researchers don't operate by searching all of one type of resource, then all of another and so on. When we seek a certain piece of information, we use many resources at once – websites, email, newsgroups or whatever's available. This book helps you to take this more open approach. Third, few genealogy books tell you how to actually use the resources on the Internet. Often they list resources and where to find them, but rarely do they guide you through. We do the opposite: we don't go into detail about every resource that we mention, but we discuss the major tools in great, but simple, detail, so you can use them properly and to your best advantage.

We've tried to avoid the mistakes that we think appear in some online genealogy books. We've taken care not to become bogged down in computer-heavy detail at the expense of the broader picture. Our focus is on genealogy rather than computer technology or the obsessive ins and outs of the Internet and its resources – although we do assume a familiarity with basic computer technology. Neither do we pretend that everything you need during the course of your research is available online. We've tried to achieve a balance, and we hope this book helps you make the most of what's available without leading you down false avenues or creating false expectations. We tell it as it is.

Finally, we'd like to induct you into the world of genealogy. Hold your head up high and say in a loud clear voice, 'I declare myself to be an official genealogist!' And there you have it. You can even call in witnesses if it helps you to play your part. Whatever you choose, we emphasise that you don't need any formal qualifications to call yourself a genealogist: you don't need a degree or a diploma. You don't have to know all the kings of England or name the Scottish Clans. And you don't have to memorise the contents of this book to prove yourself to your genealogically minded friends. You simply need an interest in your ancestry and a willingness to devote lots of spare time to gathering information to illustrate it.

Foolish Assumptions

In writing and updating this book, we made a few assumptions. If you fit one or more of the following assumptions, this book's for you:

- ✔ You've done at least a little genealogy groundwork, and now you're ready to use the Internet to pursue and prepare yourself for your genealogy research both online and offline.

- ✔ You may have carried out research years ago without using the Internet and the online census indexes now available. Using the information in this book you hope to find the ancestor that eluded you all those years ago and take your research further than you previously thought possible.

- ✔ You have at least a little computer experience, are now interested in pursuing your family tree, and want to know where and how to start.

- ✔ You have a little experience in genealogy and some experience with computers, but you want to learn how to put them together.

Of course, you can have a lot of computer experience and be a novice to genealogy or online genealogy and still benefit from this book. In this case, you may still find it useful to read some of the basic sections on computers and the Internet in case you find an alternative to use.

How to Use This Book

We don't expect you to read this book from cover to cover. Nor do you need to approach the chapters in numerical order. You can read the book in this way if you wish, and you won't regret your investment. But you won't miss out on vital info if you skip through the sections looking only for the stuff that you're interested in at any particular moment. We want this book to be useful and a little entertaining – but how you use it is up to you. In fact, when writing this book we've tried to accommodate your every need. The sections within each chapter stand as separate entities, so you can turn directly to a section that deals with what you want to find out. If something in one section's relevant to something somewhere else, we cross-refer you to the relevant bits of the book – but we've tried hard to do this referencing in a manner that isn't distracting if you're reading the book from cover to cover.

We use a couple of conventions in the book to make it easier for you to follow a set of specific instructions. Commands for computer menus appear with arrows between each selection. For example, the command File⇨Print tells you to choose the Print command from the File menu. And if we want you to type something, we use **bold type** to indicate what you need to type.

How This Book Is Organised

To give you a better picture of what this book offers, we tell you a little about how we organised it and what you can expect to find in each part.

Part 1: Starting at the Roots

You need to establish a good foundation before you begin your online genealogical research. That way you have something solid to build on. Part I explores the fundamental family information that you need to collect, how to form an online research plan and how to organise your research and place it in a genealogical database.

Part II: Focusing on Your Ancestors

Searching online for information about your ancestors can be a little daunting. Part II examines the resources you can use to locate your ancestors by name and offers advice about placing your ancestors geographically on your ancestral map.

Part III: Rooting Around in the Past

Here we come to the fundamental section of the book. In this part, we guide you through the key online genealogical resources, from civil registration to the census, from parish records to wills. We describe a host of online resources and databases to speed you on your way. We also discuss offline resources and how to find them when you've reached the limits of the online collections.

Part IV: Share and Share Alike

One of the most important and rewarding aspects of genealogical research is joining other researchers to achieve your mutual goals. This part introduces you to the online resources that you need to make the most of sharing. We show you how to cooperate with other genealogists, coordinate with groups and societies and share the fruits of your research with the genealogical community online.

Part V: The Part of Tens

The infamous Part of Tens: Every book in the *For Dummies* series has one. Each section in this part bristles with profound advice and lists of things to do. Here you find a series of quick-reference chapters that give you useful genealogical hints and reminders. We include a list of online databases that you should be aware of, some tips for creating a genealogical web page, hints on keeping your online research sailing smoothly and a list of sites offering help to genealogists. The appendix defines many of the terms you're likely to encounter during the course of your genealogical research.

The Researching Your Family History Online For Dummies Internet Directory

The Internet directory in the middle of this book lists a number of Internet sites of use and interest to genealogists. You find sites dedicated to a whole range of topics, from surnames to comprehensive genealogical indexes, from big search engines to commercial endeavours (sites selling their services or software). For each site that we identify, we give the name, web address and a brief overview of what the site offers.

We want you to be able to see immediately whether a site in the directory has a particular type of information or a service that interests you. For this reason, we've created some mini-icons – or, if you prefer, *micons*. See *The* Researching Your Family History Online For Dummies *Internet Directory* for details.

Icons Used in This Book

To help you get the most out of this book, we've created some helpful icons that indicate at a glance whether a section or paragraph contains important information of a particular kind.

Here we refer you to other books or materials that you can look at to get additional information.

Here we describe concepts or terms unique to genealogy.

This icon marks important genealogical info.

When you see this icon, you know we're offering advice or shortcuts to make your research easier.

Here we walk you step by step through an example of something.

Look out! This is something to be aware of and you need to be on your guard.

Where to Go from Here

What next depends on where you are at the moment. If you're browsing in a bookshop, you need to remember to pay for the book before rushing home to your computer. If you're at home, simply turn the page and start reading, following the steps for the online activities in the book as they come along. You're ready to give your research a go. Good luck!

Part I
Starting at the Roots

'We've hired a complete team of researchers
to work out our family tree.'

In this part . . .

You're about to become an official genealogist – and you need to prepare yourself for the world of online genealogical research. This part sets you off in the right direction by introducing you to the basics of genealogy and helping you to form a coherent research plan. This part also shows you how to organise and preserve your finds, both online and offline.

Chapter 1

Laying the Groundwork and Planning Ahead

*H*old on tight! You're about to embark upon the journey of a lifetime – the journey of many lifetimes, in fact. The greatest journey begins with the first step. Well, although this book's about online genealogy, the first step in this adventure doesn't actually involve a computer – first, you need to lay the foundations of your research. Before you switch blindly into research mode, you need to decide what you're looking for – and to do that you need to take stock of what you already know. In this chapter we guide you through your genealogical research from the very beginning. You start by gathering basic information about your family in the old-fashioned way – interviewing relatives, rummaging through forgotten boxes in the attic and using your finds to draw up a research plan.

We don't pretend that every piece of information you need about your ancestors is available online. It isn't. The online collections are magnificent and constantly expanding. Advances in technology mean that more and more diverse sets of records are now available at the touch of a button. These records set you galloping hard in the right direction, lay solid foundations for your research and help you build upon them. But online genealogy is just one of many tools that you can use to put together the pieces of your family puzzle.

In this chapter we cover the basic points to bear in mind when you plan your research journey and offer tips on what you can do when you run into problems along the way. We also discuss several resources that you can rely on for genealogical information and provide a brief overview of a number of other resources you need to continue your research.

Making a Start: Taking Stock of What You Know

Taking the time to lay proper foundations for your research pays dividends later on: gathering basic information at the outset enables you to get going on the right foot and to construct a research plan based on your findings. However, lots of first-time genealogists make the same initial mistake. They become so excited at the prospect of finding their great-grandfather that they approach the task quite blindly. They switch on the computer, go online and type their ancestor's name, such as Eric Davies, into one of the many genealogical websites. And the result? Three hundred entries for Eric Davies. Their faces fall and they give up on that particular line of research. Or worse, they pick up on a possible Eric Davies without verifying and cross checking the information and then spend years following a completely incorrect line.

We show you here how to lay proper foundations so that you can distinguish your Eric Davies from the dozens of others. All you need is to know a little bit more about him, and then you can make an informed decision – both about which Eric is the magic one and whether the website you've chosen can provide sound information to further your research.

We'll share a little secret with you now. If you're in the fortunate position of having family archives with full sets of birth, marriage and death certificates, so you have good, verified information, you could by all means start with a particular ancestor, as long as you're certain the information is correct. However, if you're starting out on your family history for the first time, or if you know nothing about your family tree, your starting point for your genealogical research project shouldn't be a distant ancestor like Great Grandfather Eric. Instead, begin with someone you know – yourself.

Making notes about yourself: the biographical sketch

You already know a great deal about yourself – probably more than anyone else knows about you. You probably know your date of birth, place of birth, parents' names and where you've lived. But the first step of your research project is to write down everything you know about yourself. This can be done in a number of ways. You may choose to begin in the here and now and to work back through your life, recording details such as places of residence, occupations, birth dates of children, marriages, dates of military service and other significant events in your life. Don't forget to record your birth date and the names of your parents.

Alternatively, you may begin with your birth and work chronologically through the events of your life, up to the present day.

You may find that your thoughts and memories come in a flood and end up rather jumbled. It is, therefore, a good idea to compile your biographical sketch on your computer so that you can rearrange your entries at a later stage.

Whichever method you choose, take time and care over this initial stage. In the weeks and months to come, you'll probably see just how valuable this information is – and wish that all your ancestors had recorded their details in the same way. If you have time, try expanding your biographical sketch into something resembling an autobiography. This document can be an invaluable insight into your life if you ever become the focus of a research project conducted by any of your descendants. We expect the popularity of genealogical research to last!

Locating primary and secondary sources

As you complete your biographical sketch, you may be surprised at just how much you know about yourself – just look at the sheer number of dates, places and statistics that define your life. Writing them all down can sometimes be quite a task. Read through your sketch again and ask yourself how sure you are of the facts laid before you. How do you know they're true? We're not trying to spark a philosophical debate here, but are you sure that you haven't misremembered or been misinformed? Can you be absolutely certain of your birth date? You were there, but you were in no condition to be a reliable witness. We recently met a woman in her 60s who'd just discovered she was a year younger than she'd always supposed. Naturally, she'd believed what other people had told her about her date of birth. Only when she discovered a copy of her birth certificate was the truth revealed. This case is rather unusual, but it does illustrate the need to verify your information and highlight the value of a central feature of genealogical research – primary sources.

Primary sources are documents, oral accounts, photographs and other items created by witnesses at the time an event occurred. For example, a primary source for your birth date is your birth certificate. Usually, a birth certificate is prepared within a few weeks of the actual birth and is signed by one or more people who witnessed the event. Because the record was created soon after the event, the information contained on the certificate, such as the date, place and parents' names, is usually a reliable first-hand account of that event.

However, even if a record was prepared at or soon after a particular event, the information that it contains isn't automatically correct. Sometimes typographical errors occur or incorrect information is provided – deliberately or mistakenly – to the creator of the record. Always try to find other primary records that can corroborate the information found in any single record.

Secondary sources are documents, oral accounts and so on created some time after an event or for which information is supplied by someone who wasn't an eyewitness to that event. A secondary source can also be created by a person who was an eyewitness to the event but recalls it only after a significant period of time.

Some records contain both primary and secondary information. A good example is a death certificate. The primary information is the date and cause of death. These facts are primary because the certificate was prepared soon after the death. The secondary information on the death certificate includes the date and place of the individual's birth. These details are secondary because the certificate was issued at a time significantly after the birth (assuming that the birth and death dates are at least a few years apart). Secondary sources don't always have the degree of reliability that we attribute to primary sources. Often, secondary source information, such as that found on death certificates, is provided by an individual's children or descendants, who may or may not know the exact date or place of birth and who may be providing information during a stressful time. Given the reduced reliability of secondary sources, always try to back up your secondary sources with reliable primary sources.

Although secondary sources aren't as reliable as primary sources, that doesn't mean that secondary sources are always wrong or not distinctly useful. Often, the information in secondary sources is correct, and such records provide valuable clues for locating primary source information. For example, you can use the birth information contained on a death certificate to provide a place and approximate time frame as a starting point when you want to search for a birth record.

Familiarise yourself with primary sources by examining the information in your own biographical sketch. Try to match up primary sources for each event in the sketch – for example, birth and marriage certificates. For more on finding these documents, see the sections 'Looking for love letters, diaries and other important documents' and 'Browsing birth, marriage, divorce and death records' later in this chapter. If you can't find primary source documents for each event in your life, don't fret: much of your biographical sketch can serve as a primary source document because *you* wrote it about *yourself*.

To find out more about primary and secondary sources, have a look at these websites:

- Heather Wheeler's *History on the Net* site at www.historyonthenet.com/ Sources/primary_or_secondary_source.htm
- The University Library of California's 'How To Distinguish Between Primary and Secondary Sources' at http://library.ucsc.edu/ref/ howto/primarysecondary.html

Selecting someone other than yourself to begin your search

Making a start by tackling yourself first is always best if you don't know much about your family tree or if you're a newcomer to family research. However, if you can gather information from your family archives which enables you to start with an ancestor, and if you feel confident enough to do so, this can work well, too.

Selecting a person might sound easy, but if your chosen ancestor has a common name, such as John Smith, your research can quickly become very difficult. You may encounter millions of sites with information about John Smith, and unless you know a few facts about the John Smith you're looking for, we can almost guarantee that you'll have a frustrating time online.

Trying a unique name

The first time that you research online, try to start with a person whose name is, for lack of a better term, semi-unique. This means a person with a name that doesn't take up ten pages in your local phone book, but which is still common enough for you to find some information on it the first time you conduct a search. If you're feeling confident, you can begin with someone with a common surname such as Smith or Jones, but you have to do a lot more groundwork up-front in order to determine whether any of the multiple findings relate to your ancestor.

Consider any variations in spelling that your ancestor's name may carry. Often, you can find more information under the mainstream spelling of his or her surname than under one of its rarer variants. For example, if you research someone with the surname Barratt, you may have better luck finding information under the spellings *Barrat* or *Barrett*. The further back in time that you go, the more flexible and interchangeable the spelling of names can become. And if your relatives immigrated to the United Kingdom during the last two centuries, they may have anglicised their surname. *Anglicising* a name was often done so that the name could be easily pronounced in English, or to gain acceptance during turbulent times. Many immigrants from Eastern Europe adopted English versions of their surnames during the First and Second World Wars. A common example of this is the surname *Braun*, which people sometimes changed to *Brown*.

To find various spellings of the surname, you may need to dig through family records or look at a site such as the Guild of One-Name Studies (`www.one-name.org`).

Some search engines allow you to do what's known as a *wildcard search*, where you only type in the first few letters of a name and the search sends back lots of variants. For example, typing in **Newb*** to a name search engine gives results for 'Newbery', 'Newberry', 'Newbury', 'Newbert' and so on.

Too many ancestor irons in the research fire

You have a name that you want to research, and you're ready to see how much information is currently available on the Internet concerning that individual. Because this is just one step in a long journey to discover your family history, bear in mind that you want to begin slowly. Don't try to examine every resource right from the start. Keep things simple and look for one piece of information at a time. You're more likely to become overloaded with information and confused if you try to find too many resources too quickly. You could even become discouraged and not feel like jumping back into your research, which would be a shame because you can find a lot of valuable research help online.

Your best approach is to begin searching a few sites until you get the hang of how to find information about your ancestors online. Don't forget to make a note of the websites that you visit and the databases that you search in case they change the look and feel of the site. Many genealogy websites also update their information and databases regularly, so keep a note of the dates you visit each site, so you know to visit the site again in a few months, when more information may be available. Remember, too, that you can always bookmark sites so that you can easily return to them later, when you're ready for more in-depth research.

Using a person whom you know about

In addition to picking a person whom you're likely to have success researching, try to use a person whom you already know quite a lot about. You may never have considered the idea of researching your parents or grandparents, but finding information on these people is a good way to ease you into your genealogical research and to familiarise yourself with the records available. You can practise your research skills by finding online details that you already know. This gives you the confidence and the know-how to move beyond your immediate ancestors and begin your journey into the unknown. Starting in this way may also awaken the interest of some of your relatives who know or remember the people with whom you begin your research; it may spur them on to assist you with your research or to produce family documents that you never knew existed.

The more details that you know about a person, the more successful your initial search is likely to be.

Introducing the Family History Research Cycle

No book about research would be complete without some sort of model to follow, and the following suggestions are drawn from a combination of years of research experience and common sense. Figure 1-1 shows the five phases of the family history research cycle: planning, collecting, researching, consolidating and distilling. This section goes on to look at these phases in more detail.

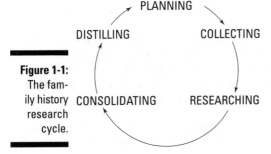

PLANNING

DISTILLING

COLLECTING

Figure 1-1:
The family history
research cycle.

CONSOLIDATING

RESEARCHING

Planning your research

Planning ahead is crucial to the success of any project, and a genealogical project is no exception. Not everyone considers this planning to be an enjoyable part of family history; after all, finding your ancestors is the fun part. However, carefully crafting a *research plan* – a common-sense approach to searching online for information about your ancestors – can be an invaluable step. A research plan entails knowing what you're looking for and what your priorities are for finding information, and having one can save you hours of work and keep you focused on the goals that you've set for a particular task, be it finding an elusive ancestor or looking for clues about when, where and how they lived.

You've heard, no doubt, that the Internet puts the world at your fingertips. And true enough, you can find literally millions of names, listed on thousands of family history websites, all waiting for you to discover them. However, the multitude of online resources can leave you feeling a bit dizzy as you navigate from one site to another for hours at a time. Recording everything that seems even remotely relevant to your family tree is also incredibly tempting, regardless of whether it actually relates to one of your family lines.

Because of the immense wealth of information available to you, putting together a research plan before going online is very important: it can save you a lot of time and frustration by keeping you focused on the task in hand. Tens of thousands of genealogical sites are available on the Internet. If you don't have a good idea of exactly what you're looking for to fill in the blanks in your genealogy, you can get lost online. And getting lost is even easier when you see a name that looks familiar and start to follow its links, only to discover hours later (when you finally get round to pulling out your existing genealogical notes) that you've been tracking the wrong person and the wrong family line. To avoid this, you should approach online research in exactly the same way you would when visiting an archive. Having a research plan and making notes of the websites you visit and what you find there saves you repeating research later down the line. Websites often change their appearance, and you may not recognise them on a return visit.

If you're the kind of person who likes detailed organisation (such as lists and steps that you can follow), you can write your research plan on paper or keep it on your computer. If you're the kind of person who knows exactly what you want and need at all times, and you have an excellent memory of where you pause during the course of your projects, your research plan can exist solely in your mind. In other words, your research plan can be as formal or informal as you like – as long as it helps you to plot what you're looking for.

For example, suppose you're interested in finding information about your great-grandmother. Here are some steps that you can take to form a research plan:

1. **Write down what you already know about the person whom you want to research – in this case, your great-grandmother.**

   Include details such as approximate dates and places of birth, marriage and death; spouse's name; children's names; and any other details you feel may help you to distinguish your ancestor from other individuals.

2. **Write down what you hope to find out about the person you're researching.**

   Getting sidetracked when researching is easy, with the excitement of uncovering new family facts, and you may well lose sight of why you decided to research your family tree in the first place. For this reason, writing down your aims in your basic plan is important. You may wish to look into an old family story or myth, or focus on finding out as much as you can about one particular side of the family, for example.

3. **Conduct a search using a genealogically focused search engine to get an overview of what's available.**

   Visit sites such as English Origins (www.englishorigins.com), Genealogy Portal (www.genealogyportal.com) and Ancestry.co.uk (www.ancestry.co.uk) to hunt for information about your great-grandmother, using her name and where she lived to narrow down the research results. The data that you obtain gives you an indication of the range of resources available.

4. **Prioritise the resources that you want to use.**

   Your search on a genealogically focused search engine may turn up several different types of resources, such as newsgroups, mailing lists and one-name study sites. We recommend that you prioritise which resources you plan to use first. A great starting point is to visit a website that provides access to civil registration documents, such as Ancestry. co.uk (www.ancestry.co.uk), Family Relatives (www.family relatives.com) or FreeBMD (www.freebmd.org.uk) so that you can start trying to verify dates of birth, marriage and death.

5. Schedule time to use the various resources that you identify.

Genealogy is truly a lifelong pursuit – you can't download every bit of information and documentation that you need all at once. Because researching your genealogy requires time and effort on your part, we recommend that you schedule time to work on specific parts of your research. Genealogy is addictive; breaking it down into scheduled research time – perhaps a couple of evenings a week – enables you to get the best out of your research plan and without getting bogged down with information.

Collecting useful information

The second phase of the cycle – *collecting* – is the process of gathering information, such as dates and locations of births, marriages and deaths, about the family that you're researching before starting your detailed research. You can do this by conducting interviews in person, on the phone or through email, and by finding documents scattered around the family – from well-known heirlooms to forgotten boxes of papers and photos in attics, basements and other home-front repositories. You may also need to look up a few things in an atlas or *gazetteer* (a geographical dictionary) if you aren't sure where certain places are located. (Chapter 4 provides more information about online gazetteers.)

Table 1-1 shows a few online resources that identify items to collect for your genealogy.

Table 1-1	Helpful Family History Websites
Websites to Get You Started	*Key Resources to Use Online*
www.genuki.co.uk	www.findmypast.com
www.bbc.co.uk/familyhistory	www.ancestry.co.uk
www.familyrelatives.com	www.nationalarchives.gov.uk/familyhistory

Chatting with Dad and Aunty Doris: Interviewing members of your family

Your first genealogical goldmine is often a close relative. You may never have thought of asking members of your family about their lives or what they remember of the generations that came before them. Few of us have, in any depth. Sometimes, the opportunity has been there to ask questions, but by the time we realise we're interested in the answers it may be too late to ask. Now is the time to put chatting with family as a priority. Interviewing your relatives is an important step in your genealogical research process.

Your great-grandmother may no longer be alive, but you may have parents, brothers, sisters, grandparents, aunts, uncles and cousins, all of whom can be good sources of information about recent generations of your family. They can provide names, dates, locations, photographs, diaries, gossip and family heirlooms. They may also be able to suggest other people to whom you could talk, who may have known your departed relatives. And, of course, they may have copies of primary source material to contribute to your genealogical file.

Wouldn't it be great to extract from your relatives the same type of information you provided about yourself when you wrote your biographical sketch? So turn your relatives' thoughts to the realms of memories, rumours and other information that may just provide a valuable clue or show you which of two records is correct.

We strongly recommend that you conduct interviews with your family in person. Receiving a questionnaire in the post or by email is very off-putting for certain people. The information your relatives give may be highly personal, evocative and closely guarded. You're likely to discover much more by conducting the interview face-to-face, displaying your interest in whatever your relatives say and taking care to reassure them of your honourable intentions.

Never misuse the information you uncover, and always remain discreet. The material you gather from these interviews relates to living people or people within living memory. To encourage your relatives to disclose what they know, reassure them that you won't broadcast the information to the rest of the family, disclose sensitive details or disprove ideals and memories heartlessly. For you, the information is useful genealogical data, but for your relatives the information is a lifetime of valued memories – so treat it with profound respect.

When your relatives are comfortable with your motives, they may provide all kinds of detail that you never dreamed they knew. Your interest may spark more memories or lead to further revelations. Always leave lots of time for these interviews. After all, who knows how long Aunty Doris will talk for when you get her going?

To start you off, here are a few tips to help you prepare for a family interview:

> ✔ **Prepare a list of questions that you want to ask:** Knowing what you want to achieve during the discussion keeps your interview focused. Check out the sidebar 'Good interviewing questions' in this chapter for ideas. Be flexible, however, and let your relative lead the conversation where he or she wants it to go. Some of the best information comes from memories that your interviewee dredges up mid-conversation rather than in response to a question.

TIP

Good interviewing questions

Simply letting your relatives chatter about what they know and remember is a good and often very useful idea. It's here that you begin to uncover real characters in your family, and to develop mere names into interesting people. But certain information is essential in order to proceed with your research, so have a list of questions such as the following prepared and work your way through them as and when you can:

- What is your full name? Do you know why your particular name or names were chosen – for example, were you named after someone else in the family?

- When and where were you born? Have you been told any stories about your birth?

- What do you remember about your childhood?

- Where did you go to school? Did you finish school, go to university or receive any further education or training?

- What were your brothers and sisters like?

- When and where were your parents born? What did they look like? What were their occupations?

- Did your parents tell you how they met?

- Do you remember your grandparents? Do you recall any stories about them, or details about their lives? What did they look like?

- Did you ever hear stories about your great-grandparents? Did you meet them? Do you know where they lived or died?

- When you were a child, who was the oldest person in your family?

- Did any relatives (other than your immediate family) live with you?

- Did your family have any particular beliefs or traditions, or did they celebrate any special holidays?

- Have any items, such as stories, traditions and heirlooms, been handed down through several generations of the family?

- When did you leave home? Where did you live?

- Did you join the military? If so, which branch of service were you in? Which units or regiments were you a part of? Did you ever serve overseas? For how long did you serve?

- What occupations have you had?

- Where have you worked?

- Where and in what circumstances did you meet your spouse?

- When and where did you get married? Did you go on a honeymoon? To where?

- When were your children born? Do you have any stories about their births?

- Do you know of anyone in the family who immigrated to this country? Where did they come from? Why did they leave their native land?

You can probably think of lots more questions to draw responses from your family. If you want further suggestions, have a look at genealogy.about.com/cs/oralhistory/a/interview.htm.

✔ **Bring a tape or video recorder to the interview:** This saves your having to frantically scribble notes and lets you relax, develop and display your interest and really get a flavour of what the interviewee is saying. Always ask the interviewee's permission before you start recording. If you both agree a video would be better, consider videotaping the session. That way you create a fuller record of the interview because you can see the expressions on the interviewee's face as he or she talks. You also have a valuable lasting record of the interview that can be seen and understood by generations to come.

Remember to keep your audio and visual recordings stored in an up-to-date format. If you don't keep pace with changing technology, you may quickly lose access to part of your most valuable genealogical material.

✔ **Use photographs and documents to help your family members recall events:** Often photographs can help to jog memories and have a dramatic effect on the stories that the interviewee remembers. If there's a lull in the conversation, producing a photo album is an excellent way to re-establish the flow. Thanks to the fact that copying photos is a lot easier than it once was, you can take copies of your old photos using a digital camera or a scanner, print off as many copies as you need and keep the originals safely at home.

✔ **Recognise and respect the feelings of the interviewee:** If your relative isn't forthcoming about certain pieces of information or you sense that he or she is becoming tired or losing enthusiasm, don't push for more, however interested you are. Sometimes people find they're not in the right frame of mind to talk about the past, or they may want to stop and consider before revealing certain pieces of information. You can always arrange another interview at a later date or ask the same questions to other members of the family. You don't want to cause any ill feeling.

✔ **Show some gratitude:** Thank your relatives for their time and patience after the interviews. And if they're interested in your research, keep them up-to-date with your discoveries.

Looking for love letters, diaries and other important documents

Have you ever been accused of being a hoarder? Is your attic, basement or spare room piled high with possessions that other people refer to as 'junk' and of which you alone can see the value? Well, we sympathise – and we're thoroughly convinced of the value of these items. In fact, we hope the hoarding characteristic is in your genes. There's nothing more valuable to a genealogist than being descended from a whole family of hoarders who make a point of saving every scrap connected with their lives. These collections contain hidden treasures, and if you do a little digging you may stumble across some gems. You only have to be let loose in your grandmother's attic to find old passports, driving licences, ration cards, identity cards, school certificates, letters, photographs and goodness knows what else. These documents help you reconstruct your ancestors' past.

When you search through family treasures, keep your eyes open for things that can serve as primary sources for facts that you want to verify. For more on primary sources, see 'Locating primary and secondary sources' earlier in this chapter. Here's a list (although not an exhaustive one) of a few things you may like to look out for:

- Family Bibles – often these are signed by various generations of the family
- Legal documents, such as mortgages, titles and deeds
- Insurance policies
- Wills
- Family letters, cards and postcards
- Obituaries and newspaper articles
- Diaries
- Naturalisation records
- Baptism certificates and other church records
- Copies of birth, marriage, death and divorce certificates
- School reports
- Occupational records
- Membership cards

For a list of other items to look for around the home, have a look at Treasures in the Attic at www.ancestry.com/library/view/ancmag/673.asp.

Dusting off old photo albums

'A picture's worth a thousand words' – so the saying goes – and this is certainly true in genealogy. Photographs are among the most valuable documents for genealogists. Not only do they tell you what your ancestors looked like, but they reveal a lot about your ancestors' lives. When you study an old photograph, you can see what kind of clothes your ancestors wore and make a guess at their wealth and social standing. You may see parents photographed with their children or with members of their extended family. Perhaps you can see a house in the background in which your ancestors lived. If you're lucky, you may find a name, date, location or message scribbled on the back of a photograph, providing crucial information.

Photographs are also useful as memory-joggers when you interview your family members. Photos help people recall the past and trigger long-forgotten memories. But be warned – not all the memories are good! You may stimulate delightful reminiscences of moments long ago, but you may also open a can of worms when you ask Grandma about a particular person in a picture. It could be a lover, a villain, a friend or a relative. If Grandma's willing to talk about her memories, she may give you the low-down on the person in the picture and every other member of the family who's ever crossed her path – giving you lots of genealogical leads.

You may discover several different types of photographs during the course of your research. If you know when the various kinds of photographs were produced, you can place your pictures within a specific time frame. Here are some examples:

- **Daguerreotypes** were taken between 1839 and 1860. They required a long exposure time and were taken on silver-plated copper. The photographic image appears to change from a positive to a negative image when tilted.

- **Ambrotypes** were produced from 1858 to 1866. They used a much shorter exposure time than daguerreotypes. The image was made on thin glass and usually had a black backing.

- **Tintypes** were produced from about 1858 to 1910. They were made on a metal sheet, and the image was often coated with a varnish. You usually find them in a paper cover.

- **Cartes-de-visite** were produced between 1858 and 1891.They are small, paper prints mounted on a card and often bound together into a photo album.

- **Cabinet cards** were manufactured primarily between 1865 and 1906. They were larger versions of cartes-de-visite and sometimes included dates on the borders of the cards. The pictures themselves were usually mounted on cardboard.

- **Albumen prints** were used between 1858 and 1910 and were the type of photographs found in cartes-de-visite and cabinet cards. They were produced on thin pieces of paper that was coated with albumen and silver nitrate. They were usually mounted on cardboard.

- **Stereographic cards** were prevalent from 1850 to 1925.They were paired photographs that rendered a three-dimensional effect when used with a stereographic viewer.

- **Platinum prints** were produced largely between 1880 and 1930.They have a matte surface that appears to be embedded in the paper. The images were often highlighted with artistic chalk.

- **Glass-plate negatives** were used between 1848 and 1930. They were made from light-sensitive silver bromide immersed in gelatine.

For more about dating your photographs, have a look at `genealogy.about.com/cs/photodating`.

When dealing with old photographs, bear in mind that too much light or humidity can damage or destroy them. As a way of electronically preserving them, and to add some colour to your family tree as you begin to build up a picture of your ancestors, you may want to scan your old family photographs into your computer. We talk more about preserving photographs in Chapter 2.

Researching: Through the brick wall and beyond

The next step is to leave the family environment and start hunting for sources elsewhere. You spend the *researching* phase of the cycle digging for clues, finding information that supports your family tree and obtaining documentation. You can use traditional and technological tools to uncover nuggets of information hidden in archives, libraries, registry offices and museums, as well as data placed online. Of course, researching your family history online is the topic of the whole book, so you can find the necessary resources to do a great deal of your online research amongst these pages.

But a time will undoubtedly come when you run into what genealogists affectionately call the *brick wall* – when you think you have exhausted every possible means of finding an ancestor. The most important thing you can do is to keep faith – don't give up! Websites are known to change frequently (especially as more people come online and begin sharing their information): although you may not find exactly what you need today, you may find it next week at a site you've visited several times before or at a new site altogether.

Fortunately, a few people post suggestions on how to get through that brick wall when you run into it. One of the best sites for this is Cyndi's List (www. cyndislist.com), which provides a range of subject headings to search under. You may also like to look at Genuki (www.genuki.org.uk).

You can also attempt to break through the brick wall by sharing a problem with like-minded people at a family history society. People there are usually available to answer queries and to give free advice. For a list of online family history societies, check the Federation of Family History website at www.ffhs.org.uk.

Browsing birth, marriage, divorce and death records

Birth, marriage and death records are amongst the most important primary sources used by genealogists. They were compiled and kept by the government through the process known as *civil registration* (the compiling of birth, marriage and death records by the state. For more on civil registration, have a look at Chapter 5). You may already possess copies of a number of these documents, and your relatives may hold copies of others. Or you may find them while you're digging around in the attic. You can also obtain copies of documents that you don't already have. Indexes to these records are available to the public both on and offline, and you can also order copies of the actual certificates online. In Chapter 5 we discuss in detail what you can expect to find on these certificates, but we tell you a little bit about them now just to whet your appetite:

- ✔ **Birth certificates:** At the very least, a birth certificate tells you the full name of the child, his or her date and place of birth, the names of both parents and the father's occupation. (If the child was illegitimate, you usually only get the mother's name and her occupation if she had one.)

✔ **Marriage certificates:** A marriage certificate tells you at least the full names of the bride and groom, their ages, current marital status, occupations and the names and occupations of their fathers.

✔ **Death certificates:** A death certificate tells you at least the name and age of the deceased, his or her occupation (if applicable) and the place and cause of death.

You may be asked to show some form of identification before ordering certain certificates. For example, if you want to order the birth certificate of someone born in the 1950s or later, you may have to prove that you're related to the person or justify why you want the certificate. This precaution aims to stop you obtaining documents with the purpose of impersonating someone. Because your aim as a genealogist is to work your family tree back, rather than to collect documents of your own or later generations, this rule is unlikely to present a problem for you.

Perusing parish records

When researching ancestors in the years before civil registration, genealogists rely heavily on *parish records*. These are the primary records of baptisms, marriages and burials that were compiled over the course of many centuries in each and every parish as and when these ceremonies took place. The information contained in these records varies, and tends to be less detailed than civil registration certificates. Parish records include the following:

✔ **Baptism records:** These give the name of the child and his or her parents, the date of baptism and the parish in which the ceremony took place. Sometimes you find more details, such as the mother's maiden name, the occupation of the father and the date of the child's birth.

✔ **Marriage records:** These can appear in several forms. You may find records of the following:

- **Marriage bond:** A financial guarantee that a marriage was going to take place.

- **Marriage banns:** Proclamations before a church congregation of a couple's intention to marry.

- **Marriage licence:** A document granting permission to marry.

- **Marriage records:** Entries in the parish records of at least the names of both bride and groom, the date of the ceremony and the name of the parish in which the wedding took place.

A single marriage may generate several records, so be careful when you record the date of a marriage. It's easy to confuse the date of the actual ceremony with the date of the marriage bond, banns or licence. A marriage licence may be filed several weeks before the actual marriage date, and banns tend to be read in the parish church on three consecutive Sundays before the happy day. Remember that just because you've found a record of a bond, banns or a licence, you still don't have proof that the marriage actually took place. Occasionally people get cold feet and back out of the marriage at the last minute.

If you have trouble finding a marriage record in the area in which your ancestors lived, try searching in the surrounding parishes. Traditionally, the wedding ceremony takes place in the bride's parish, but there's certainly no compulsion for this. You can also look in the parishes in which the couple's parents or other relatives lived.

✔ **Burial records:** A burial record reveals at least the name of the deceased, the date of the funeral ceremony and the name of the parish in which the funeral took place.

For more information about parish records, have a look at Chapter 5.

Dealing with divorce records

Genealogists often overlook divorce records. Later generations may not be aware that an early ancestor was divorced, but the surviving records can be quite valuable. They may contain important information, including the details of the marriage, any children, addresses, occupations and the grounds upon which the divorce was granted. For more on divorces, turn to Chapter 7.

Coming to your census

A census is a snapshot of a population taken on a single night. It captures details about the inhabitants of a country, including who spent the night where, their names, ages, occupations, places of birth and disabilities – all of which makes the returns invaluable to the genealogist. In the UK, censuses are taken every ten years. The returns for 1841–1911 are available online to the public, so you can get the information at the touch of a button. In this census you find family groups together and get an idea of your ancestors as real people, with brothers and sisters, friends, neighbours, houses, jobs and all the characteristics of living, breathing people. We discuss the census and how to use it in more detail in Chapter 5.

Searching for another religion

Methodists and similar Christian religions kept records in the same way as Church of England records. Online, non-Conformist records often appear in the International Genealogical Index (IGI) at www.familysearch.org along with Anglican records. Offline, some records are held at The National Archives, and some on a local level. Many Catholic records are still held by the churches, and have not made it as far as the IGI. Jewish records often appear in the online IGI and offline parish records simply as a means of registering an event, although local synagogues may also hold records. Very few Muslims or other faiths existed in Britain before the 1830s, but applying to your relative's local place of worship is a starting point to trace any records.

Further online sources of information

The deeper you delve into this book, the more websites you'll discover that can give your research project a new lease of life. Hundreds of online resources exist, dealing with civil registration, the census, parish records, military, criminal, immigration and apprenticeship records, wills, trade directories, newspapers and all kinds of resources that we don't have space to mention here. Throughout this book we guide you in the direction of these websites and show you how to find others for yourself. Have a look at Chapter 6 for more about online resources.

Visiting libraries, archives and historical societies

An important part of your genealogical research project is placing your ancestors in their social and historical context. Your mission to collect additional information about where your ancestors lived, and details about their lives and times, may inspire you to visit a range of libraries and archives, both local and national. At a local level, you'll be able to find sections devoted to the history of that particular area. You'll likely find local historical directories, newspapers, maps and a variety of records and documents that may mention your ancestors by name. You may even discover a historical society devoted to the history of that area, and you can possibly join or approach its members for further sources of information. And at both a local and a national level, you may find collections of books and documents that expand upon the events in which your ancestors played a part – for example, the General Strike, the Industrial Revolution or the First World War. For a fuller guide to using these offline resources, check out Chapter 7.

Getting involved with the online genealogical community

Dealing with all of the different records and resources tends to set your mind spinning, and you may need someone to point you in the right direction. Or you may have reached an apparent dead end in your research, and you're wondering if any other resources could further your cause. One solution is to become involved with the online genealogical community. You can send and receive messages from researchers all over the world; you can post messages on the Internet asking for information and advice; and, in turn, you can use your developing expertise to lend others a helping hand. We discuss these steps in more detail in Chapters 9 and 10.

Finding family history centres

Family history centres are wonderful places to get help and advice and meet other people doing the same thing as you. Some of these centres are located in London (for example, the Society of Genealogists), but dotted around the country are the family history centres run by the Church of Jesus Christ of Latter-day Saints (LDS). There's always someone in these places who can guide you in your research and point you in the direction of untapped resources.

You don't need to be a member of the LDS to use a family history centre. The resources contained within them are available to everyone. Bear in mind that the staff at family history centres can't research your genealogy for you, although they're usually willing to point you in the right direction. To find your nearest family history centre, have a look at www.familysearch.org/eng/Library/FHC/frameset_fhc.asp. For more about family history centres, check out Chapter 7.

Consolidating your information using a database

When you get started on your research, you may find so much information that you're overwhelmed. Starting to organise this information at an early stage, and incorporating later findings into your existing research notes, is vital. This is the *consolidating* phase of the cycle, where you take your findings and store them on your computer-based genealogical database or in your filing system.

A *genealogical database* is a software program that enables you to enter, organise, store and use all sorts of genealogical information on your computer. These programs protect your findings by keeping them in a central location, and provide an environment in which you can see the fruits of your labour. As well as programs that you can buy in the shops, many genealogical databases are available online. Websites such as Ancestry (www.ancestry.co.uk) or Family Relatives (www.familyrelatives.com) offer software for downloading or have protected areas on their websites to which you can upload your information. This option is sometimes best when you're first starting out, because it can be the easier and cheaper option, enabling you to test a few websites out and get a feel for your family tree before you rush out and buy your own software package.

Where possible, try to set aside time to update your database with information that you've recently acquired. This process of putting your information together in one central place, called *consolidating*, helps you to gain an overview of the work that you've completed and provides a place for you to store all those nuggets of information that you'll need when you begin researching again. By storing your research notes in a database, you can always refer to them for a quick answer the next time you try to remember where you found a reference to a marriage certificate for your great-great-grandparents. For further information about online storage, check Chapter 8.

Distilling the information that you gather

The *distilling* phase of the cycle is where you use your computer-based gene-alogical database to generate reports, charts or a detailed research log of the information you've gathered, showing the current state of your research. You can use these reports to remove any individuals that you've proved don't belong to your family tree and start new branches that you've discovered during your research and that you want to follow up.

Most available genealogical software programs allow you to generate reports in a variety of formats. For example, you can produce a *pedigree chart* at the touch of a button or the click of a mouse (a pedigree chart shows a primary person with lines representing the relationships to his/her parents, then lines connecting them to their parents and so on), or an outline of descendants from information that you've entered into the database about each ancestor. You can use these reports to see what holes still exist in your research, and you can add the missing pieces to the planning phase for your next research effort – starting the whole cycle over again.

Another advantage of genealogical reports is having the information readily available so that you can toggle back to look at the report while research-ing online, which can help you to stay focused. (*Toggling* is flipping back and forth between open programs on your computer. In Windows you press Alt+Tab to toggle, or you can click the appropriate item on the taskbar at the bottom of the screen. On a Macintosh, you can use the Application Switcher in the upper right-hand corner of the screen.) Of course, if you prefer, print-ing copies of the reports and keeping them next to the computer while you're researching on the Internet serves the same purpose.

Chapter 2

Fine-Tuning Your Organisational and Preservation Skills

....

In This Chapter

▶ Constructing good record-keeping habits

▶ Using a numbering system

▶ Looking at preservation methods

....

*A*fter you've collected a lot of great genealogical data, your findings won't do you much good if they're not easily accessible when you need them. You don't want to be running all over the house trying to locate your precious scraps of paper – the notes in your desk from your research at the library, letters from relatives in your mail-to-be-sorted basket and photocopies of pedigree charts which somehow got mixed up with your magazines. You may forget where you placed a particular document and miss something important because your documents aren't organised and kept in a central location.

This chapter examines ways of organising and preserving genealogical information and documents using traditional storage methods and preservation techniques.

Getting a Firm Foundation in Traditional Methods of Genealogical Organisation

No finer tradition exists in genealogy than collecting unmanageable quantities of paper and photographs. Until now, you've probably used any means possible – from notebook paper to crumpled receipts or even stick-on notes – to take notes whilst talking to relatives about your ancestors or looking up information in the local library. You may have used your camera to take pictures of headstones in the graveyard where some of your ancestors are buried, or of the house in which your ancestor lived that may since have been demolished or converted. And you've probably collected some original source documents such as your mother's birth certificate, inherited from your grandmother, the family Bible given to you by your aunt and the old photograph of your great-great-grandfather as a child that you found whilst rummaging in the attic. Now what are you going to do with all these things? Organise, organise, organise!

Even if you decide to use genealogical software to track your research progress, you're always going to have paper records and photographs that you want to keep. The following sections offer tips to help you become well organised (genealogically-speaking, anyway).

Establishing good organisational skills

You've probably already discovered that taking notes on little scraps of paper works adequately at first, but that the more notes you take, the more difficult it becomes to locate, organise and understand the information contained on each. To avoid this situation, establish good note-taking and organisational skills early on. Where you're using software or an online family tree to record your findings, stay organised from the start when uploading and storing information.

The key is to be consistent in how you take notes. Record the date, time and place that you do your research, along with the names of the family members that you interview, at the top of each page of your notes. This information can help you later on when you return to your notes to look for a particular fact, or when you try to make sense of conflicting information.

You need to be as detailed as possible when taking notes on particular people, events, books and so forth and to include the who, what, where, when, why and how. And most importantly, always cite the source of your information, keeping the following guidelines in mind:

- **Person:** Include the person's full name, relationship to you (if any), the information, contact details (address, phone number, email address) and the date and time at which you and this person communicated.

- **Record:** Include the name or type of record, record number, book number (if applicable), the name and location of the archive or library at which you found the record and any other pertinent information.

- ✔ **Book or magazine:** Include all bibliographic information, including the name of the publication, volume number, date of issue, the publisher's name and page number of the relevant article.

- ✔ **Microfilm or microfiche:** Include all bibliographic information and make a note of the type of document (microfilm roll, microfiche), document number and repository name.

- ✔ **Website or other Internet resource:** Include the name of the copyright holder for the site (or name of the site's creator and maintainer if no copyright notice appears on it), the name of the site, address or uniform resource locator (URL) of the site and any notes with traditional contact information for the site's copyright holder or creator. Also include the date at which the information was posted or copyrighted – this can be very useful when checking the same website again, especially if it's been recently updated. This can save you time searching for the information twice.

A useful idea is to print a copy of the web page or other Internet resource that contains information about your research interests to keep in your paper files. Websites may disappear with time, so print out the relevant pages while you can.

Genealogy software packages usually allow you to record detailed references so that you're able to see at a glance all the information about the source you're using. Some packages include *wizards* – programs that prompt you what to do – to make the process of recording sources easy. (We explore software features in more detail in Chapter 8.)

If you really want to go to town when you're citing your sources, check out *Evidence!: Citation and Analysis for the Family Historian*, written by Elizabeth Shown Mills and published by Genealogical Publishing Company. The book gives you some useful tips, although it contains more detail than you need – unless you're especially keen!

Getting hold of genealogical charts and forms

Before computers became widely used by genealogists, researchers would use various charts and forms to manually record information, organise their research and to make findings easier to understand – both for themselves and for those to whom they showed their results. Examples include pedigree charts that show the relationships between family members, ancestry charts that allow you to record all the ancestors from whom you directly descend and census forms in which you can record information enumerated about your ancestors at particular moments in time.

In the computer age, these charts and forms remain essential pieces of kit, and can be useful for keeping track of your research as it progresses. You can download a number of blank versions from websites such as:

- ✔ **Ancestry:** www.ancestry.co.uk/charts/familysheet.aspx
- ✔ **BBC Family History:** www.bbc.co.uk/history/familyhistory/get_started/record_sheets.shtml

A more common practice these days, though, is to generate completed charts and forms from the information you've uploaded to the genealogy software on your computer. At the click of a button, your software can collate and organise your information to produce detailed and varied charts and forms, saving you the work of filling them out. Some even enable you to customise and create your own. (Chapter 8 contains more info on the different types of charts and forms available.)

Assigning unique numbers to family members

If you have ancestors who share the same name, or if you've collected a lot of information on several generations of ancestors, you may have trouble distinguishing one person from another. To avoid confusion and the problems that can arise from it, you may want to use a commonly accepted numbering system to keep everyone in their place.

The ahnentafel (Sosa–Stradonitz) system

One well-known numbering system is called *ahnentafel*, which means 'ancestor' (*ahnen*) and 'table' (*tafel*) in German. You may also hear the ahnentafel system referred to as the *Sosa–Stradonitz* system of numbering because it was first used by a Spanish genealogist named Jerome de Sosa in 1676, and was popularised in 1896 by Stephan Kekule von Stradonitz.

The ahnentafel system is a method of numbering that shows a mathematical relationship between parents and children. Ahnentafel numbering follows this progression:

1. **The child is assigned a particular number: *y***

   Of course, we recognise that *y* is a letter and not a number, but in our mathematical (that is, algebraic) example, *y* represents a unique number for that particular person.

2. **The father of that child is assigned the number that is double the child's number: $2y$**

3. **The mother of that child is assigned a number that is double the child's number plus one: $2y + 1$**

4. **The father's father is assigned the number that is double the father's number: $2(2y)$**

   The father's mother is assigned the number that is double the father's number plus one: $2(2y) + 1$

5. **The mother's father is assigned a number that is double the mother's number: $2(2y + 1)$**

   The mother's mother is assigned a number that is double the mother's number plus one: $2(2y + 1) + 1$

6. **Continue this pattern through the line of ancestors.**

The mathematical relationship works the same way as you go forward through the generations – a child's number is one-half of the father's number and one-half (minus any remainder) of the mother's number.

In a list form, the ahnentafel for Philip John Bridges looks like this (go to Figure 2-1 for the chart):

1 Philip John Bridges, b. 15 June 1920 at Bradford, Yorkshire; d. 31 March 2002 at Camberwell, London; ma. 18 July 1946 in Lambeth, London.

2 George Bridges, b. 7 January 1893 at Doncaster, Yorkshire; d 16 December 1960 at Lambeth, London; ma. 16 May 1918 at Bradford, Yorkshire.

3 Joan Annie Hall, b. 20 April 1898 at Bradford, Yorkshire; d. 16 November 1940 at Bradford, Yorkshire.

4 Samuel Bridges, b. 23 September 1860 at Doncaster, Yorkshire; d. 2 October 1932 at Bradford, Yorkshire; ma. 25 December 1890 at Brigg, Lincolnshire.

5 Lucy White, b. 15 August 1870 at Brigg, Lincolnshire; d. 16 February 1893 at Doncaster, Yorkshire.

6 Steven Hall, b. 11 October 1870 at Ludlow, Shropshire; d. 3 June 1915, France; ma 29 May 1896 at Barnsley, Yorkshire.

7 Florence Jane Mead, b. 1 March 1873 at Barnsley, Yorkshire; d. 31 December 1919 at York.

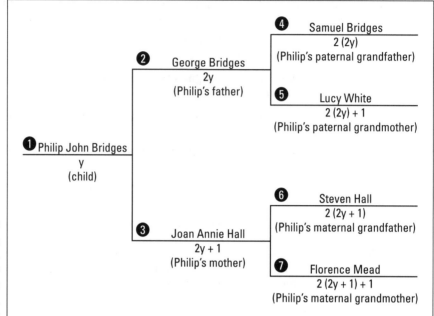

Figure 2-1:
An ahnen-
tafel for
Philip John
Bridges.

Philip John Bridges is number one because he's the base individual for the ahnentafel. His father (George Bridges) is number two (because $2 \times 1 = 2$), and his mother (Joan Annie Hall) is number three ($2 \times 1 + 1 = 3$). His father's father (Samuel Bridges) is four ($2 \times 2 = 4$), and his father's mother (Lucy White) is five ($2 \times 2 + 1 = 5$). George Bridges' number (2) is one-half of his father's number ($4 \div 2 = 2$), or one-half minus any remainder of his mother's number ($5 \div 2 = 2.5$; 2.5 minus remainder of 0.5 = 2). Well, you get the idea.

As you can imagine, after a while you begin to tire of all these calculations, especially if you do them for ten or more generations. So, if your genealogy software lets you, we highly recommend that you run an ahnentafel report, thereby saving you a lot of time and trouble. (We discuss software packages and some of their capabilities in the *Genealogy Online For Dummies Internet Directory* in this book.)

The Henry system

The *Henry* system is another well-known numbering system. This system assigns a particular number to the *progenitor*, or the ancestor farthest back (that you're aware of) in your family line. Then each of the progenitor's children is assigned a number in a sequence that starts with his number and adds the numbers one, two, three, and so forth through to number nine.

(If the progenitor had more than nine children, the tenth child is assigned an X, the eleventh an A, the twelfth a B, and so on.) Then the children's children are assigned the parent's number plus a number in sequence (again one to nine, then X, A, B, and so on). For example, if progenitor number one (1) had 12 children, then his children would be 11, 12, 13, . . . 1X and 1A. The eleventh child's children would be assigned the numbers 1A1, 1A2, 1A3 and so on.

For example, say that one of your ancestors, John Jones, had 12 children. The names of these children were Joseph, Ann, Mary, Jacob, Arthur, Charles, James, Maria, Esther, Harriett, Thomas and Sophia. Joseph had one child named Gertrude and Thomas had three children named Lawrence, Joshua and David. Under the standard Henry system, the children's children are numbered like this:

1	John Jones		
11	Joseph Jones		
111	Gertrude Jones		
	12	Ann Jones	
	13	Mary Jones	
	14	Jacob Jones	
	15	Arthur Jones	
	16	Charles Jones	
	17	James Jones	
	18	Maria Jones	
	19	Esther Jones	
	1X	Harriett Jones	
	1A	Thomas Jones	
		1A1	Lawrence Jones
		1A2	Joshua Jones
		1A3	David Jones
	1B	Sophia Jones	

Alternative numbering systems

These systems are certainly not the only genealogical numbering systems around. Ahnentafel and Henry are just two of the easier systems to learn. Several others have been designed to display genealogies in book form. If you're curious about these systems, there is a great American website that can help you. Take a look at the Numbering Systems in Genealogy page at `www.saintclair.org/numbers/` where you can find descriptions of each major numbering system.

If you decide to use a numbering system, you can place the corresponding unique number for each individual on the file that you set up for that person in your paper record-keeping system, as well as in your genealogical software.

Making copies of source documents

You don't want to carry original records with you when you're out and about researching. The chances of misplacing or forgetting a document are too great. But you have several alternative options:

- ✔ You can enter the information into a database and take a notebook computer with you.
- ✔ You can copy data from your desktop computer onto a palmtop.
- ✔ You can print out your data.
- ✔ You can make photocopies of data that you must have with you for your research.
- ✔ You can scan the documents and store them on your laptop or notebook computer. (We talk more about using computers for your notes in Chapter 8.)

You can then use your notes and copies of documents out in the field and keep the original documents in a safe place such as a lock-up box, fireproof filing cabinet or safe or a safety-deposit box.

Deciding on a storage method

Even if you scan all your original records to your computer, you still need to keep, store and organise your original hard copies. You don't want to have to start all over again if your computer crashes or you accidentally delete all your files. But how are you going to store all that information? A filing system is in order! You can set up a good filing system in many ways, and no one system is right or wrong. Just use one that's the easiest for you.

If you're at a loss as to how to start a system, here's one practical suggestion that incorporates both electronic and physical components into a single filing system. To establish an electronic system, enter your ancestors' names into your database. Most genealogical programs and some websites enable you to enter numbers for each individual. Use these same numbers to file the paper documents that you collect for each individual. It is good practice to scan all of your paper documents, but if you do happen to get behind, you can store the relevant documents in temporary folders until you're able to scan them. Having scanned the documents you can then transfer them to permanent folders to keep in a fireproof container or another safe place. You may consider saving your scanned images to a notebook computer's hard drive, a website or a writable CD-ROM or DVD so that you can easily transport the images when you go on research trips.

As an alternative, you could sign up to a website that enables you to store your files online. The advantage of doing this is that you can access your files from any computer linked to the Internet. Sites such as www.livedrive.com and www.elephantdrive.com enable you to do this, but with the price of memory sticks and portable hard drives coming down, you can just as easily save your data to one of these.

Make backup copies of all your electronic documents as a safety precaution.

Preserving Your Treasured Family Documents

Time is going to take its toll on every document in your possession. The longer you want your records and pictures to last, the better care you need to take of them now. The following sections offer tips for preserving your family treasures so that you can pass them down to future generations in the best possible shape.

Storing vital records under the right conditions

Place your certificates and other records between sheets of acid-free paper in albums. Keep these albums in a dark, dry and temperature-consistent place. Ideally, store these documents in a place that is a consistent 18–21 degrees Celsius (65–70 degrees Fahrenheit), with a relative humidity of less than 50 per cent. You may consider placing these albums in a steel filing cabinet (but make sure that it's rust-free). Also, try to avoid using ink, staples, paper clips, glue and tape on your documents (unless you use archival products specifically designed for document repair).

For your precious documents (original birth certificates and family papers), rent a safety-deposit box or find another form of secure off-site storage. Of course, one of the best ways to ensure successful preservation is to make scans of your documents, and keep back-up disks at a separate, preferably fire-safe, location (again, a safety-deposit box is a good choice).

Protecting your photographs

Fight the urge to put every photograph of your ancestors on display, because light can damage them over time. As with your paper records, keep your most-prized pictures in a dark, dry and temperature-consistent environment (18–21 degrees Centigrade [65–70 degrees Fahrenheit] with a relative humidity of less than 50 per cent). If you use a photo album for storage, make sure that it has acid-free paper or chemically safe plastic pockets, and that you attach the pictures to the pages using a safe adhesive. Acid-free storage boxes and steel filing cabinets are ideal storage methods. Avoid prolonged exposure of photographs to direct sunlight and fluorescent lights. And, by all means, have negatives made of those rare family photos, and store them in clearly marked, acid-free envelopes (the kind without gumming or glue).

To continue your preservation drive, you can convert old photographs to a newer and safer kind of film. A local photography shop that specialises in preservation can do this for you. Because colour photographs fade more quickly than their black-and-white counterparts, you may want to make black-and-white negatives of your colour photographs. Also, as with documents, you can always preserve your photographs electronically by scanning them on to your computer or having a photo CD made by your photographic developer.

An electronic version isn't a real substitute for an original. Don't throw away the photos you scan (but you knew that, didn't you?).

The following websites provide more detailed tips on preserving your family treasures:

- ✔ **Care and Conservation of Old Photographs** by Colin Robinson, artist photographer: www.colinrobinson.com/care.html
- ✔ **Caring for Your Photographs** by the National Archives: www.national archives.gov.uk/documents/archivesconservation_photo.pdf

And when you're looking for the chemically safe archival materials that we've described (including albums, paper, boxes, adhesives and so on), try investigating these websites:

- ✔ **Memories & Nostalgia:** www.memories-nostalgia.com
- ✔ **Conservation by Design:** www.conservation-by-design.co.uk
- ✔ **PEL Products Preservation Equipment:** www.preservation equipment.co.uk

Even though you want to preserve everything to the best of your ability, don't be afraid to display your albums to visiting relatives and friends. On the other hand, don't be embarrassed to ask these guests to use caution when looking through your albums. Depending on the age and rarity of your documents, you may even want to ask guests to wear latex gloves when handling the albums so that the oil from their hands doesn't get on your treasures. When they realise how important these treasures are to you, most guests won't mind taking precautions.

Part II
Focusing on Your Ancestors

'Dennis has just discovered one of his ancestors was a <u>king</u>.'

In this part . . .

Here you discover resources to help you find out more about your ancestors, both by their names and by their geographical locations.

This part has a wealth of resources about the best online maps so that you can really get a sense of where your ancestors lived and worked. This part is also for you if you're interested in finding out if your ancestors were ever mentioned in the local newspapers – for good reasons or bad!

Chapter 3

Tracking Down an Ancestor: What's in a Name?

*A*s a budding genealogist, you may start to experience sleepless nights as the questions that dominate your life begin to change. Suddenly you have to know the maiden name of your great-great-grandmother, whether your great-grandfather really was the scoundrel that other relatives say he was, and just how you're related to the Queen (well, isn't everyone?). Well, okay, perhaps you won't have sleepless nights, but you'll undoubtedly spend a significant amount of time thinking about and trying to find resources that can give you answers to these crucial questions.

In the past, finding information online about individual ancestors was a question of finding a needle in a haystack. You'd browse long lists of links in the hope of finding a website that may contain a nugget of relevant information. Today, looking for your ancestors online is much easier. Instead of browsing links, you now use search engines and online databases to pinpoint information about your ancestors.

This chapter covers the basics of searching for an ancestor by name. It presents some good surname resource sites and shows you how to combine several different Internet resources to find information about your family.

Picking the Site that's Best for You

Your dream as an online genealogist is to find a website that contains all the information that you ever wanted about your family. Unfortunately, such sites simply don't exist. But don't despair: during your search you'll discover a variety of sites that vary greatly in the amount and quality of genealogical information, and some of them are likely to be useful. Before you get too deeply embedded in your research, taking a look at the type of sites that you're likely to encounter is a good idea.

Personal genealogical sites

The vast majority of genealogical websites that you encounter on the Internet are personal sites, established by individuals and families with specific research interests. These sites give information about the site maintainer's ancestry or about particular branches of several different families rather than about a surname as a whole. This doesn't mean valuable information isn't present on these sites – they just have a more personal focus.

You can find a wide variety of information on personal genealogical sites. Some sites list only a few surnames that the maintainer is researching; others contain extensive online genealogical databases and narratives. A site's content depends upon the amount of research undertaken by the maintainer as well as their computer skills. Some common things that you see on these sites are a list of surnames, an online genealogical database, pedigree and descendant charts (for information on charts, check out Chapter 8), family photographs and a list of the maintainer's favourite genealogical Internet links.

Personal genealogical sites vary not only in content but also in presentation. Some sites are neatly constructed and use soft backgrounds and aesthetically pleasing colours. Others require you to bring out your sunglasses to tone down the fluorescent colours or to use link shades that blend in with the background, making it quite difficult to navigate your way through the site. Also, remember that many personal sites use JavaScript, music players and animated icons, which can significantly increase your download times.

An example of a personal genealogical site is Graham Carter's family history site at `www.family.cleverwork.com` (see Figure 3-1). This site traces various lines of the Carter family and includes a surname list, name index, photographs and research resources used to compile the data.

After you've found a site that contains useful information, write down the maintainer's name and email address and contact him or her as soon as possible if you have any questions or want to exchange information. Personal genealogical sites have a way of disappearing without a trace because individuals frequently switch Internet service providers or stop maintaining their sites.

Figure 3-1:
Graham
Carter's
website
is an
example of
a personal
genealogi-
cal site.

Although you may find some really useful information on personal genealogical sites, remember to check up on the accuracy of the information for yourself. There's no guarantee that the maintainer of the site has got the information right. You need to look at where the information came from and to verify every name, date and location before you can accept the data into your family tree.

One-name study sites

If you're looking for a wide range of information on a particular surname, a one-name study website is the best place to start. These sites usually focus on one surname regardless of the geographical location in which the surname appears. In other words, they welcome information about people with that particular surname worldwide. One-name study sites are also quite help-ful because they contain all sorts of information about the surname, even if they don't have specific information about your branch of family with that surname. Frequently they provide information about the variations in spell-ing, origins, history and heraldry of the surname. One-name study sites have some of the same resources that you find in personal genealogical sites, including online genealogy databases and narratives.

Although most one-name study sites welcome all surname information regardless of geographical location, the information presented may be organised along geographical lines. For example, a site may categorise all the information about people with the particular surname by continent or coun-try, such as the Goodhews of England or Canada. Alternatively, the site may be even more specific and categorise information by county, town or parish. So, you're better off if you have a general idea of where your family originated or to where they migrated. If you don't know, browsing through the site may still lead to some useful information.

The Rowberry family website at www.rowberry.org is a one-name study site that includes branches of the family in England and abroad (see Figure 3-2). The site is divided into several categories, including variations in surname spelling, the origin of the name, information about the author, reports of family gatherings, maps, an email list and details of the Rowberrys residing in Cornwall, Canada, Australia and the United States.

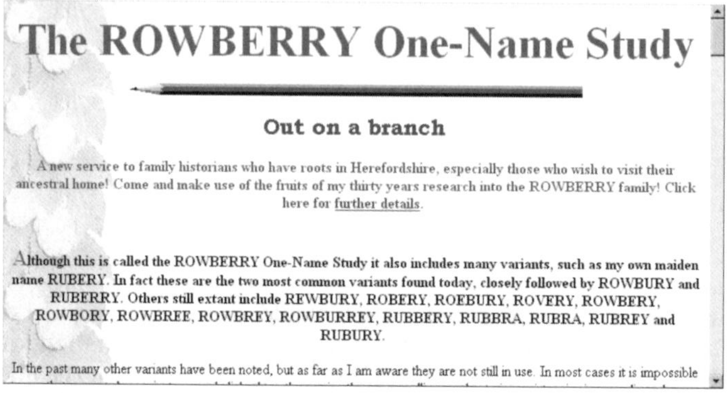

Figure 3-2:
The
Rowberry
website is a
one-name
study site
with a geo-
graphical
focus.

The ROWBERRY One-Name Study

Out on a branch

A new service to family historians who have roots in Herefordshire, especially those who wish to visit their ancestral home! Come and make use of the fruits of my thirty years research into the ROWBERRY family! Click here for further details.

Although this is called the ROWBERRY One-Name Study it also includes many variants, such as my own maiden name RUBERY. In fact these are the two most common variants found today, closely followed by ROWBURY and RUBERRY. Others still extant include REWBURY, ROBERY, ROEBURY, ROVERY, ROWBERY, ROWBORY, ROWBREE, ROWBREY, ROWBURREY, RUBBERY, RUBBRA, RUBRA, RUBREY and RUBURY.

In the past many other variants have been noted, but as far as I am aware they are not still in use. In most cases it is impossible

Maintainers of one-name study sites usually welcome any information that you have on the surname. These sites are often good places to join research groups, which can be instrumental in furthering your own lines of research.

The Internet directory in this book identifies some one-name study sites that you may like to visit. But in order to find one-name study sites relevant to you, you may have to search elsewhere. A site that can help you determine whether any one-name study sites are devoted to the surnames you're researching is the Guild of One-Name Studies at www.one-name.org.uk.

The Guild of One-Name Studies is an online organisation of registered sites, each of which focuses on one particular surname. The Guild holds information about many thousands of surnames. Use the following steps to find out whether any of the Guild's members focus on the surname of the person you're researching:

1. **Go to www.one-name.org.uk.**

2. **In the *Is your surname registered?* box enter the surname you're researching and click Search.**

   The results page contains entries from the database that match your search.

Family associations and organisations

Family association sites are similar to one-name study sites in terms of content, but they usually have an organisational structure (such as a formal association, society or club) backing them. The association may focus on the surname as a whole or on just one branch of a family. The goals for a family association site may differ from those of a one-name study site. The maintainers may be creating a family history in book form or a database of all individuals descended from a particular person. Some sites may require you to join the association before you can participate fully in their activities, but this is usually free of charge or calls for a small payment.

The Willingale family society site at `www.willingale.org/wfs/wfshome.htm`, shown in Figure 3-3, includes several items that are common to family association sites. The site's contents include a family history, the origin of the name, photographs of the village in which the earliest Willingales lived, information about their association with Epping Forest and information about Willingales overseas and other Willingale descendants.

The easiest way to find a family association website is to use a search engine or a comprehensive genealogical index. For more on search engines, see the sections 'Getting to grips with genealogically focused search engines' and 'Browsing Comprehensive Genealogical Indexes' later in this chapter.

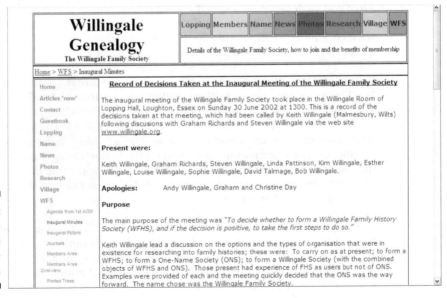

Figure 3-3: The Willingale family society site.

Surnames connected to events or places

Another place where you may discover surnames is a website that contains a collection of names connected to a particular event or geographical location. The level of information available on these sites varies greatly, even among surnames on the same site. Often, the maintainers of such sites include more information about their personal research interests than about other surnames, simply because they have more information relating to their own lines.

Typically, you need to know events in which your ancestors were involved or the geographical areas in which they lived to use these sites effectively. You may benefit from the site simply because you have a general historical interest in the particular event or location, even if the site contains nothing about your surname. Finding websites about events is easiest if you use a search engine, a comprehensive website or a subscription database. Because we devote an entire chapter to researching geographical locations (Chapter 4), we won't delve into that here.

Taking the Plunge: Using Compiled Genealogical Resources

After you've decided on a specific person to research (for more on selecting a good research candidate, see Chapter 1), it's time to research online. But as we mention frequently in this book, you need to arm yourself with a few facts about the individual before you venture online.

For example, you may decide to research your paternal grandfather's line. You know that his name was George Fletcher and that he lived in Hull, in Yorkshire. From memory and a copy of his death certificate, you know that he died in 1969. From the death certificate, you've found the year of his birth, and you can find a reference to, and order online, a copy of his birth certificate. The information contained on these documents can be used to distinguish him from other George Fletchers that you come across online. (For more information about birth and death indexes online, and ordering certificates, see Chapter 5.)

At this point, you can take what you know and use online databases and family trees to see whether someone has already completed any research on George and his ancestors. Using online databases and family trees to pick pieces of genealogical fruit is wonderful. But of course you'll always want more. Your curiosity is aroused and you're keen to find out more about George Fletcher – more specifically, perhaps, who his grandfather was.

When someone publishes their genealogical findings, whether online or in print, the resulting work is called a *compiled genealogy*.

Compiled genealogies and online family tree databases can give you a lot of information about your ancestors in a nice, neat format. Finding a compiled genealogy with info relevant to your family – or even one that contains what appear to be whole branches of your family – can give you an overwhelming feeling of gratification, and rightly so. But don't get too excited yet. When using compiled genealogies, remember that you need to verify any information contained within them. Even when sources are cited, you'd be wise to get your own copies of the sources to ensure that the author's interpretation is correct and that no errors have occurred in the publication of the compiled genealogy.

Compiled genealogies can take two forms online. One is the traditional narrative format – the kind of thing you see in a book at the library. The second is in the *lineage-linked format*, which means that the database is organised by the relationships between people. This format is where an individual has exported and posted online information from their genealogical database and is creating their family tree on a website as an ongoing process. These websites are becoming ever more popular because they are clear and easy to use.

Narrative compiled genealogies

Narrative compiled genealogies usually have more substance than their exported database counterparts. Authors sometimes add colour to the narratives by including local history and other text and facts that can help researchers to get an idea of the time in which the ancestor lived. An example of a narrative genealogy is the Fite family homepage at `www.1fite.com/8f.html`.

To locate narrative genealogies, try using a search engine or comprehensive genealogical index. (For more about using these resources, see the relevant sections later in this chapter.) Often, compiled genealogies are part of a larger personal or family association website.

Compiled genealogical databases

Although many people don't think of lineage-linked online genealogical databases as compiled genealogies, these databases serve the same purpose as narrative compiled genealogies – they show the results of someone's research in a neatly organised, printed form. Even so, finding information in these databases can sometimes be challenging. No grand database exists that indexes all the individual databases that are available online. Although general Internet search engines have indexed quite a few, a number of very large collections are still only accessible through a database search – something that general Internet search engines don't usually do. This section takes a look at a few of the larger collections.

Suppose you want to find out more about the ancestry of your grandfather, George Fletcher. You may be able to jump start your research by using a lineage-linked database in the hope of finding relevant information compiled by another researcher. From documents such as his birth and death certificates, you know that George's father was named Albert Fletcher and that George was born and died in Hull, Yorkshire. From interviews with family members, you discover that his father also lived in Yorkshire and that he was also probably born in Hull. Armed with this information, you can search a compiled genealogical database.

The FamilySearch Internet Genealogy Service at `www.familysearch.org` is the official research site for the Church of Jesus Christ of Latter-day Saints (LDS). This free website enables you to search several LDS databases, including the Ancestral File, International Genealogical Index, Family History Library Catalogue, Research Guidance, census records and a collection of related websites, all of which are free. The two resources that function like lineage-linked databases are the Ancestral File and the Pedigree Resource File. You don't have to search these resources separately: a master search enables you to search all seven resources on the site at the same time.

To search the FamilySearch site, do the following:

1. **Open your web browser and go to `www.familysearch.org`.**

   The home page for FamilySearch contains four options on the toolbar: Home (which will return you to the home page whenever you like); Search (for your ancestors); Share (your information); and Library (the Family History Library System).

2. **Click the Search Records tab.**

   The Search Records tab takes you to a dropdown list. Click Advanced Search, which then takes you to a page showing several fields that you can fill in to conduct a search on the site. The fields form a small pedigree chart.

3. **Into the fields marked First Name and Last Name, enter the first and last name of the ancestor that you're researching.**

   To continue our previous example, enter **George** into the First Name box and **Fletcher** into the Last Name box. If you decide to include information on the spouse or mother or father and you don't receive adequate results, try doing the search with only the name of the ancestor. You can also fill in optional fields such as Event, Year, Year Range, Country and Use Exact Spelling. (Bear in mind that filling in any of these fields may reduce the number of results that you receive.) If the name you're researching is particularly common, you can select the Exact Spelling option in order to limit the number of results. However, bear in mind that the same name is often spelt in several different ways, and that spelling is increasingly flexible the further back in time that you go. In this example, you can also narrow the search by selecting 'England' in the dropdown list of countries.

4. **After you've selected the search options, click the Search button.**

   The Results page contains links, with descriptions, to the resources that match your search criteria. Here, the search for George Fletcher yields 244 results. These results come from seven different resources on the site. The far-right column, Sources Searched, provides a breakdown of the number of results you received from each FamilySearch resource, as shown in Figure 3-4.

5. **Click the link of any result to see more information.**

   One result jumps out at you: at the bottom of the page you see a Pedigree Resource File (item 239) for George Albert Fletcher, who was buried in 1969 in Hull, Yorkshire.

If you select this option, which in this case comes in the section entitled Pedigree Resource File, you're taken to the Individual Record page. The amount of information revealed varies from file to file, but this page shows the sex of the individual, the names of his parents, the years of his birth and death (which matches the information provided on his birth and death certificates) and information about the submitter of the record. From this page, you can see that someone submitted a record revealing that George's parents were Albert Fletcher and Annie Elizabeth Webster. This matches the information on George's birth certificate, so you're confident that you're on the right track. The other links on the page enable people to inspect the individual records of both parents, which in turn reveal their birth and death dates and the names of their parents. And so the question is answered: George Fletcher's paternal grandfather was William Robert Fletcher (born about 1850 in Boston, Lincolnshire). These lines can be worked backwards by continuing to follow the links. Certain pages will contain a Pedigree link, which charts all generations of ancestors available in the file. However, the source information for these finds isn't here, so you may want to contact the submitter to locate the source of the information.

Although the LDS Church is well known for its large genealogical collection, don't expect to find the complete collection online – the vast majority of LDS resources reside in their library and family history centres. (These are centres run by the LDS, dedicated to helping people trace their family history. For more about family history centres, have a look at Chapter 7.) Also, you need to verify your finds with the help of the *original* records. Much of the information currently on the site has been contributed by other family-history researchers, who may or may not have been careful in researching and documenting their family history. The site may not contain *all* the information available in a particular record. For example, you may find the name of a child who was baptised, along with a date and the names of her parents, on the LDS website. This information is taken from a parish record. But if you have a look at the original record (offline), you may find extra nuggets of information, such as a more precise location or the occupation of the father.

You can find another search site for the Pedigree Resource File component of the LDS site at www.findyourfamilytree.com. The site lets you order the CD-ROM that contains the results of your search.

Other lineage-linked collections may contain useful information for your search. Because these websites enable researchers to create new trees from scratch, and upload existing GEDCOM files (see Chapter 8 for more info), you can also check them to see if any of your data match those of other researchers, and link into their trees, too. The following list gives details of some of the better-known collections:

✔ **Ancestry Trees: www.ancestry.co.uk.** The family tree section is an area where you can link your tree into other trees if they match your research, and search through other researchers' files, exclusively in the

UK or extending your search worldwide. Currently, the database contains over 400 million names.

✔ **OneGreatFamily:** `www.onegreatfamily.com`. This site hosts a subscription-based lineage-linked database. The database currently contains over 190 million unique entries.

✔ **Family Relatives:** `www.familyrelatives.com`. This fast-growing site contains over 600 million records.

Anyone can upload unverified information to these websites, so although the quality of some research is excellent, other research may contain significant errors. You need to check everything that you find before you adopt it for your family tree. For example, be wary of any reference without an exact date (genealogists refer to these as *ghost entries*) as it usually means that the researcher has found no proof. Any reference that includes the letters 'Abt' usually means that the contributor doesn't know the exact date and uses this abbreviation to mean 'about'.

Letting Your Computer Do the Walking: Using Search Engines

Imagine spending several hours clicking from link to link and not finding anything related to your research. Wouldn't it be nice to be able to just enter your ancestor's name and see whether any sites contain that name? Well, that's exactly what search engines enable you to do.

Search engines are programs that search vast indexes of information generated by robots. *Robots* are programs that travel through the Internet and collect information about the sites and resources that they find. You can access the information contained in search engines through an interface, usually through a form on a web page.

The real strength of search engines is that they can search the full text of web pages instead of just the title or a brief abstract of the site. For example, say you're looking for information about one of your ancestors, William Ramsbottom, who was born in the early 1820s in Lancashire. You can begin by consulting a comprehensive genealogical index site (for more about comprehensive genealogical indexes, see 'Browsing Comprehensive Genealogical Indexes' later in this chapter). There, you look for a website with 'William Ramsbottom' in the title or find an abstract of the site. But even if the comprehensive index contains tens of thousands of links, the chances of a website having 'William Ramsbottom' in its title or its abstract is relatively small.

However, by conducting a search through a search engine that indexes the full text of websites, you can find your William Ramsbottom on the Rhodes family website and find his date of birth and census details.

Different search engines are available, including genealogically focused search engines, general Internet search engines and general Internet meta-search engines. For a list of recommended search engines, have a look at the Internet directory in this book.

Getting to grips with genealogically focused search engines

Your first stop on a search for a particular ancestor should be a search engine set up for that purpose.

Genealogically focused search engines are sites that send out robots that index the text of only those sites that contain information of interest to genealogists. This means that you receive fewer extraneous results when you enter your ancestor's name as a search term. An example of a genealogy focused search engine is Genuki, at www.genuki.org.uk/search. This search database contains search engines covering all the website's own genealogical pages as well as those of the National Archives, the Society of Genealogists, the Federation of Family History Societies and the Guild of One-Name Studies.

1. **Go to www.genuki.org.uk/search. This page contains a field for you to fill with the relevant details. Enter one or more search terms.**

   Dropdown indexes enable you to choose whether to search for all as opposed to any of the terms, and whether to treat them as a *Boolean expression*. (A Boolean search involves using terms such as *or* and *not* to narrow your results.) You can also choose to search for your term(s) in only the title of the pages or to search both the title and a summary of the text.

2. **Enter your research details into the relevant boxes and click Search.**

   For example, by typing in the name of a distant ancestor, Thomas Peyton, you see a link to Knowlton Churchyard.

3. **Click a link that interests you.**

   By following this link, you discover the text of a monumental inscription, from which you find out that Thomas Peyton – the son of a Thomas Peyton, Baronet – was buried at Knowlton in Kent in 1667 at the age of 18. The Results page (see Figure 3-5) shows the title of the page and an abstract of the site.

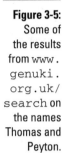

Figure 3-5:
Some of the results from www.genuki.org.uk/search on the names Thomas and Peyton.

Using general Internet search engines

General search engines send out robots to catalogue the Internet as a whole, regardless of the content of the site. Therefore, on any given search you're likely to receive a lot of hits, perhaps only a few of which hold any genealogical value – that is, unless you refine your search terms to give you a better chance at receiving relevant results.

You can conduct several different types of searches with most search engines. Looking at the Help link for any search engine to see the most effective way to search is always a good idea. Also, search engines often have two search interfaces – a simple search and an advanced search. With the *simple search*, you normally just enter your query and click the Submit or Search button. With a typical *advanced search*, you can use a variety of options to refine your search. The best way to become familiar with using a search engine is to experiment with a few searches and see what results you get.

One search engine that has proven successful for us when we search for genealogical data is Google (www.google.co.uk). To conduct a search on Google, do the following:

1. **Go to www.google.co.uk.**

   The Google home page is simple. It consists of a field where you enter search terms and two buttons marked *Google Search* and *I'm Feeling Lucky*. You can also choose to search the whole web or only pages from the UK.

2. **Enter your ancestor's name into the search field and click Google Search.** (We entered Thomas Peyton.)

   The Results page appears with a list of URLs (this stands for Uniform Resource Locator, which is the address of an Internet site) and an abstract of the site, showing the search term in bold (Figure 3-6 shows an example).

3. **Click a search result that looks as if it may relate to your ancestor.**

Figure 3-6:
Search
results from
Google.

If you're looking for additional leads, Google allows you to view other pages that are similar to the results that you receive from your original search. You can also refine your search by using quotation marks in order to search for a complete phrase – for example, you can search for Thomas Peyton using **Thomas Peyton** as your search term, which filters out results dealing with the countless other Thomases in the world. For more search hints, click the Search Tips link at the top of the Results page.

Looking at general Internet meta-search engines

Wouldn't it be nice if you never had to visit multiple sites to search the Internet? This burning question led directly to the creation of *meta-search engines*, which use a single interface or form to execute searches using several different search engines. They then return the results of all the individual search engines back to a single page that you can use to view the results. The number of results from meta-search engines can be overwhelming, so you need a good search term and to have several substantial facts about the person you're researching. Then you can quickly determine whether a result is relevant to your search. You also need to have patience because you may have to trudge through several sets of results before you find something useful. Below are some examples of meta-search engines:

- ✔ **Alta Vista:** www.uk.altavista.com
- ✔ **Dogpile:** www.dogpile.co.uk
- ✔ **Ixquick:** www.ixquick.com
- ✔ **MetaCrawler:** www.metacrawler.co.uk
- ✔ **Search.com:** www.search.com
- ✔ **Ithaki:** www.ithaki.net/indexuk.htm
- ✔ **Vivisimo:** vivisimo.com

Subscribing to Online Databases – the Gold Mines of Genealogy?

When you start researching your family history you may feel that you have something in common with some of your less fortunate ancestors – especially when you're tearing your hair out over your meagre finds in search engines. Your ancestors may have fought to put food on the table in the slums of the Industrial Revolution, but you're fighting for every morsel of information, driven by your appetite for knowledge about your great-great-grandmother's maiden name or her sister's 17 children. You're roaming from place to place in search of something to satisfy your curiosity – living from hand to mouth, occasionally receiving tantalising morsels but never seeming to strike it lucky and hit upon your genealogical feast. But don't lose hope. Riches may be awaiting you if only you can stumble upon the right site. And the right site may be in the form of an online subscription database.

Online subscription databases are repositories of information that you can retrieve by paying a monthly, quarterly or yearly fee. Some of them even offer limited free trial periods so you can get to grips with the information available.

Most online subscription databases are easily searchable and let you enter your ancestor's name and execute a search to determine whether any information stored in the database relates to that particular name. Databases can be large or small; they can focus upon a small geographical area or have a broad scope that encompasses many different areas. Each database may also have its own unique search method and present information in its own format.

You can find online subscription databases in many ways. You can find references to them through search engines (discussed in the section 'Letting Your Computer Do the Walking: Using Search Engines' earlier in the chapter), comprehensive genealogical indexes (read more in 'Browsing Comprehensive Genealogical Indexes' later in the chapter) and links that appear on personal and geographically specific websites. To give you a flavour of the types of goldmines that are available, we take a look at a couple of the major online subscription databases.

Ancestry.co.uk

Ancestry.co.uk, at www.ancestry.co.uk, is a commercial site that contains information about millions of names, focusing on England, Wales and Ireland, and constantly adds new material to its databases. The site contains a lot of free content, including message boards and compiled family trees, but in order to access the full collection you have to be a member. (The site does, however, put the majority of its new databases online for free for a few days so you can try them out.) The major collections at Ancestry.co.uk include the following:

- ✔ UK census collection (except the 1911 census)
- ✔ UK and Ireland parish and probate records
- ✔ England and Wales births, marriages and deaths indexes 1837–1983
- ✔ Pallot's Marriage Index
- ✔ Irish immigrants: New York port arrival
- ✔ British Army service records from the First World War
- ✔ UK incoming passenger lists

You can also subscribe to Ancestry Worldwide, at www.ancestry.com, to search the millions of records available in other countries, including the US Federal Census returns.

Scotland's People

Scotland's People, at www.scotlandspeople.gov.uk, is the key subscription database for Scottish genealogy. It contains constantly expanding collections of genealogical data, as well as research guides, background information about the records and how to use them, help with understanding your results, discussion groups, frequently asked questions and much more besides. Its collections include the following:

- ✔ Birth indexes 1855–2006
- ✔ Marriage indexes 1855–1932

 ✔ Death indexes 1855–2006

 ✔ Old parish registers 1553–1854

 ✔ Census collections 1841–1901

 ✔ Wills and testaments 1513–1901

Browsing Comprehensive Genealogical Indexes

If you're unable to find information about your ancestor via a search engine or an online database, or if you want to find additional information, another resource to try is a comprehensive genealogical index. A *comprehensive genealogical index* is a site that contains a categorised list of links to online resources for family history research. Comprehensive genealogical indexes are organised in a variety of ways, including by subject, alphabetically and by type of resource. No matter how the links are organised, they usually appear hierarchically and you click your way down from category to subcategory until you find the link you're looking for.

Following are two examples of comprehensive genealogical indexes:

 ✔ **Cyndi's List of Genealogy Sites on the Internet (www.cyndislist.com):** This international site contains a lot of useful resources for the UK and is used almost daily by genealogists worldwide.

 ✔ **Origins Network (www.origins.net):** This site contains a plethora of resources that would otherwise be difficult to get hold of or to search. From here, you can select links to British Origins, Irish Origins, Scots Origins or you can choose to search the whole collection at once. Searching is done by name, and you also have the option to search for 'close variants' to that name, to allow for differences in spelling.

When you're searching for your ancestors in comprehensive genealogical indexes (or anywhere else for that matter), bear in mind that they may appear in some records under abbreviated names or nicknames. Felix John Ireland may be listed in some records as F Ireland, FJ Ireland, or even as John Ireland. Similarly, his sister Charlotte may be lurking in the records as Lottie Ireland.

To give you an idea of how comprehensive genealogical indexes work, try the following example, illustrated in Figure 3-7:

1. Go to www.cyndislist.com.

 This launches the home page for Cyndi's List.

2. **Select a category, such as 'Surnames, Family Associations & Family Newsletters'.**

   Suppose you're searching for a page containing information about your ancestor William Eagle, of Norfolk. Two categories on the list may have this info: Surname Lists and Personal Home Pages. You may decide to try the Surnames category.

3. **Select a subcategory.**

   Click the link for General Surname sites and resources. This takes you to a page listing resources, websites and an alphabetical list of surnames. Click the link for the information that you're interested in. In this case, select Ancestor Guide: Genealogy and Surname search. This then takes you to another website, where you can enter the name you're looking for – Eagle, for example – and it then gives you a comprehensive list of websites and resources relevant to your particular name.

4. **Click on a promising link.**

Comprehensive genealogical indexes can be time-consuming to browse. You may need several clicks to get to the area in which the links that interest you are located. After several clicks, you may even find that no relevant links are present in that area. This may be because the maintainer of the site hasn't yet indexed a relevant site or because the site may be listed somewhere else in the index.

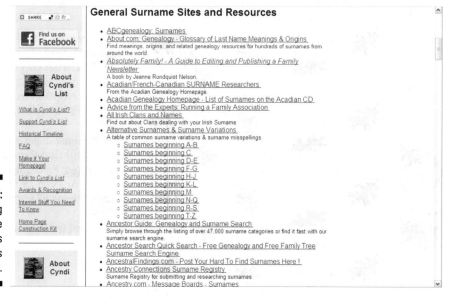

Figure 3-7:
Looking
for Eagle
resources
on Cyndi's
List.

Seeking Answers to Your Surname Questions

Even if you can't find any surname-specific sites on your particular family, you still have hope. This comes in the form of queries. *Queries* are research questions that you post to a particular website, mailing list or newsgroup so other researchers can help you solve your research problems. Other researchers may have information that they haven't yet made available about a family, or they may have seen some information about your family, even though they aren't actively researching that branch.

Web queries

One of the quickest ways of reaching a wide audience with your query is by placing it on a query site on the web. For an example of a query site, try GenForum:

1. **Open your web browser and go to** `http://genforum.` `genealogy.com/`**.**

2. **In the Forum Finder box, enter the surname you're looking for and click the Finder button.**

   Don't worry if your surname doesn't have a forum. The GenForum section is constantly growing and adding surnames, so check back every so often to see whether one's been added. Alternatively, you can request that a new forum is added for your surname: look for the link Add Forum near the bottom of the GenForum pages.

   You may also want to search other forums to see whether the name is included with a different spelling or to see whether someone else has mentioned the name in a passing reference in another forum, (more details in the next section).

3. **After you've found a forum you want to enter, click on the forum link. You can then read messages by clicking the links.**

   As soon as your browser loads the message board page, you see a list of bulleted messages to choose from. You can also navigate to other pages of the message board if the messages don't all fit on a single page. If you don't want to read all the messages, you have the option to see only the latest messages, only today's messages or any messages posted within the last seven days. These options are available at the top of the page.

4. **To post a new query, click the Post New Message button near the top of the message board page.**

   If you're not already a registered user of GenForum, you see a page containing instructions on how to register. After you've registered, a page containing the fields that generate your message pops up. This page includes the Name, E-Mail, Subject and Message fields, as shown in Figure 3-8.

5. **Complete the appropriate fields and then click the Preview Message button.**

   Make sure that your message contains enough information for other researchers to determine whether they can assist you. Include as much as you can of the following: full names, birth and death dates and places and where your ancestors lived.

   Clicking the Preview Message button is an important step because it lets you see how the message looks when it's posted. This option stops you from submitting an embarrassing message filled with factual errors and typos.

6. **If you're satisfied with the way the message looks, click the Post Message button.**

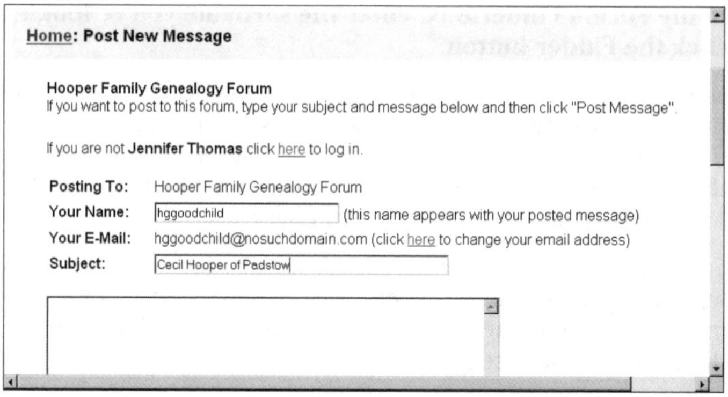

Figure 3-8:
Posting a new message to GenForum.

Home: Post New Message

Hooper Family Genealogy Forum
If you want to post to this forum, type your subject and message below and then click "Post Message".

If you are not **Jennifer Thomas** click here to log in.

Posting To: Hooper Family Genealogy Forum
Your Name: hggoodchild   (this name appears with your posted message)
Your E-Mail: hggoodchild@nosuchdomain.com (click here to change your email address)
Subject: Cecil Hooper of Padstow

Don't be put off if you don't find what you're looking for straight away when you're placing or reading web queries. An answer to your message may come within a week, a month or longer after you post your message. Also, you may find that people post some of the messages from other countries, particularly the United States. But this doesn't mean you won't find useful material amongst them. You're now getting involved with the worldwide genealogical community.

Mailing-list queries

When we mention mailing lists alarm bells may start to ring as you picture an endless stream of junk mail. Fear not! The type of mailing list that we're talking about delivers only the mail that you request. Such mailing lists provide you with a means of posting queries and messages about your surnames and genealogical research in general.

Mailing lists are formed by groups of people who share common interests. In the field of genealogy, those interests may be surnames, specific geographical areas or ethnic groups. A list consists of the email addresses of every person who subscribes to the group. When you want to send a message to the entire group, you send it to a single email address, which in turn forwards the message to everyone on the list. To join a mailing list, you send an email to a designated address with a subscription message. You receive an email confirming that you've subscribed to the list and telling you where to send an email if you want to send a message to everyone on the list.

So how do you find a mailing list that interests you? One way is to consult the extensive list of mailing lists found on the Genealogy Resources site (http://lists.rootsweb.ancestry.com/cgi-bin/findlist.pl).

To find and join a mailing list for your surname, do the following:

1. **Go to http://lists.rootsweb.ancestry.com/cgi-bin/findlist.pl and enter the surname that you're interested in in the surname box – for example, Ramsbottom. Then click on Search.**

   You're taken to a page containing the information you need to subscribe to the Ramsbottom mailing list.

2. **Follow the subscription instructions for your mailing list.**

   The instructions for the Ramsbottom mailing list tell you to send an email message to the given address, containing only the word 'subscribe'.

3. **Start your email program and subscribe to the mailing list.**

   Within a couple of minutes, you receive a confirmation message welcoming you to the mailing list. The message includes information about how to use the mailing list, how to unsubscribe and how to switch between the mail and digest modes of receiving your mail. It is worth considering this option carefully. The *mail mode* option simply forwards email messages to you every time a message is posted on the mailing list. Although mail mode works well for small mailing lists, you may end up receiving hundreds of messages every week. To avoid this, you can select the *digest mode*, which groups together several messages and sends them out as one large message. So, instead of receiving 30 messages a day, you receive only two messages, with the text of 15 messages in each.

4. **Read the messages without responding or posting your own messages for a while. Begin posting your own queries and responses to others' messages when you're ready to do so.**

   Reading messages but not posting your own messages is called *lurking*. You may want to lurk on the mailing list to see what other messages look like and to become familiar with the general culture of the list. After you get a feel for the structure and nature of the messages, jump in and begin sending your own queries and messages.

Using Email to Get Help

In the section 'Seeking Answers to Your Surname Questions' earlier in the chapter, we discussed a couple of ways to research surnames through email by using queries. You can also use email to directly contact other researchers of your surname. You just need to discover where to find them.

Identifying potential email contacts by using online directories to find everyone with the surname you're researching, getting their email addresses and then mass emailing your research questions to all of them is a bad idea. Although mass emailing everyone you can find with a particular surname generates return email for you, we can almost guarantee that the responses will be unhelpful. You have a much better chance of success if you restrict yourself to genealogical sites, where you stand a good chance of finding other researchers interested in your surname.

A number of resources are available that use email as their primary communication tool. Searching the Rootsweb site (`www.rootsweb.ancestry.com`) you may discover a number of other resources connected to the name you're interested in. For example, after entering **Ramsbottom**, you see links to Ramsbottom archives as well as to the mailing list. In the same way, you may come across email addresses of specific family associations and newsletters.

Verifying Your Information

We can't abandon this chapter without once more offering you our favourite piece of advice, whether you're researching surnames or anything else:

don't believe everything you read! A pure genealogist may go so far as to say 'Don't believe *anything* you read!' Always verify any information that you find online by referring to primary records. (For more on primary records, refer to Chapter 1.) If you can't prove it through a census record, civil or parish record or some other authoritative record, then the information may be worth little or nothing. However, just because you can't prove it immediately doesn't mean that you should discard the information. At some time in the future, you may discover a record that does indeed prove the accuracy of the information.

Chapter 4

Locating Your Ancestors (Geographically Speaking)

*W*hile browsing through your genealogical notes, you find that your Great-Uncle Peter lived with his father near the church in Loughton. But where is Loughton? What was the town like? Where exactly did he live in the town? And what was life like when he lived there? In order to answer these questions, you need to research beyond the scope of your original documents – you need to look at the geographical surroundings of your ancestor.

Geography played a major role in the lives of our ancestors. It often determined where they lived and worked, and to where they migrated. Geography can also play a major role in how you research your ancestor. Concentrating on where your ancestor lived can often point you to local record collections or provide clues about where to research next. In this chapter we look at several ways in which geographical resources can be used to provide a boost to your family history research.

Are We There Yet? Researching Where 'There' Was to Your Ancestors

What did 'there' mean for your ancestors? You have to answer this question to know where to look for genealogical information. Today, a family that lives in the same general area for more than two or three generations is rare. If you're a member of such a family, you may be in luck when it comes to genealogical research. However, if you come from a family that moved around every generation or two or in which not all members of the family remained in the same location, you may be in for a challenge.

So how do you find out where your ancestors lived? In this section, we look at several resources you can use to establish their location, including using your existing records, interviewing relatives, consulting gazetteers, looking at maps, using GPS devices and charting locations using geographical software. As we discuss these resources, we use a continuous example to show how you can use the resources together to solve a research problem – finding the house where Great-Uncle Peter lived.

Using documentation you already have in your possession

When you attempt to locate your ancestors geographically, start by using any copies of records or online data that you or someone else has already collected. Sifting through all of those photocopies and original documents from the attic, as well as printouts from websites, provides a good starting point for locating your ancestors geographically. Pay particular attention to any material that provides a definite location during a specific time period. You can use these details as a springboard for your geographical search.

If you have information about the places in which your ancestors lived, but not necessarily the time frame, you can still be reasonably successful in tracking your ancestors based on the limited information that you do have. Aids are available to help you approximate time frames, such as the Period Approximation Chart (www.pennyparker2.com/appxchart.html). For example, you may have the birth dates of your great-great-grandmother's children, but you're not sure when Great-Great-Grandma and Great-Great-Grandpa were married. You can use the Period Approximation Chart to calculate a date range in which you can look for the marriage record. The Period Approximation Chart uses average ages for events in history and typical lifespans at different eras to make the calculations.

For more info about using documents that you already have, see Chapter 1.

Grilling your relatives about what they know

Your notes from interviews with family members, or from other records that you've found relating to your ancestors, probably contain some information about where the family lived – and hopefully the approximate time frames.

Almost certainly someone has given you a clue as to location, for example that Great-Uncle Peter lived for some of his life in Loughton. Of course, whether Great-Uncle Peter himself told you this, or whether it has come third-hand from his cousin's son-in-law has an effect on the reliability of the information and therefore the time frames within which you search for records in Loughton. But these stories do at least give you a useful starting point.

For details about interviewing your family members, see Chapter 1.

Where is Loughton, anyway?

At some point during the course of your research, you're bound to find a document that tells you that an ancestor lived in a particular town or county, or was associated with a specific place, but which contains no details of where that place was – no parish or district or other identifying features. You may be able to verify your information with other documents, for example, the family rumour may be confirmed when you find Great-Uncle Peter in the 1891 census living with his father, a verderer of Epping Forest, in a village called Loughton in Essex. This gives you the information to distinguish your ancestor's Loughton from other Loughtons in the country, and is sufficient information with which to begin a search.

But how do you find out where Loughton is?

A *gazetteer*, or geographical dictionary, provides information about places. By looking up the name of the town, county or some other kind of place, you can narrow down the search for your ancestor. The gazetteer identifies every place by a particular name and provides varying information (depending on the gazetteer itself) about each. At the very least, gazetteers provide the region in which your place-name is located. Many contemporary gazetteers also provide the latitude and longitude of that place.

By adding the information that you find in online gazetteers to the other pieces of your puzzle, you can reduce the list of common place names in which your ancestor may have lived. By discovering exactly where a place is, you can look for more records to prove whether your ancestors really lived there.

Here are some gazetteers that you may find helpful in your research:

- ✔ **Gazetteer for Scotland:** www.geo.ed.ac.uk/scotgaz/
- ✔ **National Gazetteer of Wales:** homepage.ntlworld.com/geogdata/ngw/
- ✔ **Gazetteer of England, Wales and Scotland:** www.gazetteer.co.uk
- ✔ **Ordnance Survey Maps:** www.ordnancesurvey.co.uk

Most online gazetteers are organised on a national level and provide information about all the towns, cities, counties, landmarks and so on within that country. However, some gazetteers list information on a county basis. One such example is the Genuki Gazetteers collection at www.genuki.org.uk/big. Here you find a list of the English, Welsh, Scottish and Irish counties, together with the Channel Islands and the Isle of Man; by following their links, you access county gazetteers, maps, histories and a wealth of other resources relating to that county.

If you can't find a place in current gazetteers, you may need to consult an historical gazetteer, such as www.visionofbritain.org.uk/index.jsp.

As an alternative to gazetteers, you can consult town and city websites. In some cases, these sites provide lots of historic detail about the place you're researching. An Internet search engine, such as Google, can help you to locate them.

More than one village, hamlet or parish of the same name can exist even within the same county, so you need to make sure that you've found the correct one. Details from the census are invaluable here. At the top of each return (or at the beginning of each section of the census) you can find details of the location, and if you move back and forth through the census returns, you can find the names of neighbouring parishes or villages to the one in which your ancestor lived. You can check them against online gazetteers, to verify that you've found the right place. You may also be able to verify the location using the information given on birth, marriage and death certificates, which can provide details such as an address or street name, sub-district name, district name and county. And you can sometimes glean further clues from your ancestor's occupation: in our example, we would check that the Loughton we found is indeed in or near Epping Forest.

Mapping your ancestor's way

After you've discovered where your ancestor's town or village is located, you can examine the maps. Maps can be an invaluable resource in your genealogical research. Not only do they help you track the movements of your ancestors, but they also enhance your compiled genealogy by illustrating some of your findings.

Some online sites contain various maps that may be useful in your genealogical research:

✔ **Historical maps:** Several websites contain scanned or digitised images of historical maps. In many cases, you can download or print copies of the maps. Such sites include:

   • www.old-maps.co.uk

   • www.visionofbritain.org.uk

You can also find collections of maps at several library, university and historical-society sites.

- ✔ **Digitised historical atlases:** In addition to map sites, some individuals have scanned portions or the entire contents of atlases. You may like to try `freepages.genealogy.rootsweb.ancestry.com/~genmaps`.

- ✔ **Interactive map sites:** A few sites have interactive maps that you can use to find and zoom in on areas. After you have found the view that you want, you can print a copy of the map to keep with your genealogical records. Two such sites are:

  - **The UK Street Map Page (`www.streetmap.co.uk`):** This site identifies streets in the UK. Interactive maps are especially helpful when you're trying to pinpoint the location of a cemetery or a town that you plan to visit for your genealogical research. They are, however, limited in their historical value because they usually offer only current information about places.

  - **MapQuest (`www.mapquest.com`):** This site contains interactive maps for many countries, including the UK, Canada, Germany, Italy, New Zealand and the USA, although some are unable to zoom into the image as closely as you want.

- ✔ **Specialised maps:** You can view specialised maps on websites such as:

  - **Google Earth (`www.earth.google.com`):** This site offers satellite maps of the world, allowing you to zoom into the area in which you're interested.

  - **Mapsworldwide (`www.mapsworldwide.com/`):** Here you can buy topographical maps online.

  - **British Library (`www.bl.uk/collections/map_interactive.html`):** This is part of the British Library website, offering a selection of interactive maps including election, geological and demographic maps.

Zeroing in

To continue the example used in the previous sections, we are now sure that Great-Uncle Peter lived in Loughton, in the Epping Forest area. An examination of online maps has confirmed that the town lies right beside Epping Forest in Essex. You then decide that you want to visit the town for yourself to try and find the particular house mentioned in the census. To give you an idea of how to find the house, you can use an interactive atlas site.

Using the MapQuest atlas, select the United Kingdom option, enter **Loughton** into the city field and click the Search command. Three options are available for Loughton, and you know that the first one is yours – Loughton, Essex. Click on Map. The map should appear within a couple of seconds.

Crossing the line

Just as maps help you trace where your ancestors lived and their movements over time, maps can also help you discover when and where your ancestors *didn't* live or move to. Boundaries for parishes, towns, districts and counties have changed over time. Names, too, have changed. Knowing whether your ancestors really moved or just appeared to have moved because a boundary or town name changed is important when you try to locate records for them.

To determine whether a town or county changed names at some point, check a gazetteer or historical text on the area. (For more about gazetteers, see the section earlier in this chapter, 'Where is Loughton anyway?') Finding boundary changes can be a little more challenging, but resources are available to help you. For example, historical atlases illustrate land and boundary changes. You can also use online sites that have maps for the same areas over time, and a few sites deal specifically with boundary changes in particular locations. A couple of examples are:

✔ **The Counties of England, Scotland and Wales Prior to the 1974 Boundary Changes (www.genuki.org.uk/big/Britain.html):** The 1974 boundary changes were a major disruption to boundaries in the UK.

✔ **Map Seeker (www.mapseeker.co.uk):** This site has maps from all over the world, which is great if your ancestors came from somewhere other than the UK.

You can also use software designed specifically to show boundary changes over time. Programs like these can help you find places that have disappeared altogether. Try the Centennia Historical Atlas (www.clockwk.com), which tracks boundary changes in Europe.

Using global positioning systems

After you've located the street in Loughton where Great-Uncle Peter was living, you may decide that you want to go and see it for yourself. However, finding the church or house on the map is one thing, but often finding them on the ground is a completely different thing. That is where global positioning systems come into play.

A *global positioning system* (GPS) is a device that uses satellites to determine the exact location of the user. The technology is quite sophisticated, but in simple terms satellites send out radio signals, which are collected by the GPS receiver – the device that you use to determine your location. The receiver then calculates the distances between the satellites and the receiver to determine your location. These receivers come in many forms, ranging from those that plug into your car (as satellite-navigation systems) to those that fit in the palm of your hand.

On research trips, you can use a GPS receiver to locate a particular place and to document the location of a specific object within that place. For example, wandering through Loughton churchyard, you discover a grave marker to Great-Uncle Peter's father. If you take a GPS reading of the grave site and enter it into your genealogical database, you still have a means of locating the grave even if the marker is later destroyed. You can then take that information, and plot the specific location of the sites on a map using geographical information systems software (which we talk about in the following section).

Plotting your family on the map

Finding a map that shows where your ancestors lived is interesting, but even more exciting is to create your own maps that relate exclusively to your family history. One way in which genealogists produce their own maps is by plotting land records. The legal description of the land is taken from a record and placed into land-plotting software, which then creates a map showing the land boundaries. A popular program for plotting boundaries is DeedMapper (www.directlinesoftware.com) by Direct Line Software. You can also find a number of plotting programs by using a search engine such as Google (www.google.co.uk).

Another way to create custom maps is through geographical information systems (GIS) software. GIS software enables you to create maps based upon layers of information. For example, you may start with an outline map of a county. Then you may add a second layer that shows the towns of the county as they were originally plotted. A third layer may show the location of your ancestor's house based upon information from a census return. A fourth layer may show watercourses or other natural features within the area. The resulting map can give you an appreciation of the environment in which your ancestor lived.

To begin using GIS resources, you need a GIS data viewer. This software comes in many forms, including free software and commercial packages. One popular piece of free software is ArcExplorer available on the ESRI site at www.esri.com. You download or create data to use with the viewer. A number of sites contain both free and commercial data. Starting points for finding data include the Geography Network (www.geographynetwork.com) and GIS Data Depot (http://data.geocomm.com). For more information on GIS software, have a look at www.gis.com.

You can also use maps from other sources and integrate them into a GIS map. For example, when visiting graveyards, you can use GIS resources to generate an aerial photograph of the cemetery and plot the location of the grave markers on it. Back at home, you can use the aerial photograph as the base template and overlay the grave locations on it electronically to show their exact positions.

The many software packages available for purchase or download are also good for mapping your ancestors. Map My Ancestors (www.familytree assistant.com), for example, is a website that enables you to map your ancestors on the Google Earth program. You can start with new information or upload a GEDCOM file to produce a map. This website often offers free trials of its packages, so you can take a look for free and see if it's something for you.

There's No Place Like Home: Using Local Resources

At some point, you'll need to view information held at a local level – for example a copy of a record stored in a local archive, confirmation that an ancestor is buried in a particular churchyard or cemetery or a photograph of the almshouses in which your great-grandfather lived. How can you find and get what you need?

Locating this information is easy if you live in or near the county where the information is stored: you decide what you need, find out where it is and then go and get a copy. But obtaining locally held information isn't quite as easy if you live in another county or country. Although you can determine what information you need and where it may be stored, finding out whether the information really is kept where you think it is and then getting hold of a copy is another thing altogether. You can make a holiday of your research, travelling to the location to make your copy and sightseeing along the way. But you'll probably need a variety of records from several different places, and time and money may rapidly become limiting factors in your plan. Help is at hand, however.

From geographically specific websites to local genealogical and historical societies, and from libraries with research services to individuals who are willing to undertake your research in public record offices, you do have ways and means to locate local documents and obtain the copies that you want. Some resources are free of charge, some individuals charge you a fee for their time and others will claim only expenses for copying and other direct costs.

Geographically specific websites

Geographically specific websites are sites that contain information about a particular town, county, country or other locality. They often provide information about local resources, such as genealogical and historical societies, cemeteries and civic organisations. Some sites have local histories and biographies of prominent residents online. Often, they list and have links to other web pages that have resources for the area. Sometimes they even have a place where you can post *queries* about the area or families who come from there. You may find that someone who reads your query will have some answers for you.

Here are some examples of geographically specific websites:

✔ **Genuki: UK & Ireland Genealogy (`www.genuki.org.uk`):** This is an online reference site containing primary historical and genealogical information in the UK and Ireland. It links to sites containing indexes, transcriptions and digitised images of actual records. All the information is categorised by country, and then by county, and sometimes also by parish.

✔ **WorldGenWeb project (`www.worldgenweb.org`):** This site attempts to provide a central genealogical resource for information on a global scale. For more information about WorldGenWeb, go to the Internet Directory in this book.

Genealogical and historical societies

Most genealogical and historical societies exist on a local level. Historical societies attempt to preserve the documents and promote the history of their particular area. Genealogical societies sometimes do this too, but their main purpose is to help their members research their ancestors, regardless of whether they lived in the local area. (Of course, some surname-based genealogical societies, and even some virtual societies, are exceptions because they aren't specific to one particular place.)

Although historical societies usually don't have a stated purpose of aiding their members in genealogical research, they are nevertheless helpful to genealogists. If you don't live in the area from which you need a record or particular piece of information, you can contact a local genealogical or historical society to help you. Help varies from simple look-up services in books and documents that the society maintains in its library to volunteers who actually locate records for you and send copies to you.

Before you contact a local genealogical or historical society for help, take a look at its website to find out what services it offers. To find a society in an area you're researching, try the following:

1. **Go to the Federation of Family History Societies website at `www.ffhs.org.uk`.**

2. **Select the List of Members option.**

   You now have the option of viewing the members' lists in England, Wales, Ireland or overseas, by using the tabs at the top of the page. The overseas category contains links to societies in Australia, Canada, New Zealand and the United States, but further countries can be found in the 'Other' category.

3. **Select the country relevant to you, and then select the appropriate county.**

   For example, say you choose Wales. You are asked to select from a list of counties and then you get a list of societies in that particular county, with links to their own websites.

4. **Click the link to visit the group or society home page to see what services it offers to members and non-members.**

   If the group offers a service that you need, use the contact information provided to get in touch and request help.

You can also use a search engine to locate genealogical and historical societies. Usually, entering the name of the location that interests you followed by **genealogical society** or **historical society** brings up some useful results. Bear in mind that some societies are formed at a county level rather than at a town level, so you may need to search under the county rather than the town name.

Libraries and archives

Often the holdings in local libraries and archives can be of great value to you even if you can't visit the library or archive in person to do your research (and some even have free subscriptions to genealogy sites). If the library or archive has a website, you can go online to determine whether that repository has the book or document that you need. Most libraries and archives that have web pages or other Internet sites make their catalogues available online. Some even have indexes and images of documents online. If you find that a repository has what you need, contact the archivist or librarian to get a copy. Most libraries and archives have services to copy information at a minimal cost.

To find online catalogues for libraries and archives in particular places, follow these steps:

1. **Go to the ARCHON directory at `www.nationalarchives.gov.uk/archon`.**

   This directory contains contact details for archives throughout the UK. It also has a link to the list of overseas repositories.

2. **Select the area in which you're interested.**

   A list of repositories in that area appears, with links to their individual websites. If the catalogues to these repositories are available online, you can find them here.

You may find that reference books related to your research are held in the relevant local archive in order to provide a context for the documents that they hold. However, if you can't find what you want, you can arrange to borrow library material via the COPAC website at `www.copac.ac.uk`. This site provides access to the catalogues of the Consortium of Research Libraries, including the British Library, the National Library of Scotland and the National Library of Wales. Alternatively, you can enter your chosen locality and **Library** or **Library Resources** into a search engine to find information and contact details of the libraries in that region.

If you're unsure about the documents available for your particular area of research, or about where to find them, have a look at the Access to Archives website at `www.a2a.org.uk`. Here you can enter the details about what you're looking for, and the site produces a list of archival material that may be of use to you. For more about Access to Archives, check out Chapter 7.

Professional researchers

Professional researchers are people who research your genealogy or particular aspects of it for a fee. If you're looking for someone to do all of your research and to put together a complete family history, you can find professional researchers who do just that. If you're simply looking for records in a particular area to substantiate claims in your genealogy, professional researchers can usually locate the records and get you the relevant copies. Their services, rates, experience and reputations vary, so be careful when selecting a professional researcher. Look for someone with experience in the area in which you need help: ask for references or a list of satisfied customers. Chapter 9 provides a list of recommended questions to ask when seeking a professional researcher, and suggests some steps to follow in finding a professional researcher online.

Directories and newspapers

If you have a general idea of where your family lived at a particular time, but no conclusive proof, local and county directories and newspapers from the area may help. (Census records, which we discuss in Chapters 1 and 5, are helpful for this purpose, too.) Directories and newspapers can help you to confirm whether your ancestors did indeed live in a particular area and, in some cases, they can provide much more information than you expect. A true story may illustrate this point: a fellow genealogist was searching newspapers for an obituary about one of his great-uncles. He knew when his great-uncle had died but could find no mention of it in the obituary section of the newspaper. As he cast the newspaper aside in despair, he glanced at the front page – only to find a very graphic description of how a local man had been killed in a freak lift accident. And guess who that local man was? That's right: he was the missing great-uncle! The newspaper not only confirmed that the great-uncle had lived there, but also provided a lot more information than the genealogist had ever expected.

Directories

Directories provide a mine of information about the lives and occupations of our ancestors, and frequently act as a springboard to further detailed research. The beauty of directories is that you can tailor your search to the information you have. Although the exact content and detail of the volumes varies, your ancestor may be listed according to his or her profession, address or surname. A good idea initially is to select the Browse option of an online directory to get a feel for the kind of information available in these directories before you begin your own search. Although tracing male ancestors is often easier than female ancestors through directories (trade directories, for example, list those who were running the business, so historically tend to favour men over women), you may also find couples or whole families listed together, which provides an invaluable and more frequent supplement to the census. You may also find information such as business addresses and business partners, which is rarely available on the census.

Unfortunately, no central resource on the web contains transcriptions of directories or even an index to all directories that may exist on the Internet. But don't be discouraged: You can still find the info. A good starting point in your search is the University of Leicester's project at www.historical directories.org. This site doesn't include every directory that was ever printed, but provides digital images of a generous sample, which you can search according to location, date or keyword. The site covers the period 1750–1919 and is limited to England and Wales.

Other sites provide links to directories for particular geographical areas, but are by no means universal. Go to the Genuki site (www.genuki.org.uk) and select the area that you want to search: You may find a link to directories in the list of local resources. For example, London resources include a directory of London merchants of 1677 and Kent's directory of 1740. You may also find links to websites where you can buy local directories on CD or simply find a list of what is available offline if you wish to follow this avenue. Alternatively, you can use the Genuki search engine at www.genuki.org.uk/contents to obtain a list of resources online and offline.

Newspapers

Unlike directories that list almost everyone in a community, newspapers are helpful only if your ancestors did something newsworthy – but you'd be surprised at what was considered newsworthy in the past. Your ancestor didn't have to be a politician or a criminal to get his picture and story in the paper. Just like today, obituaries, birth and marriage announcements, public records of land transactions, advertisements and gossip sections were all relatively common in newspapers of the past.

Finding copies online of those newspapers from the past is a challenge. Most of the newspaper sites currently on the web are for contemporary publications. Although you can read about wedding anniversaries and birthdays taking place all over the world today, you can't necessarily access online information about your ancestor's death in the 1800s. Many researchers are beginning to recognise the potential that the web holds for making historical information from newspapers available worldwide. However, lack of time and money prevents them from doing so as quickly as we would like.

Here's what you're likely to find online pertaining to newspapers:

- ✔ **Transcripts:** A few sites contain transcripts of whole newspapers or of pages relevant to the genealogist. Here are some examples:

  - **The Times Digital Archive (**http://archive.timesonline. co.uk/tol/archive/**):** This archive contains every page of *The Times* that was published between 1785 and 1985. You can search it by name. You have to take out a subscription to the online archive, although you do have the option of a free trial before you commit your money. However, try checking with your local library first, as some boroughs offer this service for free.

  - **Genuki (**www.genuki.org.uk/big**):** Select, for example, England then Lincolnshire, then click the newspapers option and follow the link. You find information about a variety of newspapers in Lincolnshire and **Out of county** (useful if your ancestors lived near a border, because their activities may be reported in the other location). For example, transcripts (of births, marriages and deaths) from intermittent Hull newspapers are available for the period 1791–1903. These include birth, marriage and death notices and reports of local court hearings. Have a look and see what's available for your own locality.

  - **Ireland Old News (**www.irelandoldnews.com**):** This contains transcripts of some of the more eye-catching political, maritime and criminal news of the eighteenth to the early twentieth century.

✔ **Collectors' issues for sale:** Although they don't provide information directly from the newspaper for you to use online in your genealogical pursuits, these sites can help you to find out about collectors' editions of newspapers and even to buy them online. The sites that sell old newspapers generally market their papers as good gift ideas for birthdays and anniversaries. For the services to be really useful to you as a genealogist, you have to know the date and place of the event that you want to document (and a newspaper name helps, too), as well as to be willing to pay for a copy of that paper. Here are a couple of newspaper collector sites to try:

- **Newspapers Remembered:** www.newspapersremembered.co.uk/acatalog/old-newspapers.html

- **Bygone News:** www.bygonenews.com

✔ **Online newspaper projects:** Many people are beginning to recognise the important role that newspapers play in recording history, and therefore the value of putting newspaper information on the web. An increasing number of online projects to catalogue or transcribe newspapers are beginning to appear. The websites for these projects describe the purpose of the project, its current status and how to find the newspapers if they've been transcribed or digitised and placed online. Here are a few examples:

- **The British Library Newspaper Archive (www.bl.uk):** The British Library has undertaken a large project to digitise nineteenth century national and local newspapers. Some of these newspapers – editions of the *Daily News*, the *Penny Illustrated*, the *Graphic* and the *Weekly Despatch* – are available online on pay-per-view access at http://newspapers.bl.uk/blcs/. You can search them by keyword. The site is free to use at The British Library.

- **Local resources:** Go to www.genuki.org.uk/big and select the location you're interested in. The resource list that appears sometimes includes digital newspapers or newspaper name indexes for that area – just follow the link.

If you can't find a suitable newspaper online, study a comprehensive index to find out what was around at the time, even if you can't access it online. Your local library is the best place to start, as they have many copies of historic local and national newspapers. Another good place to go for this is the British Library Newspapers Catalogue at www.bl.uk/catalogues/newspapers.html, as shown in Figure 4-1. You may then decide to hire a professional researcher to examine the material that you want. Alternatively, you could travel to the British Library to view the copies of local and national newspapers that you're interested in, but you need to obtain a reader's ticket to do this, and contacting the British Library before you go to make sure they hold the newspaper you're looking for is always a good idea.

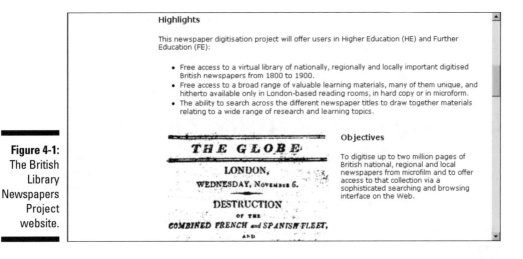

Figure 4-1:
The British
Library
Newspapers
Project
website.

Highlights

This newspaper digitisation project will offer users in Higher Education (HE) and Further Education (FE):

- Free access to a virtual library of nationally, regionally and locally important digitised British newspapers from 1800 to 1900.
- Free access to a broad range of valuable learning materials, many of them unique, and hitherto available only in London-based reading rooms, in hard copy or in microform.
- The ability to search across the different newspaper titles to draw together materials relating to a wide range of research and learning topics.

THE GLOBE

LONDON,

WEDNESDAY, November 6.

DESTRUCTION

OF THE

COMBINED FRENCH and SPANISH FLEET,

AND

Objectives

To digitise up to two million pages of British national, regional and local newspapers from microfilm and to offer access to that collection via a sophisticated searching and browsing interface on the Web.

Localising your search

After you've discovered when and where your ancestor lived, you may want to find out more about what their life may have been like in that particular place at that particular time. Local histories are the key resource here. Local histories often contain information about early local inhabitants and patterns of migration, and may have biographical information on principal people within the community who have contributed to its history.

Online local histories can be tucked away in geographically specific websites, historical society pages, library sites and web-based bookshops. Here are a few more general sites that you can try:

- ✔ **Victoria County History (www.victoriacountyhistory.ac.uk):** The ongoing Victoria County History project has published 240 comprehensive encyclopaedia volumes covering historical periods from the earliest times and most English counties. A digitisation project is underway to make all of these volumes available online via their website. Many counties have an online volume already, and the collection is growing by the day.

- ✔ **Scottish History (www.scottishhistory.com):** This site offers online access to essays, articles and information about Scotland and its history. It also offers links to other publications and magazines specifically relating to Scottish history.

- ✔ **Island Ireland (http://islandireland.com):** This great website is dedicated to Irish local history and contains links to many Irish counties, as well as links to family history websites and resources.

Don't forget the standard resources to search by the location of your choice: www.genuki.org.uk and www.cyndislist.com.

Hit the Road, Jack! Planning Your Genealogy Travels Using the Web

A wealth of information is available to help you plan your travels – and it's all at your fingertips. You can find out about hotels, car rental and other means of travel, local attractions and a host of other things related to research trips and holidays. You may find the UK Travel search engine and directory (www.atuk.co.uk) helpful in planning your trip. If you need directions for driving to your destination, you can find them at the AA Routeplanner site.

Follow these steps to get driving directions from AA Routeplanner:

1. **Open the AA Routeplanner site at www.theaa.com/travelwatch/ planner_main.jsp.**

2. **Enter the details of where your journey will begin and end.**

   If the route planner doesn't recognise your destination, you can obtain a more detailed description, for example a postcode, from the website relating to your destination.

3. **Click on the GetRoute link.**

   You receive step-by-step instructions on how to get there, and an estimate of the distance and the time that your journey will take. You can also view and print out a map of your journey.

Part III
Rooting Around in the Past

In this part . . .

Here we reach the heart of the matter. In this part of the book you discover the fundamental documents used in genealogical research, including birth, marriage and death certificates, the census and parish records. We also introduce you to more specialised resources, both online and offline, to help you build a fuller picture of your ancestors and their lives and times.

Chapter 5

Basic Genealogical Resources in the UK

This chapter takes a close look at the keystones of your genealogical research project. You'll probably come back to this chapter again and again as your journey into the past progresses. The chapter covers in detail how to use and make the most of the central genealogical resources online. The key to using these resources is practice, experimentation and play. Simply have a go. See what you come up with. You may be surprised at how quickly you start to feel at home with these resources and how invaluable they are to your research.

Exploring Civil Registration

You're now uncovering the building blocks of genealogical research. No matter who you are, how expert or inexperienced you're feeling or which line of your family you're tracing back, the indexes of births, marriages and deaths – also known as *BMD indexes* – will be amongst your greatest friends. For once, you can be grateful to those government officials, with their love of paperwork, who created and preserved these records: without them, genealogists would be a great deal worse off.

So what does civil registration actually mean? The term is nothing to do with our ancestors being courteous. Civil registration is the recording of births, marriages and deaths by officials of the state. Today, registering all such events is compulsory, but in the past things were rather different. Civil registration began only in 1837 in England and Wales, and in 1855 in Scotland. In Ireland, much of the civil registration began in 1864, although a number of Protestant records go back to 1845. Before those dates, these events were recorded locally, but not compulsorily, and records are patchier. (See 'Going Beyond Civil Registration: Finding Parish Records' later in the chapter for more about these records.)

What do these records tell me?

By searching the civil registration indexes and obtaining references for certificates, you can order copies of the birth, marriage and death certificates of your ancestors. These documents are packed full of useful information:

- ✔ **Birth certificate:** This gives you the full name of the person and his or her parents, including the mother's maiden name. The certificate also tells you the date, place and (in the case of multiple births or a birth in Scotland) the time of birth, the occupation of the father, the name of the person who registered the birth and that person's relationship to the child. In Scotland, from 1861 a birth certificate also gives the date and place of marriage of the parents. If you're lucky enough to find an ancestor born in Scotland in 1855, the certificate also tells you about the person's siblings, the ages and places of birth of the parents and the date and place of their marriage. After 1855, the authorities decided that too much information was being asked for, and it was reduced.

- ✔ **Marriage certificate:** This reveals the full names, ages, marital status (bachelor, spinster, widow and so on), occupations and addresses of the bride and groom, together with the date and place of their marriage, the rites under which their ceremony took place (Church of England, Catholic, Jewish, Methodist and so on) and the names of the officials and witnesses. The certificate also gives the names and occupations of the fathers of the bride and groom. In Scotland, the mothers of the bride and groom are listed too, with their maiden names. A marriage certificate in Scotland in 1855 is a genealogist's dream come true because it also provides the birthplace of the bride and groom, the number of previous marriages of the bride and groom and the number of children that resulted from these marriages.

- ✔ **Death certificate:** This gives the full name, sex and age of the deceased, the address at which they died, the date and cause of death and sometimes the duration of the final illness. In the case of a man, it was usual (until 1969) to provide his occupation; for a woman, the name of her husband or late husband; and for a child, the name of the father. The informant of the death is also recorded, along with their address and their relationship to the deceased. Scottish records also record the time of death, the marital status of the deceased, the name of the spouse and the names and occupations of the parents. In 1855, Scottish certificates reveal the birthplace of the deceased and the names and ages of their children. Until 1860, Scottish certificates reveal the place of burial, the name of the undertaker and the time at which the doctor last saw the deceased alive.

Using online BMD indexes

Okay, so you're convinced of the value of these documents and want to start searching for your own family's details. The good news is that you don't have to leave the comfort of your own home: many of the BMD indexes are available online.

One of the key subscription websites for England and Wales is the Ancestry site at `www.ancestry.co.uk/search/rectype/vital/freebmd/bmd. aspx`. This site contains BMD indexes for the years 1837–2005 and also a search aid called FreeBMD (more on this under 'Searching the indexes for free' later in the chapter). Ancestry.co.uk is a subscription website, but (in our opinion) is worth every penny. (Have a look at Chapter 3 for more about Ancestry.co.uk and other subscription databases.) We discuss the websites for Scotland and Ireland later in the sections 'Looking North: Searching Made Quick and Easy in Scotland' and 'Heading Over to Ireland: A Project for the Future'.

The indexes are arranged alphabetically by year and within each year by quarters. The March quarter of each year contains all the births, marriages and deaths that were registered in January, February and March of that year; the June quarter contains April, May and June, and so forth. Thus you have to search four volumes before you can cross any particular year off your search list. You also need to remember that because parents have up to six weeks in which to register the birth of a child, if a child was born in December then it may be that the birth entry comes under January of the following year.

Searching the indexes

Suppose you're searching for the birth record of your maternal great-grandfather, Sydney Victor Hall. From an interview with members of your mother's family, you discover that he was born around 1890 in Lichfield. Here's how to find him:

1. **Call up the Ancestry web page at `www.ancestry.co.uk/search/ rectype/vital/freebmd/bmd.aspx`.**

   You see two links: Births 1837 to 1915 and Births 1916 to 2005. The births from 1916 are fully transcribed, which means that you can call up the exact entry you're looking for without having to search through the online indexes. Just type in the name and you should bring up the exact birth entry for your ancestor. However, if you're looking for an ancestor born before 1916, click on the link for 1837 to 1915.

2. **Enter the name of your ancestor in the search boxes, and select an approximate year of birth. (If you're absolutely certain that the name you're looking for is correct, you can tell the search engine to look for the exact terms you enter, with no variations, by ticking the 'Match all terms entirely' box.)**

   In this case, you enter Sydney Victor Hall's name and 1890.

3. Select Search.

You're given a list of relevant entries (see Figure 5-1). Remember, although some of these entries are fully transcribed, some aren't, and you may still have to search through online registers, depending on the ancestor you're searching for.

4. Click on the small magnifying glass icon at the end of the row to view the image of that page.

You now see a digitised image of the page you want. (It may take a few seconds to load.) You can enlarge this image by clicking on the magnifying glass with the + sign. Scroll up and down the page, and from side to side, using the scrollbars at the bottom and right-hand side of the screen.

5. Search the alphabetical lists to see whether the name you want is there.

You need patience, but as a genealogist you know all about that. The name you want may appear right away, or you may have to search 20 volumes. In this case, you see plenty of references to Sydney Hall as you search the various quarters, but no Sydney Victor Hall appears until the December quarter of 1887. You discover that his birth was indeed registered in Lichfield.

6. Note the name and its reference.

The information that accompanies the name is vital because it identifies the correct birth certificate. Write down the name and the information contained in the three columns that follow: the *district* in which the birth was registered, the *volume number* and the *page number*. The columns are labelled clearly at the top of every page. In our example, you write down the following:

- **Name:** Sydney Victor Hall
- **District:** Lichfield
- **County:** Staffordshire
- **Volume number:** 6b
- **Page number:** 423
- **Quarter:** Dec 1887
- **Type of record:** birth

By now you're entitled to give yourself a pat on the back – there's nothing more satisfying than a successful search.

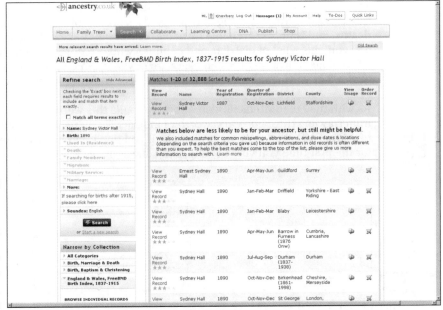

Figure 5-1:
Ancestry.
co.uk
search
results for
Sydney
Victor Hall.

Sometimes you find further information given in the indexes that can help with your research. For example, birth indexes from 1911 onwards include an extra column giving the mother's maiden name, marriage indexes from 1911 give the names of both partners and death indexes from 1866 give the age of the deceased. The information given in the actual certificates before and after these dates remains the same – only the amount of information provided in the indexes changes.

Searching the indexes for free

Many projects are underway to transcribe the entire birth, marriage and death indexes. If you have an existing Ancestry.co.uk subscription, you can search some of the birth, marriage and death indexes on that site by name and date, meaning that you don't have to trawl though pages and pages of records. This subscription is the best option, because these records, along with the census returns, are all on one website, saving you lots of time and effort.

However, as well as being a feature of the Ancestry subscription website, the FreeBMD transcription project has its own dedicated website (www. freebmd.org.uk), so you can see sections of their transcriptions without having to subscribe to Ancestry.

This free-to-use website gets updated continually with new transcriptions, with the aim of eventually having fully indexed records of births, marriages and deaths, and is fully searchable by name. The FreeBMD search page (see Figure 5-2) contains a list of districts and counties whose records are included on the site and an indication of which years are covered, which gives you a good idea of whether your ancestor is likely to have been included in these records.

As with the FreeBMD facility on Ancestry.co.uk, this website can save you from trawling through years' worth of indexes, if you're lucky. Remember, too, that FreeBMD is an ongoing project, so if you don't find what you're looking for the first time you visit the site, keep checking back.

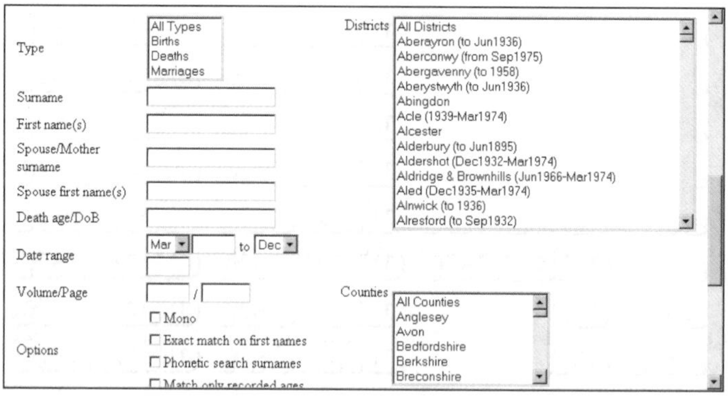

Figure 5-2:
The
FreeBMD
search
page.

Type	All Types / Births / Deaths / Marriages	Districts	All Districts / Aberayron (to Jun1936) / Aberconwy (from Sep1975) / Abergavenny (to 1958) / Aberystwyth (to Jun1936) / Abingdon / Acle (1939-Mar1974) / Alcester / Alderbury (to Jun1895) / Aldershot (Dec1932-Mar1974) / Aldridge & Brownhills (Jun1966-Mar1974) / Aled (Dec1935-Mar1974) / Alnwick (to 1936) / Alresford (to Sep1932)
Surname			
First name(s)			
Spouse/Mother surname			
Spouse first name(s)			
Death age/DoB			
Date range	Mar ▾ to Dec ▾		
Volume/Page	/	Counties	All Counties / Anglesey / Avon / Bedfordshire / Berkshire / Breconshire
Options	☐ Mono / ☐ Exact match on first names / ☐ Phonetic search surnames / ☐ Match only recorded ages		

FreeBMD is particularly useful for matching up marriage partners in the years before 1911. Say you're searching for the marriage of your great-uncle, Samuel John Leonard. You found him on the 1901 census (for more on census returns, check out 'Finding Your New Best Friend: Census Records' later in this chapter), along with his wife Jane and two small children, all living in Gloucester. You want to find the marriage of Samuel and Jane and trace both of their family lines – but you don't know Jane's maiden name.

FreeBMD is a good solution here: you fill in the details that you have about both bride and groom and run a marriage search for Samuel John Leonard to Jane in the ten years before 1901. You find a possible candidate in the June quarter of 1896 in Gloucester, and write down the quarter, district, volume and page number, as you would for any other search.

Now you can run a second search.

1. **Return to the search page by clicking Back in the top left-hand corner of the screen and clear all information boxes of names or any other details.**

Doing a good turn

Many websites, such as FreeBMD, and especially local family history societies, are always on the look out for volunteers to help update their databases. Helping with this work is a great idea, as not only are you helping the wider genealogy community by adding to the online resources, but it's a great way to meet other amateur genealogists and get involved with the wider online community.

2. **At the bottom of the page, fill in the date range (in our case, June 1896 to June 1896) and the volume and page number (6a in the first box and 537 in the second) of the marriage that you found.**

3. **Click Find.** And there you have all the marriage partners who correspond to that reference.

Hold on a minute, though – the search has thrown four names up. What's going on? In this period, marriage certificates are stored two to a page, so two sets of brides and grooms have the same reference. (Earlier on, you may find even more names on the same page.) By looking at the names, you can't tell who married whom. But that isn't a problem for you because you have your 1901 census return. You know that Samuel married someone called Jane, and so you can correctly identify the marriage partner here: her name is Jane Oakley. Equipped with her maiden name, you can now trace her line back.

But what if your couple aren't there? In the absence of any other clues as to the woman's maiden name, the best solution is to order the marriage certificate. You can do this under the name of the groom or bride – you don't need both names. The marriage certificate gives you a lot of useful information apart from the bride's maiden name (see 'What do these records tell me?' earlier in this chapter), which may come in handy as you continue your research.

Overcoming common stumbling blocks when searching BMD indexes

The best way to become familiar with the BMD and FreeBMD indexes is simply to use them. Make a start by finding your own birth reference, and then those of close members of your family. After you've practised a bit and come to grips with the structure of the websites, begin to search for the unknown – who knows where it may lead? Many people come across the same problems and queries when they're searching the indexes, so we've drawn up a list of handy hints to help you avoid the regular pitfalls and speed you on your way:

✔ **I know my grandmother was born in this quarter, but her name isn't in the indexes.** Remember that the quarter listed in the indexes refers to the date when an event was registered, not necessarily when it took place. A marriage was usually registered on the day of the ceremony, so it should be in the correct quarter. A death would have to be promptly registered in order for the burial to take place. But several weeks may have elapsed before a birth was registered, so if you don't find what you're looking for in one volume, take a look in the next volume. The solution to your problem probably lies there.

✔ **I may have found my great-grandmother's birth reference, but how do I know whether it's the right one?** You can do several checks. First, always do a full search – that is, search all the possible years in which your great-grandmother may have been born. You may know from her marriage or death certificate, or from a census record, roughly when she was born and possibly where she was born. But don't abandon your search part way through – you may have one hit, but there may be other candidates waiting to be found. Choose the most likely candidate from a comprehensive list and then order the certificate itself. If the father's name and occupation on the birth certificate match those on the marriage certificate, then you have the right one. (See 'Ordering BMD certificates online' and 'Piecing It All Together: Using Your Certificates to Build Your Family Tree' later in this chapter for more on this.)

✔ **I can't find my grandfather's birth reference, and I've searched all possible years.** This is a common and frustrating occurrence. Sometimes, people got away without registering births, although the proportion of people who registered increased gradually over time. Other people slipped through the net when the indexes were made. But go over everything else you know about your grandfather and see whether you can find any clues. Can you find him in the death indexes? If so, you can find an age, which may give you a more exact date for his birth. Another possibility is that he wasn't born in England or Wales, or that the name you always knew him by wasn't his real name. For example, Great Uncle Jack may have been born at sea or abroad, and it could be that he wasn't registered under the name Jack at all. It may be time to interview other members of the family and put these ideas before them.

✔ **I think I've found the right reference, but it isn't the name I was expecting.** This can be disconcerting but is by no means disastrous. Sometimes people change or adjust their names. A girl born Lilian O'Sullivan may appear as Lillian, Lilley, Lilly or Lily O'Sullivan on her marriage certificate. Henry George Cooper may marry as George Henry Cooper or Harry George Cooper. But that's all part of the fun, isn't it? Middle names may also throw you off the scent. It was fairly common for children, particularly girls, to acquire a middle name (which they were not given at birth) at the time of their confirmation, so the middle name appears on the marriage certificate but not on the birth certificate. Sometimes brides, grooms and parents choose not to declare their middle names on marriage or birth certificates. But middle names can be an asset too. Apart from making an individual more traceable, especially if the rest of the name is quite common, a child's middle name may turn out to be the mother's maiden name, or another important family name. This can be an important clue as you trace these lines further back.

Ordering BMD certificates online

You've searched the indexes and found references to the certificates that you want. Now you can order the certificates themselves and uncover the mine of information that they contain. These certificates are legal documents and you can order them from the General Register Office. Here's how to do it:

1. **Open your browser and call up the website of the General Register Office:** `www.gro.gov.uk/gro/content/certificates/Login.asp`.

   This is the Login page: you must log in before you're allowed to use this site.

2. **Register your personal details.**

   You need to enter details such as your name, address, email address and phone number. You also need to create a password: choose something that you can remember easily. When you've filled in this page and clicked Submit, the system stores your details. You simply have to confirm your identity each time you visit. If you prefer, you can log on as a guest user, but this means you have to enter your details every time you order a certificate from the site. You can register fully right away to save yourself time in the future.

3. **Enter the preliminary details for the certificate you want.**

   After you've happily logged in, the website prompts you to fill in the reference details for the certificate that you want. The website asks the following questions (see Figure 5-3):

   - Which certificate type would you like to order (birth, marriage, death, adoption or overseas)?

   - Is the General Register Office Index known?

     This is the reference that follows each name in the indexes (the volume and page number), for example 7b 236. Your answer is likely to be Yes.

   - For which year would you like to order a certificate?

   After you've submitted this information, you need to complete a second page detailing your delivery address (so that the General Register Office can post the certificate to the correct place) and your email address. Any boxes marked with an asterisk are essential – you have to complete these in order to proceed. Boxes without asterisks are optional. After you've entered the necessary details, click Submit.

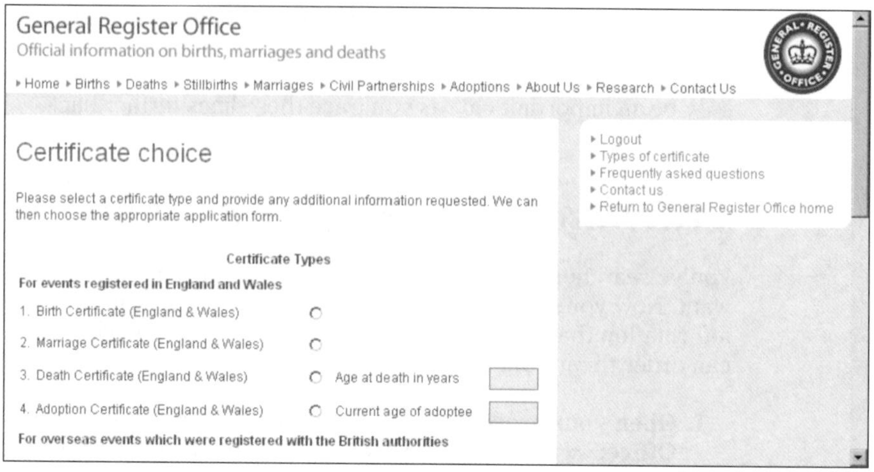

Figure 5-3:
Ordering
your certifi-
cate online.

4. Enter the particulars of the person whose certificate you require.

Again, only the asterisked boxes are compulsory. Sometimes, especially with birth certificates, details such as the mother's maiden name are marked as compulsory. This information is required to ensure that people don't order certificates to commit fraud or identity theft.

Fill in the details required for your ancestor. Then scroll down and complete the boxes for quarter, district name, volume number and page number.

5. Choose the delivery service you'd like.

This is the tricky bit – a test of your patience. *Standard delivery* costs £7; with this, the office usually sends you the certificate on the fifteenth working day after you place your order. (Delivery time changes periodically, so check out the latest information given on the website.) If you're bouncing up and down with impatience, you can have the certificate dispatched on the next working day as a *priority delivery* – but this costs £23. You may have to battle with your conscience (not to mention your bank balance), but the better option is the standard service. You can find plenty to get on with while you wait for the standard delivery, and there's nothing more frustrating than ordering a priority certificate only to discover that it's wrong or not as helpful as you'd hoped.

6. Decide on the number of copies that you want.

You almost certainly want only one copy. We recommend that you wait for the certificate and check that it's what you want before you order multiple copies. If one of your relatives or genealogical partners is desperate for an original copy rather than just the information that it contains, you can always order another copy at a later date.

7. Choose a reference number to identify your order.

This identifies your order just in case there's any confusion or problem with it.

8. Decide whether you want your reference to be checked.

A reference check acts as an optional safeguard to ensure that you get the right certificate. When you click on the Reference Checking box, you're asked to fill in one or more other details about the certificate that you already have from your existing research. For example, for a birth certificate, you may list the place or date of birth, the parents' surnames or forenames or any other checking point that you know of. For a marriage certificate, you may give the date of marriage, place of marriage, the surname or forename of the father of the bride or groom. And for a death certificate, you may give the place of death, the date of birth or death, the occupation or marital status (if female). The certificate is sent only if its details match your checking points, so be absolutely sure of any information that you give. If the certificate isn't produced – in other words, the details that you expect to find there aren't there, indicating that you've found the reference to the wrong certificate – you receive a refund of £4. If in doubt, don't use checking points: it's better to see a wrong certificate than to be left with no certificate and wondering what if . . . ?

After you've filled in the details that you have, click Submit. If you decide against using checking points, click Resume Application. When you've returned to the previous page, click Submit.

9. Check the details on the summary page and select Add to Order.

You can then order more certificates or select Checkout to finish your shopping, enter your method of payment, and wait to receive your certificate in the post – delivery times vary, so check out the latest news on the website for further info.

If you have problems using the website, a box in the top left corner of the screen links to some frequently asked questions. If this online aid doesn't answer your query, the box also carries the option Contact Us so you can put your question to the experts.

When the certificate arrives, read it, copy it and add it to your document file. It contains important information, so you don't want to lose it. If you have any difficulty reading or making sense of the certificate, check out the following list for tips:

✔ **Handwriting:** Some of the handwriting on certificates is impeccable, but on others it's barely legible. If you can't read something, have a look at other words on the page – you may see the same word or letter again in a more legible form. Sometimes you can confirm a name or date from the indexes or an occupation from the census or other records. Be especially careful with words that can be hard to distinguish from one another when they're sloppily written: for example, was Great-Uncle Samuel a tailor or a sailor? Trade directories and seamen's records can help to clarify this (check out Chapters 4, 6 and 7 for more). You can also make use of the many websites that offer information and advice about old handwriting. Cyndi's List offers a treasure trove of links to such websites at www.cyndislist.com/handwrit.htm.

✔ **Formerly/late:** On most birth certificates, you see something like this to denote the name of the person's mother:

Jane Hartwright formerly Cromwell

This means that the person's mother was born Jane Cromwell and married a Hartwright. But you may also see this:

Jane Hartwright, late Hudson, formerly Cromwell

In this case, you can deduce that Jane Cromwell married twice, first to someone called Hudson and then to someone called Hartwright.

✔ **No father on the birth certificate:** This sometimes occurred if the father didn't turn up in person to register the birth of the child, and was therefore not included on the certificate. However, the absence of a father's name more often implies that the child was born outside wedlock, and the child has therefore taken the mother's name. This can be an interesting find. If you want to investigate it further, look at the census to see who the child was living with, and in what circumstances. Also look at the child's marriage certificate to see whether a father is declared there.

✔ **Thomas Jones X his mark:** This is a good indication of literacy levels among your ancestors. Brides, grooms, witnesses and informants were asked to sign their names on these official documents. Those who were unable to write made their mark – an X.

✔ **Of full age:** This means that a bride or groom was over 21 years. But you don't know how many years over 21. Your great-grandfather may have been 'of full age' at the time of his second marriage – in fact he was 64. And remember that occasionally people recorded an incorrect age on a marriage certificate, either in order to appear of full age when they weren't, or to make the bride appear to be the same age as or younger than the groom. You may even find that your great-grandmother knocked several years off her age each time she married, so as always to appear younger than the groom.

✔ **Deceased:** Sometimes on a marriage certificate the father of the bride or groom is recorded as deceased. This is a useful piece of information, because it narrows the margin that you have to search for this person in the death indexes – and perhaps explains why you can't find him on the census (for more about the census, see 'Finding Your New Best Friend: Census Records' later in this chapter). But you need to remember that a person may be deceased even if it doesn't say so on the certificate – the fact that a person was deceased was an additional rather than a compulsory piece of info.

✔ **Inquest:** A death certificate may carry a note stating that an inquest followed this particular death. An inquest happens in cases where an investigation is considered necessary into the circumstances of a death. Inquests are useful for genealogists because they point you to other sources of information: For example, the results of inquests are sometimes printed in the local newspaper, along with details of the case and other info that may be useful in your research.

✔ **Errors:** If a word on a certificate is crossed out or corrected, don't worry. Mistakes were sometimes made as the certificates were written out, and the procedure for putting them right was to draw a line through the mistake and to insert a little number beside it. The number indicates the number of mistakes made by that particular person.

Looking North: Searching Made Quick and Easy in Scotland

Here's some good news: if any of your ancestors came from Scotland, your life is about to become rather easy. A large collection of Scottish records is available online at www.scotlandspeople.gov.uk. This marvellous website holds many of the Scottish BMD indexes (called *statutory registers* in Scotland) and lets you call up images of the original documents on screen (see Figure 5-4). You don't need to wait for copies to arrive in the post as you can access them – for a fee – right away. The following BMD indexes and certificates are available on the site:

✔ Births: 1855–2006

✔ Marriages: 1855–1932

✔ Deaths: 1855–2006

The site also holds a large collection of parish registers, wills and testaments and census materials, and the collections are constantly expanding. The site charges a fee for each record that you look at, but the information that you get is well worth the cost. For more about subscription databases, have a look at Chapter 3.

Lucky Scottish researchers may notice that some Scottish BMD certificates contain a lot of extra useful information, depending on the year of the certificate (see 'What do these records tell me?' earlier in this chapter). For more information about what is contained on Scottish certificates, and for images of sample certificates, have a look at www.scotlandspeople.gov.uk/content/help/index.aspx?r=554&402. You can navigate your way from birth to marriage to death information by clicking the links in the Record Types and Examples box on the left-hand side of the page. Figure 5-5 shows an example of a marriage certificate from 1880.

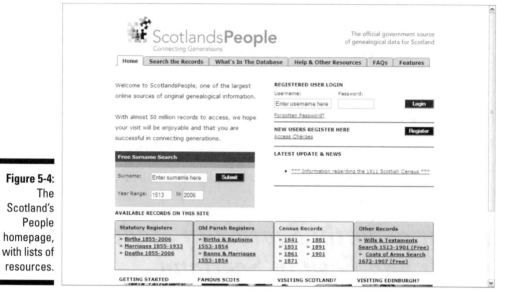

Figure 5-4:
The
Scotland's
People
homepage,
with lists of
resources.

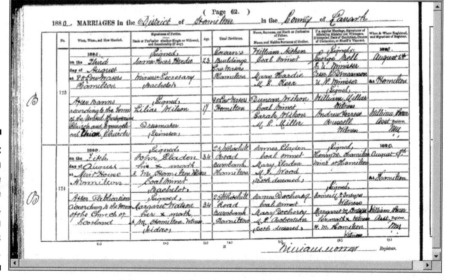

Figure 5-5:
A Scottish
marriage
certificate
from 1880,
taken from
Scotland's
People.

Heading Over to Ireland: A Project for the Future

You may have noticed how quiet we've been about genealogical records in Ireland. We've revelled in the English and Welsh records and sung the praises of Scottish resources – so what can we say about tracing your Irish ancestors? This area of research is a bit more challenging, for two reasons: many of the records (including much of the census material gathered before 1901) have been destroyed, so little of what remains is online. However, the census material is extremely informative (see the nearby sidebar 'The luck of the Irish...genealogist'). To trace your Irish ancestors, check out the following websites, which give info about civil registration:

- **The General Register Office (GRO): www.groireland.ie**

  The GRO contains records for all of Ireland until 1921 and for the Republic of Ireland after 1921. These records aren't available online here, however a pilot scheme offering some online civil registration has been launched at http://pilot.familysearch.org/recordsearch/start.html.

- **The General Register Office of Northern Ireland: www.groni.gov.uk**

  This office contains records relating to Northern Ireland, but the records aren't online.

- **The National Archives of Ireland: www.nationalarchives.ie**

  The Irish national archives website is a good source of general information about genealogical research and resources in Ireland. It also includes a free online search facility for the 1911 Ireland census.

- **Origins Network: www.origins.net**

  This resource is a subscription website, but has lots of records that relate specifically to Ireland, such as Griffith's Valuation Records and passenger lists. The site also contains lots of information about searching in Ireland for ancestors.

Short of visiting the record offices yourself, your best bet if you want to trace your Irish roots is to hire a professional researcher who can examine the relevant records for you and report back on what they find. The National Archives of Ireland website provides a list of professional researchers willing to undertake research in Northern Ireland and the Republic of Ireland. To find them, go to www.nationalarchives.ie/genealogy/service.html. Alternatively, you could undertake a web search for research agencies that have teams based in Ireland. Sticks Research Agency (www.sra-uk.com/ireland) is a good example of one such agency.

The luck of the Irish . . . genealogist

Whatever direction your research is heading, don't let the lack of online resources put you off researching your Irish ancestors. You'll get more information about your ancestors from the Irish censuses than from their English or Scottish equivalents. The 1901 Irish census gives the name of your ancestor, their relationship to the head of household, their religion, their literacy, occupation, age, marital status, the county of their birth and whether they spoke English or Irish. You can even build a picture of your ancestor's domestic situation, because the census records several details about their house, including the number of walls and windows, whether the roof was made of slate or thatch, how many outhouses the property included and the name of the person who owned the property. The 1911 census for Ireland is also available. You find the same sort of information on the Irish 1911 census as on the Irish 1901 census, but with one useful additional feature: married women were asked to declare the number of years they had been married, how many children had been born alive from this marriage and how many children were still alive at the time of the census.

For more about choosing and hiring a professional researcher, check out Chapter 9 of this book.

Piecing It All Together: Using Your Certificates to Build Your Family Tree

Now you know how to search the indexes to find the certificates you want and how to order or view the certificates online. And now you can build your family tree. To do this, you need to piece together the information on the various certificates that you find during the course of your research. You may have gathered generations' worth of genealogical information from interviews with your family (for more about interviewing your family members, have a look at 'Chatting with Dad and Aunty Doris: Interviewing members of your family' in Chapter 1). Alternatively, you may have very little info. But don't worry: you can start your research as close to the present day as you like. In fact, it's always a good idea to check what other members of the family have told you, because people often misremember or get their facts confused over time.

Making a start

Suppose you're beginning your research by finding the marriage certificate of your maternal grandparents, Donald and Ann Elizabeth Hemmings. You may remember them from long-ago family parties, watching you running about on the lawn or helping you tie your shoelaces. Or perhaps you never met them at all and know them merely through photographs or other people's memories. Well, you're about to find out more than anybody else is able to tell you, and here's how to do it.

You need to search the marriage indexes to find a reference for the marriage certificate. You probably have a rough idea of when the marriage took place, or can estimate it from the birth dates of Donald and Ann Elizabeth's children. If the eldest child was born in 1950, for example, the marriage likely took place within a few years prior to 1950. So you can begin your search at 1950 and work back until you strike gold. Remember that in England and Wales in the years after 1911, you can cross-reference one marriage partner with the other in the indexes (see the section 'Using online BMD indexes' earlier in this chapter to discover more about cross-referencing). When you've found what you're looking for, you can order the certificate if the marriage took place in England or Wales, or you can call it up on screen if it was a Scottish ceremony. If your grandparents were married abroad, it may take a little longer to track down the certificate. As with all international genealogical research, you have to track down where and in what form the records are held, and contact the appropriate organisation to see whether you can obtain a copy of the record that you want. Have a look at the Internet Directory in this book for more about locating records overseas.

The certificate: Your stepping stone into the past

So you have the marriage certificate of your grandparents. You may find it difficult to imagine your grandparents as young newly-weds, just starting out in their married life together. But finding characters in your family's past is part of what your research is about. Perhaps you can picture them signing the register, creating the record that you have in front of you, and walking away arm-in-arm. You may now have a burning desire to search through that box of assorted paraphernalia in the loft to try and find a photo of the happy day. For the moment, though, examine the marriage certificate and use it for the next stage of your research.

The certificate is full of interesting info. The occupations of one or both partners, and those of their fathers, give you an idea of the stock from which your grandparents came. You can see whether they were married in a church, and if so under which rites, and where each was living at the time of the union. Most importantly, the certificate gives your grandparents' ages on the day of the wedding, and by doing a bit of simple maths you can work out when each of them was born and begin to search for their birth records.

But is the maths really so simple? Yes – if you bear a couple of simple points in mind. It is easy to slip up and assume that because Donald Hemmings was 25 when he got married in 1950, he must have been born in 1925. Donald *may* have been born in 1925, but also he may have been born in 1924. If the wedding took place in the early part of 1950, Donald may not yet have celebrated his birthday for that year. So look carefully at the date of the ceremony. Also, remember that it was not at all unusual for one or both marriage partners to use a touch of poetic licence when declaring their ages on marriage certificates – ancestors often had 'flexible' ages! For the bride to be older than the groom was often considered bad form, and occasionally a year or two is removed from her age or added to his to avoid this. One or both partners may also have added a few years to their age in order to appear to be 'of full age' – in other words, over 21 and able to marry without parental consent. Others may have tweaked their ages to avoid raised eyebrows or probing questions: we recently came across a case where the bride claimed to be 20 and was in fact only 15.

If you don't find the birth record you're looking for right away, search a few years either side in the indexes. You're then in a position to order the birth certificates of both Donald and Ann.

Building and building: Putting rungs on your ladder

Obtaining grandparents' birth certificates can lead you back to *their* parents' generation, and so on back. Here's how it works. Equipped with birth certificates for Donald and Ann Elizabeth, you have the full names of both parents, including the maiden names of their mothers. You know what to do now: search for the marriage certificates of your great-grandparents, then their birth certificates, and so on. Your workload increases with each generation, as you have four grandparents, eight great-grandparents, 16 great-great-grandparents – we'll stop before this gets ridiculous, but you get the idea. You may find it useful to sketch the family tree in the form of a chart (for more about different types of chart, check out Chapter 2) to help you visualise the generations as you work backwards. But you're now in a position to take your family lines back to the beginning of civil registration. And in the next section we introduce you to another marvellous resource that will help you on your way: the census.

Finding Your New Best Friend: Census Records

Why do genealogists make such a fuss about the census? Did you hear a distant drum-roll and shift in anticipation in your seat as you started to read this section? We try to give you an idea of why genealogists get so excited about the census in this section. But be warned: the excitement is infectious. Soon you'll be enthusing about the census to anyone who'll listen, especially when you find your ancestors hiding amongst its returns. You may even convert your less excitable relatives to take an interest in your research as you show them your findings on the census.

A *census* is a snapshot of the population taken on a single night and recorded household-by-household, institution-by-institution, street-by-street, all over the country. A census records who was in which house, vessel, school, prison, workhouse – anywhere in fact – and with whom. You find family groups together with their lodgers, servants, visitors and neighbours. The information provided on the UK census return has gradually increased with time, but on censuses later than 1851 you find the name of each person who spent the night in each household, their relationship to the head of house (for example, wife, son, mother, servant and so on), marital status (married, single, widowed) and age, occupation, place of birth and whether the person in question had a disability. In Wales, the census tells you whether each person spoke Welsh or English, or both.

The value of these returns is twofold. You get the facts about the family and the circumstances of their lives. The census is first and foremost a mine of information that helps you to further your research. Not only can you find your great-grandmother as a little girl, but you find her brothers and sisters and parents, and their occupations and places of birth. You find your great-grandmother's address, and from the size of the house and household estimate the relative wealth of her family. You see whether she was still living with her parents at the time of the census and whether her father was unemployed.

But you find more to a census return than just this basic information. You may find that your ancestors use pet names, middle names or nicknames to identify themselves on the census. You gain an idea of the community in which they lived and their own interpretations of where, and sometimes when, they were born. In other words, you start to see the identities of your ancestors through their census returns. Suddenly your ancestors are more than just names: your predecessors are people looking back at you.

And the best bit about the census? From 1841 to 1901 all surnames on the census are indexed alphabetically so that you can search them quickly and easily.

Using the census: A practical guide

This section answers a few of your burning questions.

Which census?

First, you need to find out what's available. The UK census is taken every ten years, and returns are available from 1841, 1851, 1861, 1871, 1881, 1891, 1901 and 1911. Earlier census material than 1841 exists, but it isn't so useful to genealogists because it doesn't rely on names: early censuses were largely head counts. Later census material exists (you've probably filled in census returns yourself – they're still taken every ten years), but this is the annoying part for genealogists: the material gathered remains confidential in the UK for 100 years.

Finding the census

The census returns for England and Wales are available on many subscription websites. For example the National Archives website at `www.national archives.gov.uk/census/` contains a full list of available census material and will redirect you to the appropriate subscription website. Simply click the link for the census that you want to look at – for example, 1851 Wales or 1881 England – and you're taken to the appropriate website. If you visit the National Archives in person, you can access the online material for free in their search rooms.

For Scottish censuses, go to `www.scotlandspeople.gov.uk` and click on the census that you want to use.

Searching the census

Continuing with our example from previous sections of this chapter, assume that you've traced your Hemmings ancestors a couple more generations back through birth and marriage certificates. The earliest certificate you have now is the marriage of a certain David Hemmings to a Julia Irons in 1897. You're now burning with curiosity to find David on the census both before and after his marriage. Here's how to do it:

1. **Open your browser and call up `www.ancestry.co.uk`.**

2. **On the left-hand side of the page, scroll down to the UK census collection heading and click View All.**

3. **Scroll down past the search boxes to Search a Specific UK Census by Year and click the census year and country that you want.**

   Begin by finding David and Julia in 1901. You have the option to search in England, Wales, Scotland, the Isle of Man and the Channel Islands. From their marriage certificate you know that they married in Staffordshire, so click the England 1901 option. This takes you to the search page for England in 1901.

4. **Enter the name you're looking for, and other relevant details.**

   To search the 1901 name index, enter **David** in the First Name box and **Hemmings** in the Last Name box (see Figure 5-6). When you click Search, the index produces several options – all the David Hemmings who were living in England at that time.

   You need to narrow down your options. You've discovered from the marriage certificate that David was 24 in 1897, which gives you an approximate birth year of 1873. You can therefore enter **1873** in the Birth Year box, and select +/– 1 in the dropdown list. This gives you a bit of leeway and means you don't have to worry about when *precisely* he was born (working out the month in which the wedding took place and then comparing it with the month in which the census was taken gets a bit complicated). You also see from the certificate that the marriage took place in Staffordshire, so you can enter Staffordshire in the Lived In (Residence) box. It is likely (although not certain) that the couple was still living there in 1901.

5. **Click Search.**

   Now you have a list of options for David Hemmings. The index gives basic but important information about each option: the first name or initials of the person, surname, estimated year of birth (based on the age declared on the census), birthplace, relationship to the head of household and the civil parish and county in which the person spent the night of the census. The information provided in the index varies slightly from census to census, but there is always enough to guide you in your search. In this case, only one likely match arises for your David Hemmings – the first one on the list. All your details match: the index tells you that David was born in 1873 in West Bromwich, Staffordshire, and that he was still living there in 1901. He is also head of household, as you would expect a married man to be in those days.

Figure 5-6:
Entering the search terms for David Hemmings in 1901.

6. **Click the View Record link at the start of the row, and View Original Image on the subsequent page, to view the digitised image of the census return.**

   And there you have it. You can scroll down and across this image using the blue bars at the bottom and right side of the screen. You can also zoom in and out of the image or any part of it using the + and – icons at the top-left corner of the image. Scroll down until you come to David Hemmings. If the entry is correct, David should be living with his wife Julia . . . and he is in Figure 5-7! The couple are living together in West Bromwich, Staffordshire. And you can see other checking points as well. David Hemmings' profession – a canal boatman – matches that on his marriage certificate, and Julia has given her age as 28 – the same age as David, which again matches the information on the marriage certificate. This return is almost certainly the correct one, but best to view the other options too, just in case a coincidence of names or details exists.

7. **Print the image or save it on your computer.**

   Nothing is more frustrating than finding the correct census image only to lose it again because you forgot to take a copy. We recommend that you print out a copy of the return and save the image or transcribe the info it contains on to your computer:

   • **Print the image:** Click the printer icon at the top right of the image. You may want to change the image from portrait to landscape to get a better image on paper: click File at the top left of the screen and then Page Setup, and then change the orientation of the page.

   • **Save the image:** Click the disk icon to the right of the print icon.

   • **Share the image:** Click the envelope icon to the right of the disk icon. This option enables you to send the image to your research partner so that you can gloat about what you've found.

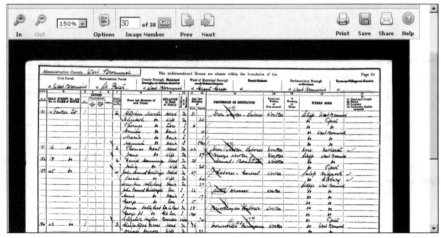

Figure 5-7:
David Hemmings on the 1901 census.

8. **Work back through the censuses to find the younger David Hemmings, first in 1891.**

   You now have the details that will help you correctly identify David Hemmings on earlier census returns. From his marriage certificate, you see that his father was William Hemmings, a labourer at the ironworks. From the 1901 return, you discover that David was born in West Bromwich. Select the 1891 census from the options on Ancestry, and enter the following details:

   - **Name:** David Hemmings
   - **Birth year:** 1873 +/– 1
   - **Residence:** Staffordshire

   This time, David is listed as a lodger in somebody else's house. This detail about his life is interesting, but what you really want is to see him listed with his parents, brothers and sisters. Print out and save a copy of the 1891 return anyway, so that you have the complete set.

9. **Find David Hemmings in 1881.**

   This time you strike gold (see Figure 5-8). David is here, with his father William, his mother Sarah and several siblings, whom you knew nothing about until now. William is still working at the ironworks, which matches the information on David's marriage certificate. David is still a scholar, but his elder brother Thomas is working as a boatman. The family is living in West Bromwich, as you'd expect. Don't forget to make and save a copy of this return.

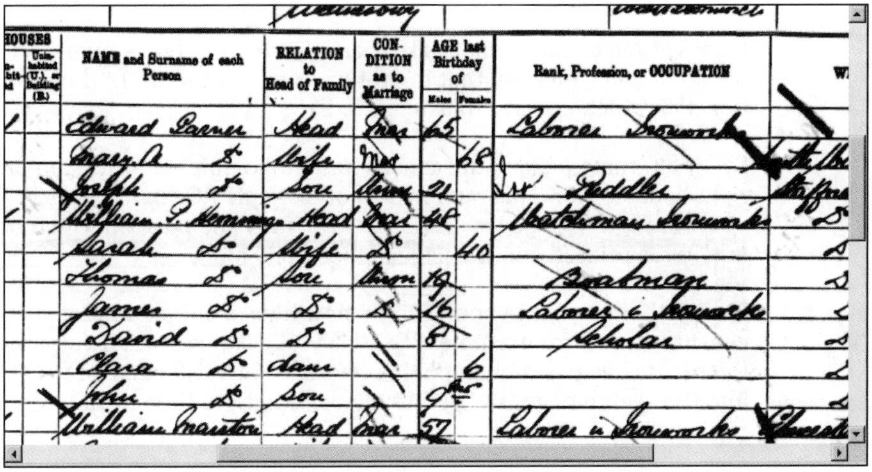

NAME and Surname of each Person	RELATION to Head of Family	CONDITION as to Marriage	AGE last Birthday of Males	AGE last Birthday of Females	Rank, Profession, or OCCUPATION
Edward Parner	Head	Mar	65		Labourer Ironworks
Mary A. Do	Wife	Mar		68	
Joseph Do	Son	Unm	21		Iron Puddler
William P. Hemmings	Head	Mar	48		Watchman Ironworks
Sarah Do	Wife	Do		40	
Thomas Do	Son	Unm	19		Boatman
James Do	Do	Do	16		Labourer in Ironworks
David Do	Do		8		Scholar
Clara Do	daur			6	
John Do	Son		9 mo		
William Marston	Head	Mar	57		Labourer in Ironworks

Figure 5-8: David Hemmings and his parents in 1881.

10. Use the census returns as a launching pad.

You now have masses of information with which to continue your research. You can look for the birth record of not only David but also those of all his siblings. You can hunt for the marriage of William and Sarah, and trace them back on earlier censuses. You can return to 1891 and 1901 and find out what happened to all their children by tracing their families forwards. And you can start to investigate the social context in which your ancestors lived, finding information about iron workers and boatmen, and the town of West Bromwich when David and his parents were living there. Now is the time to let your imagination take off, and to put your research skills to the test.

Each census, and each page of each census, carries its own unique reference number to help you identify it and to help you find it again. These reference numbers are unique to the National Archives, who own the census material. The reference for the census as a whole is printed automatically at the side or bottom of your page as follows:

- ✔ HO 45 indicates the 1911 census.
- ✔ RG 13 indicates the 1901 census.
- ✔ RG 12 indicates the 1891 census.
- ✔ RG 11 indicates the 1881 census.
- ✔ RG 10 indicates the 1871 census.
- ✔ RG 9 indicates the 1861 census.
- ✔ HO 107 indicates the 1851 and 1841 censuses.

Each section of each census also has a further reference number. For example, RG 13/455 tells you that the return comes from the 1901 census, from section 455, which covers a particular area.

Every alternate page of the census has a folio number at the top or on the right-hand corner. This reference – for example RG 13/455 folio 34 – narrows your return to two pages of the 1901 census – the page on which the folio number is printed and the page immediately after.

Finally, there is a page number. You now have a unique reference for your census return – for example, RG 13/455 folio 34, page 22. If you want to call up the record again, simply type this reference and the name of your ancestor into the search page, and you're taken straight to the relevant return.

Losing your census: When you can't find what you're looking for

Searching the census can be an exhilarating experience. Sometimes, the person or family that you're looking for almost leaps out from the indexes and you complete your entire search in minutes. But other times, things don't go quite so smoothly. Some families are more difficult than others to pin down. You may find yourself accusing long-dead ancestors of hiding from you, so frustrated are you at their absence. When searching the censuses, our advice is this: don't give up! Tales abound of suspicious Victorians spending the night of the census on boats on the Thames or in railway carriages to avoid being counted – and of equally scrupulous officials rowing out on the river or patrolling railway stations and demanding details to complete their returns. Chances are, however, that your ancestors are there somewhere: if you're persistent, you're likely to find them. You just have to play detective.

When you search the census, remember that the information on the returns isn't necessarily going to be absolutely accurate. The information has passed through many hands and many stages of administration before you get to see it, and errors have inevitably crept in.

Did your ancestors tell the truth?

Our first word of caution concerns your ancestors themselves. People commonly declared an incorrect name, age or place of birth on the census. If your great-grandmother was born Amelia Jane Short but was known in the family as Emily, then she may appear on the census as Emily (with or without her middle name). Similarly, ages on the census may be approximate. You're likely to find ancestors who have aged rather more or rather less than ten years from one census to another. We came across one man who was apparently 42 on one census and 56 on the next, and a child who wasn't born in 1871 but was listed as 12 years old in 1881. Often such information was given in good faith – or at least without any underhand intentions. Look at it from your ancestors' point of view: What did it matter if your great-great-grandmother tweaked her age so she appeared younger than her husband on the census? Who really minds whether their son Daniel was 14 or 15, so long as he could find a good job? And who can remember exactly how old Great-Great-Great-Aunty Mary was – she couldn't quite remember herself. Take this into account when you consider the accuracy of your census return. Finding information that you think is wrong can be a bit disconcerting, but the crucial question is whether you've found the correct family. Based on the certificates and other information you have, ask yourself whether the members of the household are present and correct as they should be, or whether there's so much wrong info that you may have the wrong census return.

There's another twist in the tale too. Sometimes mistakes were made when our ancestors declared their information, and sometimes a spot of wishful thinking crept in. But at other times our ancestors deliberately lied, usually to hide something that they would rather not admit to. A common case in point concerns illegitimate children. We discovered a family whose several sons and daughters ranged in age from 25 to 15, apart from a little girl of 3, listed as a daughter. This was an interesting find. Why a 12-year gap between the two youngest children? The gap may indicate that several children were born and died before they reached the census. But in this case the parents were both in their 50s – probably beyond childbearing age. Something didn't make sense here. We ordered the birth certificate of the little girl and discovered that she was the illegitimate daughter of one of the other daughters. This situation was considered so shameful at the time that the family attempted to cover it up. We may have been the first to uncover the secret for more than 100 years.

Were details miscopied?

The version of the census return that you call up on your computer screen is not the document compiled on the night of the census. The information taken that night was gathered and copied by civil servants who may have made copying and spelling errors. Sometimes, for example, you see the same information duplicated or you uncover something quite ridiculous, such as a father listed as 20 years old and his son as 22. But don't panic and disbelieve everything you read: By and large, the clerks did a pretty good job and you can enjoy the fruits of their labours.

Compiling the name index

The census name indexes enable you to find in a few minutes what would otherwise take hours, days or even weeks of laborious searching. Be grateful that people have so energetically and successfully undertaken indexing projects and made the results available online. But also remember that human beings compiled the indexes, and human errors have crept in. Sometimes the difficulty comes with the handwriting on the returns. You soon see that the quality and clarity of the writing varies enormously from one section of the census to another. You may have found from your own research that the head of a certain household should be Joseph Biddle, but whoever indexed the census didn't have your research in front of them and had to rely on the handwriting: if the writing was pretty appalling, Joseph Biddle may be indexed as Josiah Puddle, Joseph Bidell or Josiah Diddle.

Improving your census searching

Finding relevant information on the census can be immensely satisfying. But you may also find yourself roaming for hours through the returns without hitting upon the family that you want – very frustrating! Here's a list of tips to save you time and energy, and to stop you from tearing your hair out when your research project begins to heat up.

- **Get acquainted with abbreviations.** Everyone abbreviates: it saves time and effort, and you probably do it every day without realising. The same goes for our ancestors who compiled the census. If you can't find James, William, Elizabeth or Marianne, you may find them as Jas, Wm, Elizth or Mnne. Middle names, if declared at all, may be denoted by a single initial.

  The same is true of place names, especially counties. Yorkshire may be Yorks and Middlesex Mx. If you enter the full word **Yorkshire** as a search term for your ancestor's place of birth, your ancestor who was born in Yorks, Bradford (which may also appear as Bradford, Yorks, on the census) may not appear in your list of options.

  The best way around this problem is to run a Soundex search (which I describe in the next point in this list) or a *wildcard search*: a wildcard search involves entering the first few letters of the name you're looking for, followed by an asterisk (*). Your results will include all the names that begin with this combination of letters. For example, if you enter Eliz*, your results include Eliz, Elizabeth, Eliza, Elizth, Elizah, . . . you get the idea.

- **Sound out the Soundex search.** The Soundex search is one of your most useful tools for searching the census indexes. It allows you a wider margin when you enter your search terms. For example, if you're searching for Joseph Biddle and select the Soundex option on the dropdown menu to the right of the name boxes, your search encompasses names that sound like Joseph Biddle in addition to that exact name. So your list of options includes Joseph Baddeley, Joseph Batley, Joseph Beadle and more. Sometimes a Soundex search gives too many options, but at other times it strikes gold because it allows for spelling errors on the actual return or the indexing process.

- **Understand location, location, location.** 'My ancestor isn't where he should be,' you discover. We know the feeling! People you expect to find in London turn up on the census in Derby. People who were born in Shropshire appear in deepest Lincolnshire. And your great-great-grandfather's place of birth seems to change with every census. So what's going on? And should you worry?

Remember that people did and do move around, from house to house within the same area, or to different counties or even countries. You may find that a shift in location opens up a whole new line of research: *why* did your ancestors move? Were they looking for work? Were they part of mass migration into the towns of the Industrial Revolution? As a rule of thumb, if the members of the household are all as you expected, you have found the right return and you can investigate at your leisure the reasons for their move.

✔ **Be aware of birthplaces.** The final column of a census return can be a mine of information. But you need to understand what you're looking at. Your ancestors supplied the birthplace info from their own point of view, without worrying about boundaries, registration districts and other paraphernalia that you uncover during your research. If your ancestor was born in a village outside Camberwell, he may well appear on different census returns as being born in Camberwell (Surrey), Camberwell (London) and London (Middlesex). People born on or near the county border of, for example, Nottinghamshire and Derbyshire may claim Nottinghamshire as their birthplace in one census return and Derbyshire in the next. Even if you have a birth certificate to 'prove' a person was born in London, it may be that his home and identity were in Essex, and that's what he put on the return.

So exercise a little caution: the Where Born column can be a blessing and work wonders if your ancestor lived in the same village all his life and declared it on every census. But if you hit a brick wall when you enter one thing, try something else – or leave this box out altogether when you search and rely on your other info instead.

✔ **Go easy on the ages.** Remember to give a bit of leeway here. You have the option of filling in a birth year on the search page. This birth year is calculated from the age your ancestor claimed to be on the night of the census and is a useful tool for narrowing down the number of hits you get, but best to allow at least two years on either side. Ages and dates of birth weren't always the exact science that they are today.

✔ **Reduce information overload.** Surprisingly, you may actually have more information at times than you need. You'll probably be more successful in your search if you don't fill the search page with every piece of info you have about your ancestor. A name, approximate year of birth, and perhaps an indication as to where the person was born or living (even if it's just a county) usually suffices. Other details can be added if the name you want is very common – for example, John Smith – to help narrow your search. You can also take away information if your search comes up with no hits at all and you need to spread your search net a little wider. We occasionally find elusive ancestors by entering no surname at all and simply using a first name and approximate date and location of birth. This tactic is especially handy if you're working with an unusual surname that may have been horribly misspelled in the index.

✔ **Broaden your search.** Sometimes you need to do a bit of lateral thinking when the census stumps you. If one of your ancestors isn't turning up, try to find other people who you expect to be in the same household. If baby Johnny was living with his parents and six siblings in 1851, he's likely to be living with at least some of them in 1861. Of course, if someone really isn't there, you can try other avenues of investigation. Has the person died since the last census? Has a girl married and changed from her maiden name? Is a father away with the army or navy or on a merchant vessel in a far-away port? You can use one census return to lead you to another and to narrow the parameters of your next searches in the BMD indexes.

✔ **Remember that not all census indexes were created equal.** Some census indexes can be searched in different ways to others. One of the most useful search features appears in the 1881 England and Wales census, where you can search by address. Say you find out from a birth or marriage certificate that your ancestor was living in a certain street in the year before the census; check whether he was still there before you run a broader search. You'll also find a facility on 1881 to search by occupation. You can use a wildcard search here: for example, if you think your ancestor was a cigar manufacturer, you can enter *cigar**, which covers any variation in his role, from cigar manufacturer to trader, merchant to dealer.

✔ **Be cautious in 1841.** The 1841 census doesn't include the same details as the later censuses. You can find the name of your ancestor, but you won't find marital status or relationships within a household, and the ages of people over 15 are often rounded down to the nearest 5. Nor do you get a detailed indication of the place of birth – merely a letter indicating whether your ancestor was born in the county in which they're currently living, or whether in Scotland, Ireland or foreign parts (or for Scottish returns, whether born in England, Ireland or foreign parts). The 1841 census can still be useful, but you need to adjust your search technique to match the characteristics of the census. For example, search for your ancestor in a wider age range than you would on a later census, to compensate for the rounding of ages. And you need to be careful not to make assumptions: just because Jane Simpson is listed just below Michael Simpson in the census, and is of a similar age, she is not *necessarily* his wife. She may be his wife, but she may equally be his sister. Common abbreviations on 1841 include NK (not known), MS (male servant) and FS (female servant).

✔ **Disregarding the deletions.** The large amounts of information apparently crossed out on your census returns can be puzzling. But enumerators made these ticks, crosses and other marks as a means of counting and rationalising the data. The marks don't mean that the information is incorrect or shouldn't be there. So don't worry if your ancestor's age is crossed out or their place of birth struck through – just ignore the marks and read whatever is underneath.

Looking in the nooks and crannies: Making the most of your census returns

What could be more satisfying than printing off a thick bundle of census returns and showing them with glee to your family and friends, waxing lyrical over great-grandma's 15 children or the fact that Great-Great-Uncle Ken has turned up in Pentonville Prison? But the difficulty starts here. When you show people your finds, they start to ask questions – and suddenly you don't know as much about your documents as you thought you did. Worry not. Here are a few guidelines to help you read, understand and make the most of your census returns:

- ✔ **Dealing with the dittos.** The squiggle that appears all over your returns and looks as though it may read 'do' is a short-hand way of writing 'ditto': in other words, 'the same as is written above'. So the first line of your census return may read:

  John Carpenter, head of household, 36 years old, brewer, born Crewe, Cheshire.

  And the second may read:

  *Alice **do**, wife, 34 years old, no occupation, born **do**, **do**.*

  This indicates that Alice also has the name Carpenter and was born in Crewe, Cheshire.

- ✔ **Reading the writing.** You quickly notice that the quality of the handwriting varies enormously on census returns. Some is so beautiful that it borders on calligraphy, but other writing is barely legible. If you're confronted with words you have trouble reading, don't panic and assume that all's lost. Look over the page slowly and decipher what you can. If you run across a letter or word that you can't read, look for a similar squiggle in a word that you can read to decipher what it is. You can also try enlarging the page or zooming in on a particular section.

  If you're having trouble uncovering a place name, look at another page of the census where the place name may be written again, or refer to a map to see whether it can shed any light. If you can't read an occupation, have a look at what the rest of the family and the neighbours were doing to see whether that gives any clues. Remember that the information may be repeated on birth, marriage and death certificates that are close in date to the census return. And you can always ask other people to help you. What one person finds impossible to read, another recognises instantly.

✔ **Making sure that you have a complete return.** Your family or household may span more than one page in the census. You may congratulate yourself for finding the parents and five children, but child number six is over the page, along with three lodgers, two visitors and a housemaid. If your family reaches the bottom of the page, always click the green Next arrow and look at the following page, just to be on the safe side. Similarly, check that you have a complete address for the family you've found before you close the census return. It is annoying to look over your copies and find that all you can see of the address is ditto, ditto, Cornwall. If you look at the previous pages, you can return to the beginning of a road or section and find the name of the street, parish, town and county.

✔ **Considering the context of your return.** You may be so bowled over with the excitement of finding your ancestor that you completely ignore everyone else on the page. But you can find out a lot from the families that share your ancestors' census return. You can discover something of the context of the return. For example, you can make a guess at how wealthy an area was by the occupations of its residents. Is there unemployment? Does everyone do the same thing, such as mining or dock work, or is there a wide variety? Are all the heads of household in the street shopkeepers, suggesting that the families were living above their shops? How many families have servants, or room for borders, lodgers or visitors? How near is young Emily Skinner living to the man she marries three years later? Can you speculate about how they met? If you just take the time to look over your census thoroughly, the possibilities are almost endless.

✔ **Using the census to guide you to other records.** You already know that the census can narrow the margins for your searches in the birth, marriage and death indexes. If your aged ancestor is on the 1881 but not the 1891 census, then the chances are that they died in the interval and you can run a search in the death indexes accordingly. If your great-great-grandparents appear on the 1871 census with a newly born child, then try looking for their marriage a year or so before this.

You may find that other records to explore are out there. You never know when a census is going to give a detail that opens up a whole new line of research. We had a case of an ancestor who was listed on his marriage certificate simply as an engineer. But on the following census, we found the initials MBW beside his occupation. After a bit of searching on Google, we realised that this stood for Metropolitan Board of Works and that the records of this organisation were held in a local archive. Then we found out precisely what he did, for how long he did it and how much he was paid for doing it.

Going Beyond Civil Registration: Finding Parish Records

After you've traced your family lines back through the BMD indexes and the census, and you've found your great-great-great-grandparents on the 1841census, where can you go from there? Is this the end of the road as far as your research is concerned? What you've done so far is pretty impressive, but the door into your family's past is by no means closing. You now have another valuable set of records open to you: parish records.

Parish records are the written records of baptisms, marriages and burials. Each time one of these ceremonies takes place in any parish in the UK, a record is made and kept. This process first began in England and Wales in 1538, although you have to be extremely lucky to find any ancestors as far back as this. In Scotland, you're considered ambitious to try to find a record earlier than the 18th century. As you would expect, record-keeping improved over time, and the later the record you want to find the greater its chance of survival. Some records were destroyed by fire or flood or simply deteriorated through age, but those that remain are a valuable resource.

Making the link from civil registration to parish records

Before you start searching for your ancestors in parish records, be clear about what you're looking for. For example, if you simply enter the name of your great-great-great-grandfather, William Joyce, into the various databases, you'll be submerged with dozens, if not hundreds, of records that may send you scuttling away in fear. So be more precise and start with what you know.

A good place to start your search into parish records is with your 1851 census returns. Here, William Joyce is head of his household, living with his wife Hannah and eight children of various ages. Here are your clues: you have an age for William – 51 – and therefore an approximate year of birth – 1800. You may be able to calculate an approximate year of marriage, based on the fact that the oldest child still at home in 1851 is 22. And you have a place of birth for every member of the family: the parents and the four eldest children were born in White Notley, Essex. Now you have a much better idea of what to look for.

Searching for families on FamilySearch

FamilySearch is the website of the Church of Jesus Christ of Latter-Day Saints. This website contains an impressive collection of genealogical data, including the *International Genealogical Index*, a vast collection of parish records from all over the world. Here's how to use this great starting point for your search:

1. **Open your web browser and go to www.familysearch.org.**

   This takes you to the website's homepage.

2. **Select Search Records in the box at the top of the page.**

   A dropdown list appears.

3. **Click Advanced Search.**

   You now see a list of options on the left side of the page.

4. **Click International Genealogical Index, and the search page appears.**

   Now fill in the details of your ancestor. You don't need to complete every box, but you must fill in the name of your ancestor, the event you're looking for (birth/christening, marriage, death/burial, other or all) and a region (British Isles, and then a country or island and a county within the British Isles if you want). Narrow your search by giving a year or year range, or, in the case of a baptism, the names of one or both parents or the name of the spouse for a marriage.

   In this case, you fill in the details of William Joyce's marriage: his name, the first name of his wife (Hannah), the event (marriage), the year range (1825 plus or minus 10), the region (British Isles), the country (England) and the county (Essex).

5. **Select Search at the bottom of the page.**

   You can now view the records that match your search terms. In this case, there is only one match because your details were quite specific. The result shows a William Joyce who was married on 20 July 1824 in White Notley, Essex. This looks good. Click the name to view further details, and you discover that his wife was Hannah Wakefield. Bingo!

6. **Continue the search: Look for the baptism records of William and Hannah.**

   This part is exciting. You're not sure at this stage how far you'll be able to work the lines back. Return to a fresh search page and enter William's details: his name, his birth/christening year range (1800 plus or minus five years) and British Isles, England, Essex.

   Four results for the search come up, but one stands out. The third option is a William Joyce, christened on the 8 February 1801 in White Notley. Click on the name and you discover that his parents were Samuel Joyce and Hannah. And so you have another generation to add to your family tree. A similar process for Hannah Wakefield reveals that she was christened on the 14 June 1801, again at White Notley. Her parents were James Wakefield and Sarah.

7. **Now look for the marriages and baptisms of *their* parents . . .**

   . . . and so on. You can also search for brothers and sisters of William, who (obviously) share the same parental details.

You may be lucky enough to find that a family tree has already been compiled for one or both lines of the family. Look out for the Pedigree icon on the right side of the results page and follow the links to view other members of the family. (For more about FamilySearch and the Pedigree link, see Chapter 3.)

The FamilySearch site only contains a limited number of parish records and isn't yet complete. If you aren't lucky enough to get a correct match on FamilySearch, you'll need to visit your local family history centre or local record office in person. Do check back on FamilySearch from time to time, though. As with all sites, information is constantly being updated.

Avoiding jumping to conclusions

We wouldn't be doing our job if we didn't point out the dangers and pitfalls of tracing your ancestors through parish records. We want to stop you falling into traps, jumping to wrong conclusions or entering into your family tree people who have no connection with you at all.

The problem genealogists find with parish records is that they don't bind the generations together in the same way as civil registration does. After 1837, you can find the birth certificate of a child with the names of both parents provided, and you can check you have the correct marriage for that child by checking the father's name on the marriage certificate against that on the birth certificate. And in case you have any doubts, census records can fill in the gaps, and confirm family relations. But this isn't the case with parish records. Although the information given in parish records varies slightly with time and geography, you may well come across the following kinds of entry:

> *Baptism of Thomas Jones in Whitchurch, Glamorgan, Wales, on 4th December 1798, son of Owen Jones and Elizabeth.*

And:

> *Marriage of Thomas Jones in Whitchurch, Glamorgan, Wales, on 31 May 1820, to Emily Davies.*

On the face of it, this looks like the same person. How perfectly possible that Thomas Jones who was born in 1798 should marry in the same place in 1820. But these records are missing crucial pieces of evidence. The marriage record doesn't give an age for either party. More critically, it doesn't give us Thomas's father's name. There may be ten other Thomas Joneses marrying in Glamorgan in the same period, and you cannot tell the difference between them through parish records alone. The same problem occurs when you look for the marriage of Owen and Elizabeth. You may find several records of an Owen Jones marrying an Elizabeth, but because you have no maiden name for your particular Elizabeth on Thomas's baptism record, you have no way of telling which is correct.

Rather than throw up your hands in horror and think about taking up an easier hobby, you just have to be a bit careful. Obviously, the more unusual the name you're searching for, the more confident you can feel that the record you've found is correct. Occasionally, you just have to decide on the balance of probabilities or the fact that there are no options other than the one you've found. You may find witnesses to a marriage who can help to pinpoint a certain family. And sometimes you can find other records that can help you to verify who is related to whom – for example, grave inscriptions, wills and Poor Law records (more on these in Chapters 6 and 7).

Many genealogists have entries at the top of their family trees that contain question marks or queries or several options for their ancestor's identity. Using such queries is a perfectly acceptable way of concluding a line of research. You don't want to pretend that you've taken your family back to 1653 when, in fact, you have gone off the genealogical rails at 1771 and since then have been researching someone else's family. There is certainly a sense of achievement in tracing your family lines back further than any of your friends, but this isn't what genealogy is about – and doing it wrong is certainly not what you or anyone else wants.

Perusing parish records online

Not all parish records are available online, although more are appearing all the time. Parish records online are what some term a hit-or-miss service: if you find who you're looking for, then great. If not, it doesn't mean that your ancestor didn't exist or that no record of them survives. It simply means that you may have to part company with your computer for a day and go to a local records office to look at the relevant parish registers. In fact, getting hold of a copy of the entry that interests you from the original register is always a good idea, because sometimes more information is given in the actual record than in an online transcription. For more about working offline and researching parish records locally, check out Chapter 7.

Before you rush off to the archives, make sure that you have exhausted the online collections; more and more parish records are appearing online all the time. Your ancestor may be hiding in a quiet corner of a database, and running a thorough search is worthwhile. You may like to explore the following resources:

✔ **Boyd's London Burial Index:** `www.originsnetwork.com/help/popup-aboutbo-blb.htm`.

This *subscription database* (you pay to subscribe) contains an index of nearly a quarter of a million entries, largely of adult males, buried in London between 1538 and 1872. You can expect to find a name, year (and occasionally age) of death and the name of the burial ground in which your ancestor was laid to rest.

✔ **Boyd's Marriage Index:** `www.originsnetwork.com/help/popup-aboutbo-bmi.htm`.

This subscription database lists over seven million names from 1538 to 1840. Every English county is covered to some degree. The information is taken from parish registers, Bishops' Transcripts and marriage licences, and can be a handy shortcut if you're searching for ancestors who married in London.

✔ **Family Relatives:** `www.familyrelatives.com`.

This subscription website is currently in the process of adding more and more parish records, county by county. Family Relatives is a good place to start when looking for marriage registers.

✔ **Federation of Family History Societies:** `www.ffhs.org.uk`.

This site includes a 'Pay to view' search for parish registers (mostly for England and Wales), and other information not available anywhere else on the web.

✔ **London records:** `www.parishregister.com`.

This growing collection of data taken from London parish registers focuses on people living and working around the docks. It can be a useful shortcut if you're searching for ancestors in the heavily populated parishes of the London docklands.

✔ **Pallot's Marriage Index:** `www.ancestry.co.uk/search/db.aspx?dbid=5967`.

This collection contains over 1.5 million marriage records from over 2,500 parishes, most of them in London or Middlesex – although some are from as far afield as Wales – between 1780 and 1837. The index is a useful shortcut when searching the vast and numerous London parishes.

✔ **Parish and Probate records:** `www.ancestry.co.uk/search/rectype/vital/epr/main.aspx`.

This collection of over 15 million names covers parishes in England, Wales, Scotland and Ireland from the 1500s to the 1800s. You may find the records of your ancestor's baptism, marriage or burial, a gravestone inscription, will, obituary and other miscellaneous documents.

✔ **Scotland's People:** `www.scotlandspeople.gov.uk`.

This site contains births and baptisms of Scottish people between 1553 and 1854, and banns and marriages between 1553 and 1854. Although the digital images of these records aren't available on the site, a project is under way to install them.

You can also find collections of parish records of specific areas by searching on Google or another search engine, by entering **parish records** and the name of the county in which you're interested. Another way to find collections is by visiting the Genuki website at www.genuki.org.uk, selecting the link for the UK and Ireland at the top-left corner of the screen, then selecting the links to the locality that you're interested in to see what resources are available for that place. Don't forget to check out existing pedigrees and one-name study sites – the information contained on these sites may save you a lot of hunting (for more on these, see Chapter 3).

Also try checking with your local family history society, as they may be involved in digitisation projects for specific counties. Many family history societies have transcribed parish registers. Volunteers have indexed these transcriptions and you can usually purchase them on CD from the society. For example, Gloucestershire Family History Society has indexed baptisms from 1813 to 1837, marriages from 1800 to 1837 and burials from 1813 to 1851, and has made them available on CD. The society has also transcribed 18th century parish registers and compiled name indexes. Many family history societies have similar resources for sale for you to use on your own computer. To search for a family history society publication, either use an Internet search engine, such as Google, or go through the Federation of Family History Societies' homepage at www.ffhs.org.uk.

Refining your search of parish registers

To help you, here are five more tips for searching the parish registers online:

- ✔ **Spelling:** Don't be put off if the spelling you find in the parish register isn't quite what you were expecting. The further back in time you go, the more flexible spelling becomes. Harrington may be interchanged willy-nilly with Herrington; Forster may become Foster; Glyde may become Glide or Glade, and so on. Try and think phonetically and you'll get the idea.

- ✔ **Parish:** If the bride and groom came from different parishes, the custom was for the couple to marry in the bride's parish. This wasn't always the case, but as a rule of thumb, search for the baptism of the bride in the parish in which she married. If you can't find the baptism of the groom in that parish, you may well find him in a neighbouring parish.

- ✔ **Birth and baptism:** When a child was born, he or she may not have been baptised immediately. There may have been an interval of several weeks, months or even years. Some parish records tell you the date of birth as well as the date of baptism, and others may indicate that a baptism was that of an older child or young adult rather than an infant. But be careful of calculating your ancestor's age from his or her baptism record: at the very least, allow a margin of at least two or three years between birth and baptism.

Baptising siblings at the same time was quite common at one time, and these occurrences don't relate necessarily to twins or multiple births. Perhaps the family had recently moved into the area or hadn't arranged the baptism of an older child before the birth of a subsequent child.

- **Extra info:** The details supplied on parish records vary enormously. If you're particularly lucky, a baptism record may give the maiden name of the mother, the occupation of the father and even the address of the family. A marriage record may specify whether the bride and groom were of the parish in which they married, and a death register may give an age. Don't be put off if the entry carries no details, though. It may still be a record worth having and help you to further your research.

- **Double identity:** You may be surprised to find more than one child of the same name in a family. More often than not, this is an indication that a child has died. The first son and daughter of a family were frequently named after the parents or given other significant family names. If such a child died, the name was often passed on to a later child in order to keep it in the family. If you come across children who appear to share a name, you may be able to clear up the mystery by searching the burial indexes between their two births.

Chapter 6

Digging Deeper into Your Family's Past

*Y*ou'll find that the longer you spend researching your family history, the more interest the other members of your family take in your investigations, the more paperwork you have to find a home for and the more intrigued you become about every new piece of information you find. Genealogy is a rewarding business, but you'll likely hit a time when you begin to wonder how much more you can actually discover. You start to worry that you'll reach dead-ends or find your ancestors disappearing irretrievably into the mists of time. But your research project isn't over.

Genealogy isn't just about finding names and dates and using them to draw comprehensive family trees. After you've exhausted the possibilities of civil records, parish records and the census (all of which we talk about in Chapter 5), your research project hasn't so much reached a full stop as a new beginning. You now have a skeleton, but you need to put meat on the bones. Now is the time to consider *who* your ancestors were: what were their lives like? What did they do for a living? What times did they live through? What events did they witness? Your research becomes a brand-new adventure – and this chapter helps you through it.

You may have learned from the census or a birth, marriage or death certificate that your great-great-uncle was a soldier in the Royal Fusiliers, that your great-great-great-grandfather was born in Germany or that your paternal great-great-great-great-grandparents lived in a mansion in Mayfair with a butler and fifteen servants. This sort of info gives your ancestors a bit of character, but you can still find out more. Census and civil registration documents act as a springboard for further research and can be full of untapped potential.

Not all the resources you need for the next stage of your research are available online, however. Collections of records and indexes to them are being added all the time, but try to be realistic when you embark upon this stage of your research. In this chapter, we look at a number of resources that are online, and in Chapter 7 we discuss offline resources and how to find them. We suggest you use the two chapters in conjunction.

Weighing Up Wills

Wills are a particularly valuable source of information for genealogists. Not only does a will confirm when your ancestor died and where he or she was living at the time of death, but it also lists the beneficiaries, including perhaps the names, professions and domestic and marital situations of spouses, children, grandchildren, more distant relatives and friends. Wills therefore are a means of binding together families and generations, which is particularly useful if all the names and dates that you possess have come from parish records (for more about the difficulties of deciding who's who on the basis of parish records, see Chapter 5). You may discover from a will whether a spouse was still alive when your ancestor died, whom the children married and who was favoured or disowned in the family. You may even find out whether your family was wealthy enough to have servants – and who they were.

A will is more than just a list of names and dates. You can unearth a great deal of information about your ancestor's situation in life from the goods and chattels that he or she left behind. You can tell whether your relative owned land, houses or plate, had servants or simply left a small sum of money to the heirs. Was there enough to go round the whole family, or were married daughters or second sons, for example, ignored? And you may learn something from the *kinds* of good that were considered important enough to be disposed of in a will. A successful cabinetmaker might bequeath the tools of his trade; a husband might leave a bed and bed linen to his widow. You will always find something to surprise and interest you, and to illustrate your ancestor's view of the world.

Unfortunately, the further back in time you go, the less likely it is that your ancestor left a will. To make a will, you need something worth leaving – land, property or whatever. Labourers and craftsmen rarely fell into this category, so don't be disappointed if you find nothing to help you here.

To find out whether your ancestor left a will, take a look at the following online resources available to you:

- **British Origins (www.britishorigins.com):** Here you can find indexes to a range of wills and (for a fee) you're able to order copies of the originals. The collection includes:
  - Archdeaconry Court of London Wills Index 1700–1807
  - Bank of England Will Extracts Index 1717–1845
  - Prerogative Court of Canterbury Wills Index 1750–1800
  - York Medieval Probate Index 1267–1500
  - York Peculiars Probate Index 1383–1883

  The indexes on the British Origins site contain over 300,000 names, and explanations of the various types of records are available by clicking on the links. You must be a member of British Origins to use this service. For more about subscription websites, have a look at Chapter 3.

  When you start looking at old wills, you may find the text difficult to read. But learning to read old handwriting is an exciting adventure – a bit like learning to decipher a secret code. To help you on your way, the National Archives has an online *palaeography* (study of old handwriting) tutorial at www.nationalarchives.gov.uk/palaeography/.

- **Death Duty Registers 1796–1811 (www.nationalarchives.gov.uk/ documentsonline/death-duty.asp):** This collection contains over 66,000 names, with details of wills concerning estates subject to death duty. It doesn't include cases dealt with by the Prerogative Court of Canterbury. You can search the registers by name, occupation, place, other keyword and date range. Searching's free, but you pay £3.50 for each document you view.

- **Irish Origins (www.irishorigins.com):** This index contains all surviving wills held at the National Archives of Ireland. The indexes contain the name and address of the person who left the will, often along with the person's occupation and the place where the will was proved. You must be a member of Irish Origins to use this service.

- **The National Archives (www.nationalarchives.gov.uk/documents online/wills.asp):** This site lists wills proved in the Prerogative Court of Canterbury (PCC, the most senior church court) between 1384 and 1858. These wills tend to relate to wealthier people. Because the court was based in London and associated with Canterbury, the wills proved there relate largely to people living in southern England and in Wales. You can search the indexes to PCC wills by name, occupation, place, keyword and date range. If you find a will you want to look at, click See details and then Add to shopping. After you've finished searching, select

Shopping basket and then Checkout to download the digitised image of the will. Searching the indexes is free, but you pay £3.50 for each document you download.

✔ **Scottish Wills and Testaments** (`www.scotlandspeople.gov.uk/ content/help/index.aspx?r=554&407`): You can search the indexes to this collection of over 600,000 wills and testaments from 1513 to 1901 free of charge, but to view an image of a will you pay £5.

✔ **Inheritance Disputes Index 1574–1714** (`www.britishorigins.com`): This lists over 26,000 cases where inheritance disputes were brought before the Chancery Court of England. Such cases tend to involve two or more members of the same family and therefore may be rich in genealogical detail.

You can find local collections of wills by searching on Cyndi's List (`www.cyndis list.com/wills.htm`), searching by location at Genuki (`www.genuki.org. uk/big`) and searching using the term **wills** and the location that interests you on a search engine, such as Google (`www.google.co.uk`).

Don't be put off if you don't find everyone you were expecting in the text of a will. Sometimes, provision was made separately for a wife, or property settled upon a son at the time of his marriage, meaning that these key individuals may not appear as beneficiaries of a will. On the other hand, you may find references to relatives that you had no idea existed before.

For more about searching offline for wills, have a look at Chapter 7.

Marching to a Different Drummer: Searching for Military Records

Chances are that one or more of your ancestors fought for king and country at some time or other, either as a career or in a time of particular need. The good news is that a large collection of military records survives, and quite a number of them are available online. This section looks at what's on offer.

Records of the two world wars

Head to the following websites to find information about your ancestor's involvement in the First or Second World War:

✔ **Commonwealth War Graves Commission** (`www.cwgc.org`): This organisation remembers, records and erects monuments to the memory of the men and women of the British Commonwealth who died as a result of the two world wars. The website includes a searchable database of 1.7

million names, which include over 60,000 civilians who died in air raids during the Second World War. In order to include those who died of their wounds after the declaration of peace, the database stretches to 1921 for the First World War and to 1947 for the Second World War.

Searching the database is straightforward (see Figure 6-1). You enter as much or as little as you know about your ancestor, including the surname and initial, whether he or she was involved in the First or Second World War, a year range for his or her death, the armed force to which he or she belonged (or whether they were a civilian) and his or her nationality.

Only give the initial of your ancestor's first name, because many of the entries contain only initials and surnames. So if you enter **Charles Shirley**, your results won't necessarily include the C Shirleys on the database.

After you've submitted your information, you get a list of matches, including all the info known about each person, such as name, rank, service number, date of death, age, regiment, nationality, the cemetery where he or she is buried or the memorial that carries his or her name. You may find that your ancestor's age is listed as 'Unknown', which indicates that the form sent to his last address by the military was never completed and returned.

This website offers a new facility that enables you to order a photograph of your ancestor's grave – very useful, especially for researchers who cannot or don't wish to travel abroad.

Clicking the links for the name you want may show more info about the memorial or cemetery, including its location, history and when and how to visit.

Figure 6-1:
Searching
the Com-
monwealth
War Graves
Commission
database.

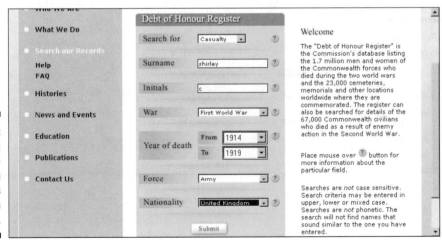

✔ **First World War Service Records and Medal Rolls Index Cards (www. ancestry.co.uk):** This website has a large collection of First World War service records and medal indexes (see Figure 6-2) which, until recently, have only been available on microfilm at the National Archives. Only 30 per cent of service records have survived to the present day, but the index is fully searchable by name and the website provides full images of all the records that do survive.

Service records are an excellent genealogical resource, containing full details about your serving ancestor, a physical description, information about where he served and any other relevant information. The detail does vary from soldier to soldier. The site is also in the process of making the service records available for those soldiers who were wounded during the war and discharged to pension.

Knowing your ancestor's service number comes in handy when searching for military records. To uncover this number, check around the rim of your ancestor's war medals, if you have them. If your relative was a casualty of the war, the Commonwealth War Graves Commission usually include the service number as part of the record, which is extremely useful when researching military service records.

Figure 6-2: Medal index search results for Robert Newbery on the Ancestry website.

✔ **First World War Diaries (`www.nationalarchives.gov.uk/ documentsonline/war-diaries.asp`):** If you've established that your ancestor fought with a certain regiment during the First World War, a war diary may give you an idea of what your ancestor's regiment was doing at the time. These war diaries rarely mention soldiers by name but are a rich source of information and illustrate your ancestor's experiences. The war diaries are for army rather than navy personnel.

✔ **WWI Campaign Medals Index (`www.nationalarchives.gov.uk/ documentsonline/medals.asp`):** If one of your ancestors fought in the First World War, he probably received a campaign medal. These medals were awarded to everyone who took part in a specific campaign, regardless of whether they displayed a particular act of heroism, provided they matched certain basic criteria. The entitlement of an individual to receive a medal was recorded on a card. You can search these cards in the Campaign Medals Index free of charge, but you pay £2.00 to download an image of the card.

You can search for your ancestor by name, corps or keyword (for example, rank or regiment number). Don't worry about completing the date range boxes, because all the documents fall into the 1914–1920 bracket.

1. Select the Search option, and you see a list of candidates matching your particular criteria.

2. If you're interested in a particular entry, click the See Details link on the right-hand side.

3. To download the image, click the Add to Shopping link. You can then return to your search results to peruse the other options and add more images to your shopping basket or click Checkout.

4. When you've finished searching and selected Checkout, you register your method of payment and then see the image.

✔ **World War II Merchant Seamen's Medals (`www.nationalarchives. gov.uk/documentsonline/seamens-medals.asp`):** This site is dedicated to merchant seamen who claimed and were issued medals for their services during the Second World War. You can search the index by name, date range and keyword (see Figure 6-3). Searching is free of charge, but you pay £3.50 for each image you download.

Awards and gallantry records

These websites have information about military honours.

- **London, Edinburgh and Belfast Gazettes (`www.gazettes-online. co.uk`):** Here you can search the online archive for editions of the Gazettes published during the 20th century. They cover the two world wars and lots more. If your ancestor received a military honour or promotion, you'll likely find him or her in the Gazettes or their supplements. You can search by name, date range and medals received. Searching and printing your own copies from the Gazettes is free.

- **Victoria Cross Registers (`www.nationalarchives.gov.uk/ documentsonline/victoriacross.asp`):** If your ancestor did something particularly heroic, you may find him in the Victoria Cross Registers. The Victoria Cross was instigated in 1856 for acts of exceptional valour in the face of the enemy. You can search the indexes by name, regiment, locale, keywords and date range. Searching's free, but you pay £3.50 to download an image from the register.

Army and militia records

Check out the following websites for army and militia information:

- **Asplin Military History Resources (`www.britishmedals.us/kevin/ intro.html`):** This site contains searchable collections of a number of military resources from the Victorian period, including a database of

40,000 soldiers who fought in the Boer War (1899–1902), casualty rolls from the Crimean War (1854–56) and profiles of soldiers and regiments. If your ancestor was in the armed forces during the Victorian era, this website is definitely worth a look.

✔ **Irish Militia Attestations Index 1872–1915 (www.irishorigins.com):** This index covers the attestation papers (produced when men were recruited into the militia) of more than 12,000 men of the Royal Garrison Artillery in Ireland. These papers list lots of useful genealogical info, including the full name, age, place of birth, residence at the time of attestation, occupation, marital status, number of children, next of kin, physical description and a record of military service (including information about the number of years to serve, service abroad, whether wounded, medals received and whether the individual was entitled to a pension). You need to subscribe to the Irish Origins website to search these records, and you can order copies of the Irish Militia Attestation Papers online at a cost of £10.

✔ **Militia Attestations Index 1886–1910 (www.britishorigins.com):** This constantly expanding index covers attestation documents for the Essex, Middlesex and Suffolk Regiments and the Suffolk Royal Garrison Artillery. The genealogical info in these records is the same as that for the Irish Militia Attestations Index described above. The original documents are held at the National Archives, but if you subscribe to the British Origins website you can order copies online at a cost of £10.

✔ **Service records of the Women's Army Auxiliary Corps (www.national archives.gov.uk/documentsonline/waac.asp):** The Women's Army Auxiliary Corps was established in 1917, and in 1918 the name was changed to Queen Mary's Army Auxiliary Corps. This series of digitised records runs from 1917 to 1920. You can search the indexes by name, place of birth and date range. The quality of the records varies, but information such as name, age, address, nationality, marital status, physical description, joining references and service record are likely to appear. As usual, searching's free, but downloading an image costs £3.50.

Maritime records

This section covers Royal Navy and Merchant Navy records. Historically, many people moved between the two navies, so you should always check both sets of records. If you think your ancestor was in one of the navies, check out the following websites:

✔ **The National Archives (www.nationalarchives.gov.uk/documents online):** The National Archives has a very large collection of maritime records available in the Documents Online section of its website. You can either search each individual record for your ancestor or perform a search of all the available online records. The Documents Online homepage has a search engine on the left side of the page that enables you to define your search criteria.

A few of the most popular maritime records available on this website are:

- **Merchant Seamen's Second World War Medals:** These records are of Second World War medals claimed and issued to more than 100,000 merchant seamen from 1946 to 2002.

- **Royal Naval Division (1914–19):** The Royal Naval Division were formed of reserve personnel from the Royal Naval Reserve, Royal Fleet Reserve and the Royal Naval Volunteer Reserve, and a brigade of Royal Marines, Royal Navy and army personnel were brought together at Crystal Palace to form the Royal Naval Division in September 1914. If you know your ancestor served at sea, but you can't find him in the main series of navy records, checking these records for information about him and his sea service would be a good idea.

- **Royal Naval Officers:** Here you can search for the service records of officers who served in the Royal Navy. The Admiralty kept these records from the 1840s onwards, and they record the service of warrant officers who joined the Royal Navy up to 1931 and commissioned officers who joined the service up to 1917. A full record usually provides you with lots of detailed genealogical information as well as details about your ancestor's time as an officer, such as enlistment dates, ships he served on and next of kin.

- **Royal Naval Seamen's Records:** Here you can search for ancestors who joined the Royal Navy between 1873 and 1923. The database contains more than half a million individuals, which you search by name, place, keyword and date range. These records list year of birth (and sometimes the day and month as well), place of birth, the ship or ships on which each seaman served and the length of time each seaman remained in the navy. The records also state those seamen who didn't complete their engagements, with reasons. For the years after 1892, you get even more information, including your ancestor's occupation, any badges he acquired, a description of his character and ability, a physical description and a note of any wounds he received.

- **Royal Naval Volunteer Reserve:** Here you can search for First World War service records belonging to those who served in the Royal Naval Volunteer Reserve and joined up between 1903 and 1919. The Royal Naval Volunteer Reserve records typically contain name, rank, details of appointments, honours and awards, dates of promotion, the officer's address and the address of their next of kin.

- **Trafalgar Ancestors:** This database is dedicated to the people who fought on Nelson's side at the Battle of Trafalgar in 1805. The site draws names and information from a variety of sources, including ships' musters, certificates of service, Greenwich Hospital *in-pensioners* records (pensioners resident at the hospital), *passing certificates* (certificates obtained (after examination) by junior officers who wished to obtain a commission) and *survey returns* (the Admiralty's forms deciding who to put in which job). The site also offers loads of background info about Nelson, the Royal Navy and the Battle of Trafalgar.

The National Archives are always adding more and more records to their online collection, so regularly checking availability is always worthwhile. You don't have to subscribe to the site, but you do need to pay a small fee (usually around £2–£3.50) to download each record that you wish to see.

✔ **The National Maritime Museum (www.nmm.ac.uk):** The NMM contains a wealth of information relating to maritime history and is in the process of digitising some of its collections. Online, you can find access to the museum's Maritime Memorials – a database dedicated to those who died at sea – as well as a comprehensive list of research guides, links to other websites and online galleries and museums about their collections.

✔ **Welsh Master Mariners, Mates and Engineers (www.welshmariners.org.uk/index.php):** This database contains an index of over 21,000 Welsh merchant seamen who served between 1800 and 1945. You can search by name, place of birth, year of birth, competency or service certificate number, county of birth and other details.

Uncovering the life and times of your military ancestor

If you find one of your ancestors in these records and discover when and where he or she served, you can start searching for background material to paint a picture of your ancestor's military life. The sites described in the preceding lists offer a substantial collection of background material, but you may also want to try the following:

✔ **First World War.com:** www.firstworldwar.com/battles/index.htm

✔ **Maritime History:** www.mightyseas.co.uk

✔ **Naval-History.net:** www.naval-history.net

✔ **BBC Family History – First World War:** www.bbc.co.uk/rememberance

✔ **BBC Family History – Second World War:** www.bbc.co.uk/ww2peopleswar

Investigating Immigration Records

Perhaps you've discovered from a census return that one of your ancestors was born outside the UK. Or maybe you've come across a name in your family tree that's obviously foreign. In this section, we show you how to find out more about how your ancestor came to be here, when and from where.

Immigration is the process of people (immigrants) coming into a country (in our case, into the UK). *Emigration* is the process of people (emigrants) leaving the UK to go to another country. In this book we are primarily concerned with immigration, although many records, especially passenger lists, contain information about both types of movement. If you have an ancestor who emigrated from the UK to another country, you can search for them on passenger lists and the various other resources listed below. But if you want to find out about their lives and family within their new country, you need to look for records within that particular country. For more on research and archives abroad, check out the Internet Directory in this book, or have a look at Genuki (www. genuki.org.uk) or Cyndi's List (www.cyndislist.com) for the area that interests you.

Britain is a society of immigrants. Your job is to find a record relating specifically to your ancestor and to work out whether he or she fitted in to the wider patterns of movement and immigration. If your info comes from census returns, you may be in luck. If the 'Where born' column on one census contains only the information that your ancestor was born in Germany, another return may pin him down more precisely. If you've found your ancestor on the 1871 but not on the 1861 census, your ancestor likely moved to Britain between those dates. You may be able to estimate the year of your ancestor's arrival by looking at where the children of a family were born: if Peter, aged 8, was born in Berlin, but his sister Ella, aged 6, was born in London, you've narrowed the move to within two years.

Various online resources are available for tracing the movement of your ancestors. For best results, use these websites in conjunction with the offline resources that we discuss in Chapter 7. Have a look at the following:

- ✔ **Ellis Island (www.ellisisland.org):** The Ellis Island website contains a searchable database for all those who entered the USA via Ellis Island from 1892 to 1925. It's free and easy to use and will give you details of your ancestor's entry to the US. The database contains some very famous names: try searching for Walter Elias Disney or Archibald Leach, just for fun.

- ✔ **Find My Past (www.findmypast.com):** Through this website you can access the National Archives' collection of passenger lists, which comprise outgoing passenger lists from 1890 to 1960 and incoming passenger lists from 1851 to 1903. You can search these lists by name, but because the lists are so large, having some idea of where your ancestor sailed from and an approximate date of departure or return is always helpful.

- **Moving Here (www.movinghere.org.uk):** This site's devoted to Caribbean, Irish, Jewish and South Asian migrants to England over the past 200 years. You can search the site by keyword (for example, your ancestor's name or a place name). The site also gives lots of background info, with links to useful websites and personal testimonies.

- **Ships and Passenger Lists (www.cyndislist.com/ships.htm):** A list of links to online resources relating to immigration and emigration to and from Britain and many parts of the world. The categories include famous and historical ships, general resources, research guides, mailing lists, professional researchers and more.

- **TheShipsList (www.theshipslist.com):** A useful resource, particularly for tracing your emigrant ancestors, this site provides passenger lists, lists of marriages at sea, information about famine emigrants, shipwrecks and a wealth of useful background information. The focus is on those heading for Australia, Canada and the United States.

Regardless of whether you track down the exact year in which your ancestor arrived or the vessel upon which he or she came to Britain, a whole new area of research opens to you. Why did your ancestor come here? Was he a merchant looking for new opportunities? Was he fleeing political or religious persecution? Was your ancestor driven by greed, hunger or the spice of adventure? Did he intend to settle here? How many people from your family came to Britain? How well did your ancestor integrate with their new community?

You can research these questions almost infinitely, but a bit of background about the migration patterns of the time may help you on your way. Here are a couple of websites to get you started:

- **A History of Immigration to Britain:** www.sovereignty.org.uk/ features/articles/immig.html

- **The National Archives Research Guides:** www.nationalarchives. gov.uk/catalogue

Don't forget to contact other researchers who are in the same boat as you. Cyndi's List (www.cyndislist.com) contains a large number of mailing lists but just to whet your appetite here are a few websites that may provide useful information about your immigrant ancestors:

- **Anglo-German Family History Society:** www.art-science.com/agfhs

- **Anglo-Italian Family History Society:** www.anglo-italianfhs.org.uk

- **Huguenot Society of Great Britain and Ireland:** www.huguenot society.org.uk/family

Coming to Terms with Criminal Records

At first glance, you may not be too thrilled to find that one of your ancestors ended up on the wrong side of the law. If you feel strongly about this, that's fine – you've no obligation to investigate further than you want to. But criminal records are extremely useful for your genealogical research. A criminal ancestor, just like a military ancestor, has an extra set of records that can help you as a researcher. You may find police, quarter-session, prison or other records about your criminal ancestor that turn other genealogists green with envy. As well as giving you lots of details about your ancestor, criminal records illustrate beautifully the society in which your ancestor lived, describing the deeds that were considered crimes, the severity of the sentences and the judicial process itself.

A lot of criminal records are held at the National Archives and aren't available online – have a look at Chapter 7 to find out more about locating offline resources. The following websites might prove helpful though:

- **Blacksheep Ancestors (www.blacksheepancestors.com/uk):** This extensive site covers all kinds of legal and criminal matters, from lists of convicts transported to Australia to information about prisons, background details, famous criminals and execution records.

- **Ireland–Australia Transportation Database (www.nationalarchives.ie/topics/transportation/search01.html):** Although only a partial index to transported criminals from Ireland to Australia is available on this site, the information is invaluable. A name search may produce such details as age, date and place of trial, crime committed, sentence passed, the name of the ship in which the individual was transported and the date of sailing.

- **Proceedings of the Old Bailey (www.oldbaileyonline.org):** This site contains details of over 100,000 cases that came before the Old Bailey between 1674 and 1834 – and not only the horrific crimes that we associate with the place, but also thefts, larceny, assault and bigamy, among others. You can peruse a background to the Old Bailey records and a bibliography of books that you can use to take your research further if you become interested in a particular aspect of the proceedings. You can search the index under a wide variety of terms, looking for defendants and others involved in the judicial process, such as jurors, witnesses and victims. The amount of info given for each case varies, but most have a date, a description of the case, witness statements, location, the verdict and the sentence.

If you find your ancestor in these records, you may also find newspaper reports about him or her – see Chapter 7 for more on using newspaper cuttings.

Looking for Significant Others – Further Online Resources

Take a peep at other useful online resources:

- ✔ **Apprenticeship Records (`www.britishorigins.com`):** Here you find London Apprenticeship Abstracts 1442–1850 and Apprentices of Great Britain 1710–1774.

- ✔ **Clergy of the Church of England Database (`www.theclergydatabase. org.uk`):** This constantly expanding database is useful for tracing your ecclesiastical ancestors. You can search by name, location or head straight to the bishops' index if you think your ancestor belongs there. If you find your ancestor on the database, you can find information such as the date and church of his ordination, his promotions, educational qualifications and whether he was dismissed.

- ✔ **Genuki (`www.genuki.org.uk`):** This great resource is useful when you're searching for resources on a local level, or by category – for example, nobility, Jewish records or medical records.

Monumental inscriptions

Tombstone and monument inscriptions are a great way of binding together family generations. Projects to transcribe, record and index inscriptions are often undertaken at a local level to preserve information in danger of being lost to weathering, or as a tool to assist genealogists and historians in the area. Genuki (`www.genuki.org.uk`) has links to local resources, or enter **monumental inscriptions** and the name of the place that interests you into a search engine such as `www.google. co.uk` and see what comes up. Check out the following websites for examples of tombstones and monumental inscriptions:

- ✔ **Memorial Inscriptions (`www.memorial inscriptions.org.uk`):** The National Archive of Memorial Inscriptions (NAOMI)

is currently digitising its database of Church of England inscriptions. You can search by name and place to locate information about your ancestor.

- ✔ **Churchyard Monumental Inscriptions (`www.kentarchaeology.org.uk/ Research/Libr/MIs/MIslist. htm`):** This resource, created by the Kent Archaeological Society, contains transcripts from churchyard monuments throughout Kent. Links take you to the churchyard that interests you.

- ✔ **Kent Archaeological Society (`www.kent archaeology.org.uk`):** This site contains links to monumental inscriptions and gravestones in and around Kent.

✓ **Local and Trade Directories for England and Wales 1750–1919 (www. historicaldirectories.org):** Here you find a selection of historical directories, searchable by location, decade or keyword. You may be able to find your ancestors who were in trade or well-known in their local area, or find where they were living in between censuses.

Delving into Genetic Genealogy

More and more genealogists and researchers are becoming interested in genetic genealogy, which is commonly known as DNA testing. *Genetic genealogy* is the study of a person's genetic makeup, and you can use it to uncover information about where your long-lost ancestors originated and how that connects you to other people on the planet. Genetic genealogy is not useful for tracing recent ancestors; only to clarify that you're related when you meet them. Think of it as a tool to use in addition to other research methods; one that helps you to build up another facet of your family tree. The interest in genetic genealogy – and genetic genealogy itself – is advancing all the time, and may be something to consider as you gain more experience in genealogy research.

Taking a genetic genealogy test is easy and pain-free. All you do is take a cotton wool swab from the inside of your mouth, pop it into a sealed container and return it for testing. The kits are widely available on the Internet, and the cost varies depending on the kind of test you want to subject your sample to! The best option is to find a website that carries out these tests and that offers information about the different types of test available and which ones will be the most useful to your research. Check out these example sites:

✓ **Ancestry (http://landing.ancestry.co.uk/offers/uk/dna. aspx):** You can buy test kits from this DNA section of the Ancestry website. Follow this web address, or you can click directly through from the homepage. Through this website, you can also upload and share your results with other people who've undertaken a DNA test.

✓ **The DNA Ancestry Project (www.dnaancestryproject.com/ydna_ intro_ancestry.php):** You can buy kits to return for testing from this website and then plot your results on a map and explore the timelines and ethnic origins of your ancestors.

Shop around when looking for DNA testing kits, as the results can vary from test to test. Make sure you use a reputable company, and know exactly what you're going to get from your results.

Uncovering the results

Many different DNA tests are available. The most popular are those that determine the paternal line using the Y chromosome. These tests can tell us lots of things, apart from who your father may be, such as revealing your ethnic origins and linking you to a specific section of the community. Perhaps your ancestors all originated from Norway, for example; you could find out how many other people share this common gene. This ability is great for pinpointing a specific location connected to your ancestors. You may know exactly where you and your parents are from, but some genetic tests can date the results much farther back to map the migration of your long-forgotten ancestors across the world.

The *Who Do You Think You Are?* website provides a great example of genetic genealogy delivering some interesting findings. This BBC television series used genetic genealogy to map athlete Colin Jackson's ancestors, and the results gave him some surprising results about his genetic makeup, helping him to get a real sense of his distant past. To read Colin's story, take a look at the website (www.bbc.co.uk/whodoyouthinkyouare/past-stories/colin-jackson.shtml).

Using the information

When you've received and excitedly read through the results of your test, you can use the information to take your research onto another level by uploading your DNA results to one of many websites. (Take a look at the Delving into Genetic Genealogy section earlier in this chapter for a couple of example websites.) There you can share your findings with other people who have common genes. Doing this enables you to build up a picture of where your distant relatives originated and can help to pinpoint your origins on a map.

Going Forward from Here

We could go on forever listing the different web resources, as more and more material becomes available online each day. The pickings are rich, and you never know what resources you may stumble across. This chapter is a starting point rather than a comprehensive list of resources. It gives you an idea of the resources available on the web and how to find them. If we haven't covered the topic you're particularly interested in, remember the five golden research questions:

- ✔ Is a research guide available for my area of interest? Do any of the websites I've looked at provide guidance for further research?

- ✔ Can I find more about my particular topic on Genuki, Cyndi's List or another genealogically focused search engine?

- ✔ Can I find out more using a standard search engine such as Google?

- ✔ Does a research group, society or mailing list deal with my area of interest?

- ✔ Are there offline resources that can help me?

Chapter 7

Looking Offline: Further Research Sources in the UK

*Y*ou're unlikely to find online all the resources you need for your genealogical research. More genealogical material appears each day on the Internet, with more records that you could once only access in the archives appearing all the time. However, you will come to a point where you reach the limits of the online resources. If you're still burning with curiosity about your ancestors' lives and times or are simply stuck and want a bit of encouragement, consider continuing your search offline. Up and down the country are archives, libraries, repositories and family history centres crammed with useful information.

Whether your ancestor was a servant or a lord, a soldier or a sailor, a criminal or a copper, shopkeeper, innkeeper, vicar, mill worker, pauper, non-conformist, teacher, preacher or agricultural labourer – or even if he's simply vanished inexplicably from the census or parish registers – you may well find something more about your ancestor in the offline records. Somewhere among the vast archival collections, your ancestor may be lurking, just waiting to be discovered.

Even if you can't find your ancestor's name in any offline records, you may still uncover a wealth of information about the kind of life he or she lived – the living conditions and the social, economic and geographical background of the day – giving the names on your family tree a bit of character.

Online tools such as catalogues, research guides and communication with other genealogists can help you locate the offline resources that you need. But in order to view these resources, you're going to have to part with your computer for a while, leave the confines of your familiar research spot and step into the unknown. In this chapter, we show you how. We suggest that you use this chapter in conjunction with Chapter 6, to get an idea of how online and offline resources can combine to further your research project.

Finding Family History Centres

All over the country are *family history centres* – centres dedicated to (you've guessed it!) family history. The centres house documents and resources useful to genealogists. The members of staff in these centres are usually happy for you to turn up with research enquiries and can point you in the direction of resources to help you on your way. Visiting one of the centres is a pleasure. Not only do you give your research project an encouraging boost, but you also get a real sense of community: you'll probably come across lots of people who are doing the same thing as you – and have encountered the same problems, resources, frustrations and delights as you.

So where are these family history centres, and what resources do they offer?

LDS family history centres

The Church of Jesus Christ of Latter-Day Saints (LDS), which we talk about in Chapter 5, has established family history centres all over the world, including over 100 throughout England, Wales, Scotland and Ireland. Check out www. familysearch.org/Eng/Library/FHC/frameset_fhc.asp for a list of LDS family history centres. Simply enter your country and county, and you get the address of the centre closest to you.

The resources held in LDS centres are varied and wide-ranging and include a vast collection of parish records, going well beyond the scope of the International Genealogical Index (IGI). Find out more about the IGI in Chapter 5. What's more, you can arrange for records held in LDS family history centres to be transferred to a centre near you – which may save you the trouble of travelling to a distant county, or even country, to get hold of the records that you want.

The National Archives

The National Archives (TNA) at Kew in London is the official archive for UK government records and holds records dating back to the Domesday Book. Since the closure of the Family Records Centre in Islington, all the microfilmed records, resources and staff have been relocated to the National

Archives, which is now the main archive in London for family history records. As well as the vast collection of family history resources, TNA is also the place to go if you have an ancestor who may have served in the forces, was a criminal or came into contact with government in one way or another during their lives.

TNA holds regular talks and workshops on subjects ranging from getting started in family history to advanced lectures on medieval history. You can visit TNA and use all of the *open access* genealogical material (meaning material available for public viewing without restriction) for free without needing a reader's ticket, but you do have to pay small fees for photocopying. You can find more information and details about opening hours, records held and personal identification requirements on their website (www.national archives.gov.uk).

The Society of Genealogists

The Society of Genealogists (www.sog.org.uk) is a charity and the oldest genealogical organisation in the UK. At its base in London, the society holds an inspiring collection of genealogical material, including Scottish and Irish resources, a large collection of surname-specific research deposited by other researchers, local information, parish records from all over the country and a great deal more. For a better idea of its collections, try searching its online catalogue at www.sog.org.uk/sogcat/access.

Staff at the society can help with your research enquiries, but you need to pay a reading fee or become a member of the society before you can use its material. Which option you take is up to you. If you think you can explore all the material you want to look at in a day, you can pay a reading fee just for that day, or even for just part of a day. Or if you find a lot of useful material in the catalogue and want to make several visits to the society to study it all, consider taking out annual membership of the society, which allows you to return as many times as you like within the year. The society also runs an array of lectures and courses – check out its website for details.

Courting County and Municipal Archives

The scope of family history centres tends to be nationwide, but often you want to search at a local level. Enter the county and municipal archives, many of which list their archive holdings on their websites. You may also come across library and archival resources combined for a particular area into a *local history* or *local study centre*. Visiting archives whose collections relate to a specific place is rather satisfying. You can peep at the place in which your ancestors lived, and the archives are often very well equipped for your genealogical purposes. Many archives and local history centres have microfilm copies of parish registers from all over the town or county and also hold documents relating to the history of the place. So if your great-great-grandfather was a brewer, you can probably find out about the brewery where he worked. If he was a clergyman, you might find a history of his church. If he was a farmer, the local archives may help you to discover where he worked his land, whether he owned it and what he grew.

Other records in which your ancestors may appear are also held at a local level, including legal documents and deeds, Quarter Sessions records (sessions of local courts that operated in each county and county borough in England and Wales from medieval times to the 1970s) and Poor Law records. Local and county histories are also available, giving you an idea of what the area was like when your ancestors were living there, together with all kinds of records that you never even dreamed of. Look at 'Locating Your Sources' later in this chapter for help on finding an archive appropriate for you.

Don't forget to make use of your local library. Many local libraries have excellent local history resources, such as village and town histories, as well as a selection of street directories. They may also have free access to many genealogy subscription websites – check with your local council for more information.

Before you dash off to the local archives though, a word of warning: not all sources relating to a particular geographical area are kept in that area. For example, as we point out in 'Getting underway with some common examples' later in the chapter, the military records of your ancestor are likely to be kept at the National Archives, regardless of where you ancestor actually lived or enlisted for service. Records for national and international businesses and organisations often work in the same way, housing their records in a single location rather than scattering them about the country or the world. The archivists who keep such records can advise you of their accessibility.

The key questions to bear in mind here are:

- ✔ How are the records organised?
- ✔ Are the records indexed?
- ✔ Do I have enough info to search the records effectively?

For example, you won't get far if you turn up at the National Archives equipped only with the information that your ancestor was in the army. You need to know *when* your ancestor was in the army and ideally in which regiment he served. The more information you have, the better, and you'll be better prepared to navigate the records more successfully.

Aiming for Archives Overseas

You can sometimes find genealogical material from other countries online. For example, much US material, including a large collection of census returns, is available at Ancestry.com (www.ancestry.com), and you can find a selection of international material at Cyndi's List (www.cyndislist.com/census2.htm).

However, if you want to embark on research abroad, we suggest you hire a professional researcher in the relevant country and get them to do the research for you. Unless you've a lot of time and money on your hands, you're unlikely to be able to travel abroad to spend your time rooting around in an archive. A local researcher speaks the language, is familiar with the relevant archives and records and knows all the little shortcuts. A professional researcher can also place your ancestor within the right social and historical context.

So how do you go about finding and hiring a professional researcher overseas? You can take a number of approaches. Many UK-based research agencies have overseas sections and can liaise directly with the overseas team on your behalf, so check these first. If you want to find an overseas researcher yourself, however, have a look at Cyndi's List at www.cyndislist.com/profess.htm, which offers an extensive list of overseas researchers in a variety of countries. Another option is to visit a family history centre, many of which hold lists of researchers willing to take on work abroad. But we've also found that simply typing your request into a search engine (such as Google) tends to yield results. For example, if you enter **professional genealogical researcher Poland** into Google, you get a list of several websites with useful contact information.

Make sure that you follow the guidelines for hiring a professional researcher; you want to ensure that you're getting the best possible service. For more information about what to look for when hiring a researcher, have a look at Chapter 9.

Locating Your Sources

As you become excited about the possibilities open to you, you may also find yourself thoroughly confused about how to decide which ones to choose. Here's the good news. Although you can only consult offline many of the records that you need to extend your research, you can consult a variety of online catalogues and resources to help you decide which archive, library or family history centre you need to visit. You may also find detailed descriptions of the holdings of various archives on their websites to help you narrow your choice. Read on to discover some of the major resources that you may find useful.

Finding an appropriate centre

You need to do a bit of groundwork before you rush out to visit your local record office or travel hundreds of miles to an archive in the hope of finding a treasure trove of information about your ancestors. Dashing over to an archive in Aberystwyth to find out about your ancestor who worked on the railway there, only to discover that the records are held in London, is really frustrating. And you'll kick yourself if you turn up in London on the hunt for his Union records, only to find that they're kept in Coventry.

The section that follows helps you to create a sensible and coherent research plan. So, firstly decide what you're looking for, and then decide where you're likely to find it. To get going, try the online catalogues in this section.

If you look through these online catalogues and are still a bit unsure about where to find the records you want or whether they even exist, try directing your enquiries to the experts. Contact the local archives by phone or email and ask what kind of records your ancestor may have left behind and what facilities you can use to find out more about your ancestor's life and times. Then decide whether you need to visit the archive. Similarly, if you can't find a research guide or any promising looking documents in the online catalogues, try asking the National Archives to point you in the right direction.

The National Archives' catalogue

The National Archives is the major repository for government documents in the UK. You can search its catalogue online at www.nationalarchives.gov.uk/catalogue/search.asp. Here you can run a standard search by entering a search term and narrowing it down with dates, a department or series code (for example, HO for Home Office, which contains convicts' transportation records. You become familiar with certain department and series codes the more you use the documents and read the research guides, but you don't need to worry about using them at all if you don't want to.) Or you can try a more specialised search using the category Subjects, Places and Prominent People.

You can also find detailed research guides at www.nationalarchives.gov.uk/catalogue/researchguidesindex.asp, which tell you about the records available to you in your specific area of interest, including how and why the records were created, for which dates and the series or department code allocated to those particular records. For instance, suppose you know that one of your ancestors was convicted of a crime and ended up being transported to Australia. You want to find out more about him and how he ended up in Australia but you can find no information on the Internet. So where do you start? First, see whether the National Archives has a research guide to give you a bit of background information. In the list of research guides (see Figure 7-1), you find a general guide *Sources for Convicts and Prisoners*. This sounds good, so click on the link and have a look. Here you discover that the National Archives houses a wealth of records that may relate to your ancestor and that many of the records fall within the HO (Records of the Home Office) series. By following the links on the page, you read more about the series of records mentioned in the text.

C
Cabinet Committees
Cabinet Office Records
Canals: Administrative and Other Records
Captured Enemy Documents: Films of German Foreign Ministry (GFM) Archive and Other Sources
Catholic Records for Family History
Catholic Recusants
Census Returns
Census, 1801-1901: Statistical Reports
Chancel Repairs
Chancery Masters' and Other Exhibits: Sources for Social and Economic History
Chancery Masters' Reports and Certificates
Chancery Proceedings: Equity Suits before 1558
Chancery Proceedings: Equity Suits from 1558
Change of Name
China, Records relating to, in The National Archives
Citing Documents in The National Archives
Civil Servants
Civil War Soldiers, 1642 - 1660
Coal Mining Records in The National Archives
Coastguard
Colonial Office: Advisory Committees
Colonial Office: Registers of Correspondence, 1849-1926
Colonial Office: Registers of Correspondence, 1926-1951
Colonies and Dominions, Researching British
Companies and Businesses: Registration
Convicts and Prisoners, 1100-1986, Sources in The National Archives
Copyright Records: Stationers' Hall
Coroners' Inquests
Court of Requests, 1485-1642: A Court for the Poor
Court of Star Chamber, 1485-1642
Court of Wards and Liveries, 1540-1645: Land Inheritance
Court, Funds in
Crime and Law in England, Sources for the History of
Criminal Courts in England and Wales from 1972

Figure 7-1:
Alphabetical list of research guides on the National Archives website.

When you've read the research guide, you can see that the records you want are under code HO11, so call up the catalogue and type **HO11** in the reference box in the top-left corner (see Figure 7-2).

The result tells you that the transportation records at the National Archives in HO11 cover the period 1787–1870. From here, you can view the full catalogue entry by clicking on the Browse from here button, and then HO11 link, which brings up a list (Figure 7-3) of places and transportation ships in chronological order. If you know that your ancestor sailed on a particular date, but don't know the name of the ship, you'll have to take a look through a few documents in order to track him down, but that's half the fun of genealogy. In this example, you'll see that the dates the ships set sail are clearly listed on the right side, with the destination and ship's name in the catalogue description. If you find one that looks particularly promising, for example, the fourth option, click on the link. You then clearly see that the records for the prisoners who sailed on the convict ship *Guardian*, which sailed to New South Wales in July 1789, are within this document. Make a note of the unique HO reference number, which in this case is HO11/1/23. If you're unsure of what you've found, return to the research guides for a fuller explanation (see Figure 7-4). In the case of this document, you'll have to make a trip to the archives or enlist the help of a researcher in order to view and copy it.

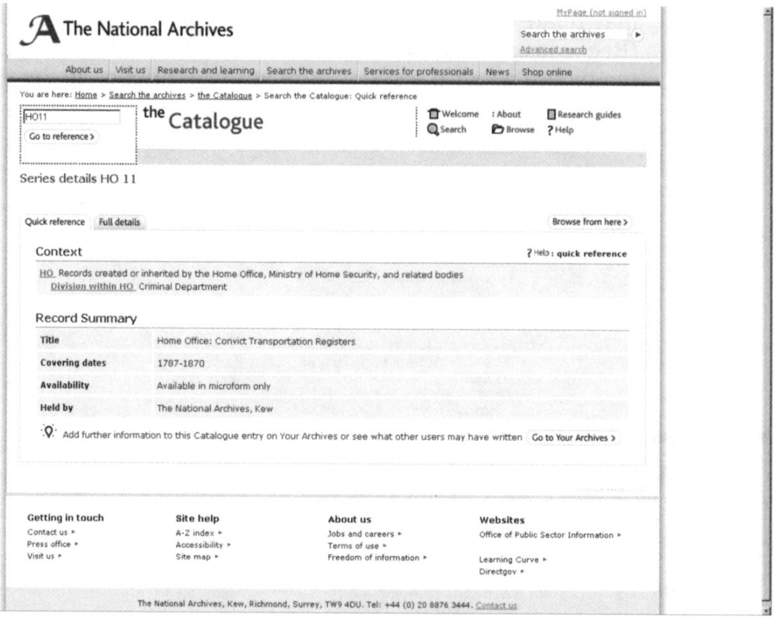

Figure 7-2: Searching for transportation records in the National Archives' catalogue.

Reproduced under the terms of the Click-Use Licence.

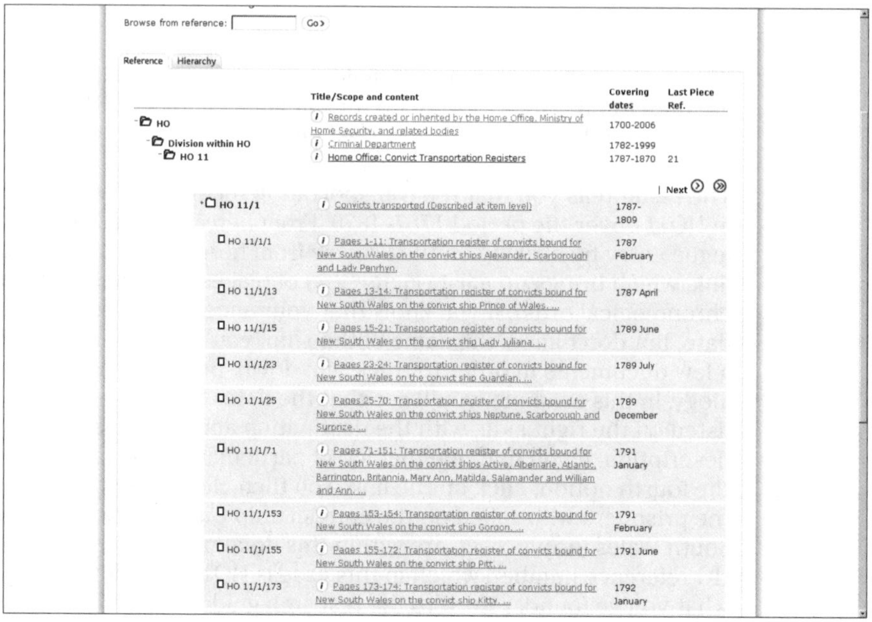

Figure 7-3: Results of a search for transportation registers in the HO series.

Reproduced under the terms of the Click-Use Licence.

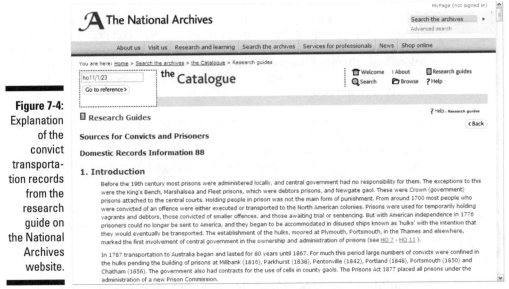

Figure 7-4:
Explanation
of the
convict
transporta-
tion records
from the
research
guide on
the National
Archives
website.

Don't forget to read the rest of the research guide thoroughly, because you may find even more. The research guide gives you not just a great starting point for searching the online catalogue, but is invaluable for helping you follow up leads or explore other research avenues, making the hunt for ancestors in original documents all the more exciting. You can see, for example, that you may be able to search for prison and trial records for your ancestor, and that ships' medical registers can be a great source of information about individual convicts and their health whilst on board.

When you've finished searching for documents, and have chosen which ones you want to see in person, you can begin to arrange your trip to the archives. For more on visiting the archives, check out 'Taking a Trip to the Archives' later in this chapter. The National Archives (like many) enables you to order documents online in advance, so you don't have to wait around on the day for the document you want to be brought up from the repository.

Access to Archives (A2A)

The constantly expanding Access to Archives (A2A) database (www.national archives.gov.uk/a2a) holds the details of over 9 million records located in over 400 repositories in England and Wales, with the exception of those housed at the National Archives. You can search the database by keyword or phrase, location of the archives (specific or limited to a particular region), the date of the archives and the date of the catalogue (so that you can search only new additions to the database). You can also run an extended search including info such as the creator of the archive, the catalogue reference, the archive category (for example, military records, Poor Law Union records or Quarter Sessions), the theme of the records that interest you (for example, Images of Suffolk, Church, State and People, and Religion and Rebellion), or search under People, Places and Subjects.

Give yourself plenty of time to experiment and play with A2A. At each stage in your search, follow the links to see what's available. If you get no hits for your particular word or phrase, choose a similar phrase or cut out unnecessary words and then try again. The search page offers help with your searching.

The A2A site has links to information about the repositories featured in your search results, including location, contact details and opening hours. You can find similar info in the National Archives' ARCHON directory (www.national archives.gov.uk/archon).

National Archives of Scotland Online Public Access Catalogue

At www.nas.gov.uk/onlineCatalogue/ you can search much of the vast collection held at the National Archives of Scotland. You can also browse a list of the categories that haven't yet been added to the online catalogue. You get a reference number and a brief description of the document that you want, but you need to visit the archive to view the complete document.

Scottish Archive Network (SCAN)

This database (www.scan.org.uk/aboutus/indexonline.htm) is similar to Access to Archives (described earlier in this section) and enables you to search over 20,000 collections of documents housed in over 50 repositories throughout Scotland. The catalogue gives a brief description of the documents contained in the archives.

For an excellent collection of research tools, check out www.scan.org.uk/researchrtools/index.htm. Select the Knowledge Base link and you can choose a record type, subject or place that you want to know more about, and discover where the relevant records are held. The site also has a glossary of terms and a family history guide.

Archive Network Wales

Archive Network Wales (www.archivesnetworkwales.info) is an access point to collections in archives, museums, universities and libraries in Wales. Its focus is on collections of documents rather than individual documents.

Getting underway with some common examples

Tracking down the records you need can be great fun – but also a little time-consuming. To make your life a bit easier, we list here a few of the major genealogical resources and where to find them:

- ✓ **Wills proved in England and Wales after 1858:** The indexes to these wills are held at the Principal Registry of the Family Division, First Avenue House, 42–49 High Holborn, London, WC1V 6NP (www.hmcourts-service.gov.uk/cms/1226.htm).

  Searching the indexes is easy and you can order copies of wills for a fee. You don't have to make a trip especially to search the indexes or to order the will that you want: you can request that the staff make the search for you and send you a copy of anything that they find. Alternatively, if you find in indexes elsewhere a reference to a will that you want, you can pass this information to the staff, who can send you a copy of the will (have a look at the website for more information and relevant fees). You can search indexes and order copies from any of the local probate offices listed at www.hmcourts-service.gov.uk/cms/1226.htm#addresses, but check (before you visit) that they hold the records for the year and location that you want. Several archives, county record offices and family history centres also hold copies of the indexes in the form of *National Probate Calendars* (probate is the official proving of a will) to wills proved 1858–1943, and in certain cases, indexes are held almost up to the present day. A number of Family History Societies have online indexes to wills proved within their county (see www.ffhs.org.uk for more).

  Wills proved before 1858 at the Prerogative Court of Canterbury are available online via the National Archives website at www.nationalarchives.gov.uk/documentsonline.

- ✓ **Scottish wills after 1901:** These wills are held at the National Archives of Scotland (NAS) at HM General Register House, 2 Princes Street, Edinburgh, EH1 3YY (www.nas.gov.uk).

  The NAS holds both the indexes and the wills. The Mitchell Library in Glasgow also has an index for the years up to 1936. To look at a will, contact the archives before you visit, because many of the wills aren't held on site. The NAS also has a handy research guide to wills and testaments at www.nas.gov.uk/guides/wills.asp.

- ✓ **Irish wills:** These wills are a bit more difficult to find than UK wills because many early Irish wills were destroyed in a fire at the Public Record Office in 1922, along with numerous other Irish genealogical records. However, information has been pieced together from various sources, including Inland Revenue administration books, Prerogative and Consistorial will books, charitable bequests and pedigrees prepared from wills before 1922. The documents that survive (including documents relating to Northern Ireland) and their indexes are held at the National Archives of Ireland at Bishop Street, Dublin 8, Ireland (`www.nationalarchives.ie`).

Wills after 1916 weren't kept at the Public Record Office and so survived the 1922 fire. You can request these wills from the National Archives of Ireland. For more info, check out the research guide at `www.nationalarchives.ie/genealogy/willsandadmin.html`.

✔ **Naturalisation and denization records:** If you uncover evidence that your ancestors came to the UK from another country, check whether they applied for a grant of British nationality. A grant of *naturalisation* meant that the recipient enjoyed the same rights as a British-born subject (protection under the law, the right to inherit land, serve in the military and so on). A grant of *denization* meant that the recipient was protected by the law, but did not hold the rights of a British-born subject and was subject to a higher rate of tax. Those who wished to apply for grants of naturalisation or denization made an application to the government, which would examine the individual's details and consider the worth of their case. From the records that this process produced, you may learn where your ancestor came from, what he or she did before coming to the UK and details about their family. The relevant records are held at the National Archives. Check out the research guide at `www.nationalarchives.gov.uk/catalogue/RdLeaflet.asp?sLeafletID=242`. You can search for your ancestor by name in the online catalogue, but this index is not comprehensive.

✔ **Railway records:** Some staff and individual records for ancestors who worked on the railways are held locally or with the railway companies themselves, and these records can give a good insight into what life was like for these workers. For information about the railway companies, view the National Archives' research guide at `www.nationalarchives.gov.uk/catalogue/RdLeaflet.asp?sLeafletID=114`.

✔ **Labour history records:** A large collection of labour, industrial relations and trades union records have been gathered together at Warwick Modern Records Centre (`www2.warwick.ac.uk/services/library/mrc`). Check out their introductory guide to genealogy at `www2.warwick.ac.uk/services/library/mrc/subject_guides/family_history` and the summary of what the centre holds at `www2.warwick.ac.uk/services/library/mrc/holdings`.

✔ **Poor Law and workhouse records:** Most of these records are held at a local level, often at the local or county record office. Check out the superb introduction to this area of research and the resources available at `www.workhouses.org.uk`.

✔ **Divorce records:** These records are held by the National Archives although divorce indexes are sometimes available at family history centres and at local and county record offices. Have a look at the research guides at `www.nationalarchives.gov.uk/catalogue/RdLeaflet.asp?sLeafletID=260` for the period before 1858 and at `www.nationalarchives.gov.uk/catalogue/RdLeaflet.asp?sLeafletID=53` for subsequent records. Particularly useful to genealogists are the *divorce case files*, which provide invaluable information, including details about the marriage, children, residences of the couple and the reason for the divorce. However, very few divorce case files have been kept for the period from 1938 to the present day.

✔ **Newspapers:** You usually find copies of local newspapers, often saved as microfilm or microfiche, at the relevant local record offices. Many local libraries also have access to The Times Archives online for free, and in some cases they also have microfilmed copies. The central source for historic newspapers in the UK is the British Library Newspapers Library (`www.bl.uk/reshelp/findhelprestype/catblhold/all/allcat.html`). You can search this catalogue online, but you have to visit their offices to view the newspapers themselves. However, the British Library has digitised many nineteenth century newspapers, and you can view these online for free from the main British Library.

Newspapers are a great resource for obituaries, inquest reports and any noteworthy activities on the part of your ancestors. They also provide a flavour of the life and times in which your ancestors lived. (To find out more about collections of online newspaper material check out Chapter 4.)

TRY THIS

Six key questions to help locate your records

If you're having trouble finding offline resources that are relevant to your research project, or are finding it difficult to decide which ones to use, you can find resources to help you. Ask yourself the following questions:

✔ Is there a research guide available for my area of interest? Have a look at `www.nationalarchives.gov.uk/catalogue/researchguides index.asp` or on websites related to your topic of interest.

✔ Can I find more about my particular topic on Genuki (`www.genuki.org.uk`), Cyndi's List (`www.cyndislist.com`) or other genealogically focused search engines?

✔ Can I find relevant archives or offline resources by using a standard search engine such as Google (`www.google.co.uk`)?

✔ Do any research groups, societies or mailing lists deal with my area of interest? Can I find anyone who has come across the same problems, or who may know of the best archival resources for me?

✔ Can a national or local archive or a family history centre help? If I am looking for records of a certain organisation, can I contact this organisation or visit their website to find out where their archive is located?

✔ Can I find out more information at a library? Check out Chapter 4 for more about locating library resources.

Taking a Trip to the Archives

So you've searched the online catalogues and found a record or collection of records that you want to have a look at. You now have two options: you can hire a professional researcher to visit the archive and check out the documents on your behalf (we give the low-down on using professional researchers in Chapter 9), or you can make the trip yourself.

Working in record offices can be both enjoyable and satisfying. A professional researcher can send you a pile of photocopies and a comprehensive report, but with this option you miss the thrill of the chase. Local archives are welcoming, user-friendly and thoroughly accustomed to first-time researchers walking through their doors.

A bit of planning makes all the difference between a successful research trip and a highly frustrating experience. Like any good explorer, before you embark upon your voyage of discovery, sort out the details of your trip. Take the time to arrange your expedition, organise your research strategy and iron out any potential problems before they throw you off course. Here are a few suggestions.

Planning before you go

You can lay the groundwork for your trip days or weeks in advance. Take the following steps:

1. **Decide which archive, record office or family history centre you want to visit.** Have a look at its website, where you can read about its location, collections, facilities, opening times and 101 other things you never thought of. This process gets you into the right frame of mind.

2. **Decide when you'd like to go.** Many archives have different opening times on different days of the week, and on certain days they may not open at all. You may want to select a day when the archive is open late, because you don't want to be turfed out when you're only half way through your research.

   On the other hand, if you know your stamina typically runs out by mid afternoon, a shorter day at the archive, when it may well be less crowded, will do fine.

3. **Contact the archives.** You can make contact via email, telephone or letter. Check that the archives have the records you want, and that they are open to the public on the day you want to visit. You may also need to book a seat for your chosen day. Many local archives have limited space

for readers and researchers and ask you to book in advance. If you're using parish records or other documents on microfilm or microfiche, you may need to book a microfilm or microfiche reader. If you're visiting with a research partner, you need seats and readers for two people. Ask about any reading fees that apply at the archive, whether you need a reader's ticket or other ID, and whether you can use laptops, digital cameras and other research equipment in the archive.

4. **Sort out your travel plans.** After you've booked your seat at the archive, work out how to get there. Many archives have location maps on their websites, with details of accessing the archive by public transport or car. Or check out `www.streetmap.co.uk` and your archive by typing in the road name, postcode or the name of the archive.

5. **Check out the archive's facilities.** Does the archive have disabled access? Is there a cafe nearby or somewhere to eat a packed lunch? Can you access the Internet at the archive? Can you use your mobile phone at the archive? To answer these questions, take a look at the archive's website or speak to a member of staff.

6. **Decide upon a research strategy.** This step is an important one for helping you to make the most of your day. We don't suggest that you plan every minute of your day, but you'll find it helpful to have a good idea of what you're trying to achieve. Deciding 'I'm trying to find out anything about anyone called Scully who lived in this area' isn't going to serve you very well. You can get on much better (and the archivists can better advise you) if you come equipped with a plan along the lines of 'I'm trying to find out about my great-great-great-grandfather, Matthew Scully, who owned a mill in this area, and I hope to find the names of his parents, siblings and grandparents.'

The more precise your information and intentions are, the better your chances of striking gold. If you have a friend or research partner with you, share the workload between you and cover twice the ground. But plan in advance who's going to search for which record to avoid duplication and uncertainty.

Deciding what to take

Most of what you take with you won't accompany you into the reading rooms: most archives provide lockers for your bags, coats, umbrellas and general paraphernalia and let you take in only pencils, paper and research notes with you. The less equipment you have in the reading rooms, the less chance of a document being damaged (such as by someone tripping over your bag), or of leaving something important behind.

Here are a few suggestions of what to take for your day at the archives:

- **Two sharp pencils:** You're not allowed to use ink near original documents, and most archives don't allow pens of any description into the reading rooms. You may also need a pencil sharpener, but most of the large archives provide them, as you're not allowed to use your own near original documents.

- **Blank paper:** You need enough to record your findings. Keeping all your research notes in one spiral notebook or binder is a good plan. Be sure to check what kind of notebooks, if any, the archive permits.

Write your name and address on the front of your notebook. That way, if you lose it or leave it behind, you have a much better chance of someone returning it to you.

- **Your research to date:** You'll doubtless need to refer to your current research notes as you work, so make sure that you have copies with you. Nothing is more annoying than wanting to confirm a name or date and then finding that you've left your records at home. If you're allowed to bring a laptop, you can have your entire database with you. If you're limited to papers, be sure to only print out relevant data as some archives only allow a certain number of loose pages in their reading rooms. We advise against taking original documents such as birth certificates with you: leave them safely at home, and bring copies or transcripts instead.

- **A clear plastic bag:** This is a convenient way of keeping your possessions together and carrying them about the reading rooms. Other bags aren't usually allowed and you're asked to leave them in a locker. Sometimes you can get a clear plastic bag when you reach the archive, but if in doubt take your own.

- **Reader's ticket or identification:** The documentation that you need varies from archive to archive, and you need to find out from the website or archivist what system is in operation at the archives you're visiting. Some (for example, the National Archives) have a reader's ticket unique to that particular archive. Others share a ticket. You may come across the County Archive Research Network (CARN) ticket, which gives you entry to many county archives all over the country. CARN tickets are free of charge, and you can obtain them on the spot when you reach the archives, but you need to fill in a form and to provide certain details and proof of identification. So be sure to bring the necessary documents with you. You can read more about the CARN ticket and how to get one on participating archives' websites. Check out `www.gmcro.co.uk/ftpfiles/carn.pdf` for an example, but do check with each archive directly before you go.

- **A laptop and/or digital camera:** The website or archivist can tell you whether you're allowed to use these tools in the archive. Laptops are rarely a problem. Often you have to register a digital camera when you arrive, and sometimes pay a fee for its use. But you can obtain good quality images of the documents you want without having to wait for photocopies. Digital cameras also have the advantage that the images you collect can be transferred to and stored on your computer, but be sure to take spare batteries and a large enough memory card. However, be aware that copyright restrictions mean that not all archives allow you to take digital copies of their documents.

✔ **Plenty of small change:** Change is useful for lockers, copying machines and payment for photocopying done by the archive staff.

✔ **Appropriate clothing:** Have we gone mad? Do you have to dress up to visit an archive? No, but bear in mind the following tips when choosing your wardrobe for the day. Remember that if you're handling delicate old documents, you don't want to wear your best clothes. Not only is there a certain amount of physical labour involved in carrying the documents, unpacking them from boxes and putting them back to bed, but your clothes are likely to attract a certain amount of dust, dirt, flakes of paper and stains from particularly lurid covers and bindings. You may feel more professional if you dress up smartly, but you don't want something to disintegrate down the front of your best shirt.

Also be prepared for unexpected temperatures in the archives. Often archives have rigorous temperature controls in operation to protect the documents, which means that the reading rooms may be colder than you expect. On the other hand, when lots of computers are gathered together, the temperature rises significantly and you may find your cheeks growing rosy.

✔ **Lunch:** Take plenty to eat and drink if the archive doesn't have a cafe. You don't want to be distracted from your research because you're hungry or thirsty – and you don't want to waste time wandering about an unfamiliar town trying to find a meal. Of course, you're never allowed to consume food or drink in the reading rooms (but you knew that, didn't you?)

✔ **Reading glasses:** Old writing can be difficult to read, microfilms can be faded and catalogues often written by hand. You want the best possible chance of seeing and understanding what you're doing – so bring your specs if you wear them.

Arriving at the archive

Now the fun really begins. But you don't want to waste time at the beginning of the day – you want to get straight down to researching. Here's what you need to do before you can view those documents:

1. **Sign yourself in.** An archivist usually signs in you, your laptop and your digital camera for the day, examines your reader's ticket or identification and points you in the right direction for the lockers, the reading rooms and other facilities. If you made a booking in advance, the archivist can indicate where your reserved seat is.

   Be patient: sometimes the paperwork you're asked to complete is a little cumbersome, but it helps the archive to keep detailed records of who is visiting, from where and for what purpose, which may enable them to apply for funding and other resources to keep the archive working. You may also be asked to sign a form agreeing to stick to the rules and regulations. For an experienced researcher, the rules are little more than common sense. You weren't contemplating tearing pages out of documents anyway! But have a skim through before you sign: knowing what's expected of you is always a good idea, and there may be something in there that hadn't occurred to you before.

2. **Grab a locker.** Here you can leave everything that you can't or don't want to take into the archive with you. Make sure that you take your pencils, paper and research notes with you. Don't panic if you forget something, though: you can return to your locker whenever you like during the course of the day.

Getting started

Remember that an archivist is always available to help you, so don't be afraid to ask for help. If you're unsure of what you're doing or how to access the documents that you want, ask at the enquiries desk. Part of the archivist's job is to guide you in your research, and to help you make the most of your day.

As a genealogist you'll want to search for records relating to your particular ancestor, and these may range from military records to apprenticeship records – anything that you haven't yet found online. Most of these records are popular with genealogists, and because the original records would quickly deteriorate if thousands of genealogists were allowed to leaf through them, you'll find that many have been copied onto microfilm or microfiche to protect them. This is why you may need to book a microfilm reader in advance of your trip to the archive.

Most of the more popular records have indexes, saving you from hours of trawling though every single name and making locating the exact record that you're looking for straightforward. Microfilm and microfiche are usually kept in filing cabinet-style drawers. Most archives operate a self-service system for their microfilm records, many having a small box or card next to the cabinets for you to use as a 'bookmark' when you take anything out of the cabinets. That way, any missing item can be traced back to you, and it also makes putting yours back in the right place easy to do. The microfilm readers themselves are usually easy to use, but always ask if you have any trouble, as using them for the first time may be a little tricky.

And now you're ready to search. Good luck. Don't forget to take regular breaks to give your eyes a rest – and don't forget to make a copy of anything relevant that you find. You may need to ask an archivist for help making a copy the first time you try it; getting the right part of the page to print at a readable size can take some finesse.

You may also wish to consult *original documents* during the course of your visit. For example, you may have found the records you were looking for amongst the most popular microfilmed records, but this may lead you to other records that are only available to consult as original documents. The archive always has a catalogue of its holdings. Usually the catalogue is computerised, but occasionally there may be a card index too. Taking a look at both is a good idea, but always ask the archivist for advice as you don't want to miss anything that may be important during your visit. The archivist can advise you further as to what is available.

When you find a document that you want to consult, you order it from the repository (where the documents are stored). Always ask the archivist about the procedures that apply to that particular archive. The number of documents that you can order at one time is often limited, and document ordering may finish an hour or so before the archive closes. Sometimes, you can place an order electronically, but often you need to fill in a paper slip and hand it to the archivist. Think ahead here – the document may take up to an hour to arrive, so plan something to do in the meantime.

Handling original documents

Ordering up original documents can be one of the most exciting parts of your research. Not only do you get to hold a piece of history in your hands, but nothing is more thrilling than finding the name of your ancestor hidden amongst its pages. Hang on, though. We're not going to be killjoys, but we must offer a few words of caution. We don't want you to be carried away with the excitement of what you're seeing, and inflict damage on the document that will reduce its lifespan, or make it difficult for other researchers to make the most of what's there. Always treat these documents with respect. Here are a few simple pointers to help you on your way:

   ✔ **Make sure that you have enough space to examine your document safely.** Sometimes a document that appears to be quite small turns out to be awkwardly large when you come to open, unfold or unpack it. If your desk is too small to accommodate your document, ask the archivist for a larger working space. Most archivists are more than happy to do this to protect and increase the lifespan of the documents, and the last thing they want is for you to crush or crumple them. Often an archive has *map tables* where larger documents can be viewed without their edges hanging over the side of the table, touching the wall or encroaching on the working space of other researchers.

✔ **Use foam pads or wedges to support your document.** The spines of old books may be much more delicate than the books you have at home. If you force the books open, or leave the covers hanging under their own weight, you may inflict irreparable damage to the document. So archives can provide foam pads and V-shaped wedges to support the spine and covers of such documents. These supports can also tilt the document toward you, thus making it easier to read.

✔ **Touch the documents as little as possible.** Even when clean, your hands aren't good for old documents, so touch as little as possible. If you need to hold a document in place (for example, one that is stored as a roll and won't lie flat enough for you to study it), the archive can provide weights for you to place on the edges so you don't have to hold them down with your hands. If you need to follow your place in the script with your finger, place a transparent sheet of paper between your hand and the document. And sometimes, in the case of a particularly vulnerable document, you'll be issued with a pair of gloves. You may find the regulations a little cumbersome, but they're crucial if the documents are to survive in good condition.

✔ **Leave the document exactly as you found it.** When you've finished consulting a particular document, it is important to pack it away carefully. Add nothing to it, and take nothing away. Don't bend or fold it where it wasn't bent or folded before. And don't force it back into its box with pages sticking out, or tie the string so tightly that it snags at the paperwork. Take your time. You're helping to preserve this document for the next person who wants to see it. If you're having trouble, ask the archivist for help.

Continuing your research

Yes, we've mentioned it before, but remember as you go to cite all of your sources to record all the documents you've searched (even those that yielded nothing), and to make copies of all your finds. Label the top of every page in your research notes with the date and the name of the archive in which you found the information, as well as the references of documents transcribed on that page. That way, if your notes become mixed up, you can easily put them back together again. Correct labelling also enables you to refer to your finds quickly and easily. If you remember finding a birth for Ethel Turner last week and this week you find that she really is Grandma's sister, you know where to look for the reference.

You're now well under way, and time will probably fly by. Remember to take breaks, stop for lunch and wash your hands afterwards. Be realistic: if you realise you're not going to finish everything in one trip, don't panic and rush your research. If you do, you'll miss things and have to do it all over again. Decide what you can do, and don't worry about what you can't. Spend time consulting the catalogues and the archivist to decide how much more there is to do at this location so that you can plan a future trip to the archives.

Finishing up

Finishing for the day can be one of the most important times in your research. When you're tired or bursting with excitement about your finds, notes can get mixed up, documents damaged and research notes and personal possessions left behind. So here are some simple reminders of what you need to do at the end of the day:

- Leave plenty of time to pack away your documents properly and return them to the archivist.
- Make sure that you pay for your photocopies or other expenses incurred during the course of the day.
- Remember to take with you everything that you brought into the reading room, collect everything from your locker and ensure that you have your reader's ticket when you leave.
- Thank the staff for their help.
- Congratulate yourself: you've done a good day's work.

The *Researching Your Family History Online For Dummies* Internet Directory

'It's ever since she discovered she may have royal ancestry!'

In this directory . . .

Here we give an overview of the various resources that are available online. We don't include *everything* that you could come across online – that would be impossible. Instead, this directory identifies a range of useful Internet sites and gives a brief account of what you find at each site. We also explain why these sites are so useful to you. Among our examples are search engines (genealogically focused and otherwise), comprehensive genealogical sites and resources that are surname-related, government-sponsored, geographically specific and commercial. The examples in the directory are organised in the following order:

- Booksellers and Publishers

- Compiled Genealogical Databases

- Comprehensive Sites

- Elusive Records

- Ethnic Records

- Genealogically Focused Search Engines

- Genealogical Software Databases

- General Search Engines

- Overseas and Government Resources

- Personal Websites, Family Associations and One-Name Study Sites

- Professional Researchers

- Surname-Related Websites

- Miscellany of Helpful Sites

Recognising Micons

For each site, we give the name of the site, the URL (Uniform Resource Locator, normally referred to as the web address) and a brief description of what you find there. The mini icons – or *micons* – tell you at a glance the resources the site offers. The following list explains what the micons mean:

Queries: At this site, you can post genealogical questions regarding surnames, geographical locations and research in general, and read and respond to queries left by other researchers.

Online database: This site includes an online database of genealogical information – a collection of data that may include, for example, info about a family or surname and indexes.

Online records: Here you find transcribed and/or digitised records of genealogical importance. The information at this site is either in the form of transcripts from actual records (such as civil records or census returns) or digitised (scanned) copies of actual records.

FAQs: Here you get answers to your frequently asked questions about a particular aspect of genealogical research.

Searchable: This site has a search engine so you can look for keywords and/or surnames.

Index: This site includes a section listing genealogical resources, such as other genealogical sites, types of record and information taken from actual records.

GEDCOM: This software supports GEDCOM, the standard for sharing data between genealogical programs.

Post to web: This software lets you take information from the database and post it directly on to the web.

Book: With this software you can put together your own genealogical book containing charts, forms, photographs and reports that you generate using the data that you enter into the software.

Online ordering: Here you can place online orders for genealogical books and supplies.

Multimedia: This software supports the use of photographs, sound and video in your genealogy.

Download: Here you can download software.

Charge for services: You must pay a fee to use some or all of the services at this site (or described at this site).

Booksellers and Publishers

Sometimes you have difficulty finding a book or research guide about a specific aspect of your genealogical research. As you become more focused on a particular ancestor, event or set of records, you'll probably notice that fewer and fewer people have knowledge of or interest in the same things as you. You'll also find increasingly fewer sufficiently detailed and specialised books in ordinary libraries and bookshops. At this stage, your best bet is to search online.

D-4   Booksellers and Publishers

Here's a list of online bookshops that you might like to try for both general and specific genealogical guides. Some of these shops sell other genealogical resources as well.

If you don't find what you're looking for at any of these sites, check out some of the comprehensive genealogical websites that we list in the next section.

Ancestry.com

www.ancestryshop.co.uk

At Ancestry.co.uk you find a variety of books, resources and software packages dedicated to genealogy. You can buy online or over the phone. As well as general resources, you can also buy gift packs, DNA tests and birth, marriage and death certificates. However, ordering these certificates directly from the General Register Office is cheaper, and often quicker.

GENfair

www.genfair.com/shop/system/index.
  html

This site describes itself as 'The "One-Stop Shop" for Local and Family Historians'. It contains over 15,000 items, which you can browse by supplier, country or area of interest. You can also run a quick search of the latest additions to the stock.

GlobalGenealogy.com, Inc.

www.globalgenealogy.com

GlobalGenealogy.com is an Internet-based shop for all things genealogical. The site sells books, software, CD-ROMs, maps and

archival and *scrapbooking* supplies (items for the preservation of documents and photos) for purchase online. You search by topic, product or the country to which the material relates.

Institute of Heraldic and Genealogical Studies Bookshop

www.ihgs.ac.uk/shop/index.php

This online shop is devoted to genealogy and heraldry volumes. You search using over 30 different categories, including beginners' books, Catholic records, military, occupational and non-conformity. This site is great for both novices and experienced genealogists.

National Archives' Online Bookshop

www.nationalarchives.gov.uk/bookshop

The National Archives' own publications dominate this collection. You search by keyword or category, such as 'family history', 'military history', 'academic history', 'popular history' or 'family history software'. Look out for the genealogy magazine *Ancestors*, which the National Archives publishes monthly, and a collection of genealogy books on CD-ROM.

Parish Chest

www.parishchest.com

Parish Chest supplies genealogy books, charts, CDs, maps, gifts, guides, directories, photograph-restoration services and just about anything else you can think of relevant to genealogy in the UK.

Compiled Genealogical Databases

Much like the compiled genealogies published in book form, compiled genealogical databases usually contain a lot of information about various family lines that are located in the same place. These databases show other researchers' findings in a neatly organised, published format. Unlike compiled genealogies in book form – which are often un-indexed – these compiled genealogical databases are searchable. Chapter 3 delves into compiled genealogical databases and identifies others you may wish to try.

FamilySearch

www.familysearch.org

The FamilySearch Internet Genealogy Service is the official research site of the Church of Jesus Christ of Latter-day Saints (LDS). It actually contains several of the LDS databases, including the Ancestral File, International Genealogical Index, Family History Catalogue, Research Guidance and census records.

WorldConnect

http://wc.rootsweb.ancestry.com

The WorldConnect project is a RootsWeb. com compilation of GEDCOM files submitted by researchers like you. It contains a searchable database of over 420 million names. The WorldConnect home page provides an excellent list of frequently asked questions along with information about the project and GEDCOMs in general.

Comprehensive Sites

A comprehensive genealogical website identifies a large number of other websites that may interest genealogists. These sites contain information on surnames, families, locations and a variety of other topics. Most comprehensive sites have indexes for the site names and URLs, usually broken down into categories. Some people refer to these comprehensive sites as large genealogical *indexes* or *lists*.

Most comprehensive sites are relatively easy to navigate because they categorise and cross-index their links to other genealogical sites. As long as you know the topic you're looking for, you can glance through the lists to see what's available. For example, if you're looking for information about migration to Australia, try visiting a comprehensive site and look through its sections relating to emigration, transportation and Australia.

Some comprehensive sites make searching even easier by providing a search engine. Rather than negotiating your way through a hierarchy of categories and subcategories to find a list of links relevant to you, the search engine lets you type in a keyword – the search engine then does the hard work for you. Most search engines return results as lists of possible matches to your keyword. From that list, you pick the sites you want to visit.

Here we list a few comprehensive genealogical sites to try:

Cyndi's List of Genealogy Sites on the Internet

www.cyndislist.com

This popular site by Cyndi Howells has more than 200,000 links, indexed and cross-indexed by topic in more than 150 categories. The categories are based on ethnic groups, religious groups, geographical locations, products (such as books and software), record types, learning resources (such as beginner information, how-to and writing a family history) and a range of other interests, including adoption, reunions, royalty and travel.

The Federation of Family History Societies

www.ffhs.org.uk

Most counties in England, Wales and Scotland have their own family history society and you can find out if the area that you're interested in has a site on this website. Overseas societies are listed here too. Many people join family history societies either for a link to the place they're researching or to meet other people interested in genealogy in the local area where they live. For example, Gloucestershire Family History Society (www.gfhs.org.uk) has a family history resource centre, monthly talks, coach trips direct to the The National Archives and produces a quarterly journal. They've also indexed many local records not available on the Internet, which you can purchase from the society. You may find joining a family history society useful to see what information they have for your family history even if you live hundreds of miles away. Most family history societies have a database of *surname interests* – the names that people are researching from any area. Family history societies often sell books, maps and CDs related to the local area and may give you a list of local researchers who can carry out research for you.

Membership usually costs around £10 per year and this includes a journal posted to you every quarter.

Genealogy Home Page

www.genealogyhomepage.com

The Genealogy Home Page was the first comprehensive genealogical site. The site classifies Internet genealogical sites in 15 areas, including Genealogy Help and Guides, Internet Genealogy Guides, Religious Genealogy Resources and Upcoming Genealogy Events. Two other aspects of Genealogy Home Page are the FTP (file transfer protocol – a way of sending and receiving files on the Internet) site and the 'What's New' sections. The Genealogy Anonymous FTP Site is a collection of downloadable freeware, shareware, archived ROOTS-L files and other FTP files. In the 'What's New' and 'What's Really New in WWW Genealogy Pages' sections, you find updated lists of new sites on the web and sites that are newly listed on the Genealogy Home Page. Although the site favours US genealogy, you'll likely still find lots of useful info on its pages.

UK & Ireland Genealogy

www.genuki.org.uk

This resource for Internet genealogists is popular and wide-ranging. Genuki is a charitable trust that aims 'to serve as a "virtual reference library" of genealogical information'. You can search in a number of ways, including by location, category and keyword.

Elusive Records

Some unique records and resources can be of great value to you in your genealogical pursuits. Some records relate to a particular group of people. Others are hard-to-find standard records.

Ellis Island Foundation

www.ellisisland.org

At this site you search for ancestors who arrived in the US via Ellis Island between 1892 and 1924. The database of passengers contains more than 25 million names and a wealth of background info, testimonies and photographs.

Hospital Records Database

www.nationalarchives.gov.uk/
hospitalrecords

This resource is handy if your ancestors brushed with the medical world, whether as staff or patients. The site points you in the direction of surviving hospital records.

Huguenot Society of Great Britain and Ireland

www.huguenotsociety.org.uk/history

This site gives background info about Huguenot migration from France to Britain and lists the resources available to trace your ancestors at the society.

Mayflower Passenger Lists

www.mayflowerhistory.com/Passengers/
passengers.php

This website lists the passengers who sailed from Plymouth on the *Mayflower* in 1620. The site gives genealogical and background info for all of the passengers on the boat.

Trafalgar Ancestors

www.nationalarchives.gov.uk/
trafalgarancestors/

This site contains a list of the service details and other information about all of those people who served at the Battle of Trafalgar.

Ethnic Records

If your ancestors were members of a particular ethnic group, you may be able to find online sites that have records and information relating specifically to that group. Although not as prevalent as surname-related and geographically specific websites, some ethnic resources are available to help you. The following sites are dedicated to particular ethnic groups:

Moving Here

www.movinghere.org.uk

This site's dedicated to Caribbean, Irish, Jewish and South Asian immigration to Britain over the past 200 years.

NativeWeb

www.nativeweb.org

NativeWeb is a cooperative effort to provide a community on the Internet for aboriginal and native people of the world. The Resource Centre lists the categories of information available on the site.

Genealogically Focused Search Engines

Genealogically specific search engines employ technology similar to that which general search engines use. These tools are particularly useful because they cover significantly fewer links than do the general search engines, limiting the number of indexed sites that aren't related to genealogy.

GenealogyPortal.com

www.genealogyportal.com

A joint project by the Genealogy Home Page and Helm's Genealogy Toolbox, GenealogyPortal.com features eight different genealogically focused search engines. Each search engine focuses on a particular subject area, including Archives and Libraries, Guides to Research, Historical Sites, Location-Specific Research, Names and Personal Sites, Primary Records, Research Supplies and Software and Utilities.

Origins Network

www.origins.net

  £

Origins Network is a fee-based search engine that focuses on locating individual ancestors by name in a variety of records, including census records, marriages, wills, apprenticeship records, military records and passenger lists. Searching the indexes themselves is free, but you need to be a member in order to view the actual records.

Genealogical Software Databases

Over the past few years, the area of genealogical software has expanded significantly – from commercial databases and mapping programs to freeware and software that allows you to manipulate your GEDCOM files. Whether you want to buy your first program with which to organise your genealogical information, to upgrade to a more powerful program or to enhance your genealogical files, you'll probably be interested in the software available to you and what it has to offer. Have a look at this list of genealogical software databases, including a few speciality programs, which you might like to investigate. Also, take a look at the Information-Sharing Websites section later on for details about sites that host software to which you can upload your research. These sites offer a good – and cheaper – alternative to buying one of these software packages.

Ancestral Quest

www.ancquest.com

Ancestral Quest is available for Windows 95 or later versions. You can enter information in various formats, and the software produces a variety of standard reports and family trees.

Family Historian

www.family-historian.co.uk

Family Historian is available for Windows 95 or later versions. It can customise your reports, and contains a search engine that scans the database for the specific information for which you're looking. With this program, you can generate standard reports, including Ancestor and Descendant charts, as well as an All Relatives report.

Family Matters

www.matterware.com

Family Matters is available for Windows 95 or later versions. Reports include Pedigree and Descendant charts. The software has Soundex, relationship and birth/age calculators.

Family Reunion

www.famware.com

Family Reunion is available for Windows 95 or later versions. Reports include Pedigree and Descendant charts, and Family Group Sheets.

Family Tree Legends

www.familytreelegends.com

Family Tree Legends is available for Windows 95 or later versions. It offers a large selection of charts and reports, including standard reports, a fact usage report and statistics report.

Family Tree Maker

www.familytreemaker.com

Family Tree Maker is one of the most popular genealogical programs, available for Windows 98 or later versions. Reports include Ancestor, Descendant, Kinship, Calendar and Family Group Sheets.

Personal Ancestral File

www.familysearch.org

Personal Ancestral File runs on Windows 95 or later versions. This software is distributed by the Church of Jesus Christ of Latter-day Saints, and allows you to customise the interface through which you enter information. It generates standard reports, such as Pedigrees, Family Group Sheets and lists.

General Search Engines

Search engines are programs that search large indexes of information gathered by online robots (sometimes called spiders) that get sent out to catalogue resources on the Internet. Usually, the search engine has an interface form in which you can enter keywords. The engine then searches its index for the keywords and returns its findings to you with links directly to the web pages in which the search engine's robot identified these keywords.

Although we don't recommend that you start your online genealogical research by using one of the major search engines (see Chapter 3 for the reasons), they may be the only place left to pursue some leads if you run aground in your research. Maybe you've searched the comprehensive sites and failed to find enough resources relating to your particular area of interest. Now's the time to turn to a general search engine.

Because a search on one name or word will probably produce thousands – even hundreds of thousands – of results, reading the particular engine's instructions for narrowing your search is a good idea.

Usually this means using more than one word in your search and avoiding really common words altogether. (For example, if you're using a common surname, such as Johnson, try to narrow your list by including other details that you know, such as the first name, a known or suspected location for that person and perhaps a date of birth or death. Don't include words such as 'the', 'a' and 'of' in your search: unless your search engine automatically ignores these words, you'll get an unmanageable number of results. Reviewing the information that the search engine site provides online is a good idea and a quick way to learn new methods of narrowing your searches.

AltaVista

www.altavista.com

You can use the main search box on AltaVista to search its index of Internet sites. Have a look at the Help section – or customise your settings – to further narrow your search results. If you prefer not to search by keyword, you can find links to topics that interest you by clicking through the categories listed in the AltaVista directory of categories. And if you'd like to focus your search on information from or about a particular country, or would like results in a language other than English, simply tick the relevant boxes on the search page.

Ask Jeeves

www.ask.com

At Ask Jeeves, you can either enter a keyword, search term or an actual question to submit for your search. You can also limit your search to particular areas of the search engine site, for example only pictures or news. When you search on Ask

Jeeves, you can select the option to search the whole web, or just the pages from the UK if you prefer.

Excite

www.excite.co.uk

Excite contains a directory of subjects from which you can choose to look for sites that interest you. Like the other search engines that contain directories, when you click on your subject of interest, you're taken to a submenu from which you can select a more specific topic and access links to actual sites on that topic. Alternatively, you can use the search engine to look for particular keywords in Excite's databases of websites.

Google

www.google.co.uk

The Google search engine is a no-nonsense site. The main page is simple, with a search box, one or two search options (including *Search the web* or *Search pages from the UK*) and some links to other parts of the Google site. You simply enter your search term and click on Google Search. (Of course, if you're optimistic that Google will find the perfect site for you, you might choose to select the *I'm Feeling Lucky* button instead.) If you want to narrow your search, have a look at the *Advanced Search* function. If you prefer to use the search engine's directory of links, click on the *Directory* link. Or if you're interested in checking out the latest on various newsgroups, click on the *Groups* link.

Lycos

www.lycos.co.uk

Lycos allows you to click through a list of subjects and their submenus to locate sites of interest, or to use the search engine to look for keywords. It even offers Parental Controls on its search function so that younger or sensitive users in your household can have restricted searches in which certain types of sites are weeded out of the results list. You may want to investigate the *Advanced Search* feature in order to narrow your searches. And although this main Lycos page is in English, Lycos offers its pages in several other languages. (You can select the language you want from the list at the bottom of the page.)

WebCrawler

www.webcrawler.com

WebCrawler's a one-stop shop for searching other major search engines and Internet directory sites, including Google, Yahoo!, AltaVista, Ask Jeeves, About and LookSmart.

Yahoo!

www.yahoo.co.uk

One of the most popular search engines in the UK, Yahoo! enables you to search the whole of the web, or to restrict your results by location. (The Yahoo! International link enables you to search only in the UK and Ireland, or only within India, Italy and so on.) You can choose to search under various categories, including the web, images, business finder, news and more. You can run an advanced search and adjust your search preferences according to your choice of language, display and layout and filters (you don't have to worry about this if you don't want to – the default settings suit most Yahoo! users).

Information-Sharing Websites

These websites make uploading and sharing information easy, be it a complete family tree or a scanned image of your family. You can also use these sites to find and network with other people who have similar interests, as well as to search for discussion groups and ask questions of other like-minded researchers.

Ancestry

www.ancestry.co.uk/trees

You can upload your existing GEDCOM file or create your family tree as you go on the Ancestry website. You can also link into other people's family trees and share information with other researchers as your research progresses.

BeBo

www.bebo.com

Bebo is a website to which you can upload photos, information and a personal profile page. It's free to use, although you can't form discussion and common interest groups here.

Facebook

www.facebook.com

Free to use, Facebook is one of the most popular social networking sites. You can use Facebook to create a family profile, share information and join common interest groups. You can also upload photos and documents to the site.

Flickr

www.flickr.com

Flickr is one of the largest and most popular photo-sharing websites. You can upload a certain number of pictures for free, using pictures that you've stored on your computer, mobile phone or digital camera.

Genes Reunited

www.genesreunited.co.uk

   £

Genes Reunited enables you to search for family members and ancestors, and to upload your family tree details as you go along or import your existing GEDCOM files. This website also offers message boards and discussion groups to help you in your research. Registering with Genes Reunited is free.

MemoryBank

www.memorybank.me

  $

MemoryBank is a site that enables you to share your family memories, upload photos and join specific communities to discuss certain topics. The site is free to use, and all you need to do is register your details.

MySpace

www.myspace.com

MySpace is a popular social networking site on which you can create your own profile page, upload videos and photos, and invite people who have a common interest to join your group.

Photobucket

www.photobucket.com

Photobucket is a free site to use, onto which you can upload your photos, create albums and share with family members. You can also upload videos, images and music to create slideshows of your photos, which are great for sharing with your family.

YouTube

www.youtube.com

YouTube is a social networking site that enables you to upload, view and share pictures and videos. If you register your details you can upload as many videos as you like, which can help you to create a place online for storing all your family videos.

Overseas Resources

You may grumble at having to pay taxes and complete forms to provide the government with information. But what we moan about as being annoying and time-consuming certainly have their uses for genealogists: forms create records that each generation leaves behind. Here are some sites – either created by government organisations or containing government-related information and records – that contain useful information for genealogists:

Australia

National Archives of Australia

www.naa.gov.au

The mission of the Australian Archives is to preserve Commonwealth records and to make them accessible to the public. Some of the Archives' services include public reference, an archival library and the maintaining of personnel records of those Australians who served in the First World War. The website provides information about the Archives' collections, publications and exhibitions.

Other Australian Sites to Try

State Records: New South Wales
www.records.nsw.gov.au

Queensland Government State Archives
www.archives.qld.gov.au

State Records of South Australia
www.archives.sa.gov.au

Archives Office of Tasmania
www.archives.tas.gov.au

Public Record Office of Victoria
www.prov.vic.gov.au

State Library of Western Australia
www.liswa.wa.gov.au

Northern Territory Archives Service
www.nt.gov.au/nta

Australasia

Australasian Genealogy Web Resources: Australasia

http://home.vicnet.net.au/~AGWeb/
agweb.htm

The Australasian-Genealogy Web (AGWeb) links together and provides access to regional genealogical resources. In addition to providing links to sites that are members of the network, AGWeb links to non-member sites that have information relating to Australia. Of special interest to genealogists researching ancestors in the area is the section on Categories and Records, which contains transcribed files available to view online or to download for use. The categories that have files associated with them include aborigines, civil registration, convicts, directories and almanacs, land records, local government records, manuscripts, letters, diaries, newspapers, occupational records, passenger arrivals and departures, family histories and biographies, local histories, research directories and indexes, shipping and genealogy-related resources.

Belgium

Archives of Mechelen (Belgium)

www.mechelen.be/archief

This site provides general information about the holdings and opening hours of the Archives of Mechelen. Some of the records held by the archive include birth, death, marriage, population and parish registries, property records, tax lists and a registry of abandoned children. Click the 'English' option at the top of the page to make more sense of this site!

Canada

CanadaGenWeb Project

www.canadagenweb.org

The CanadaGenWeb Project helps researchers to locate the enormous amount of Canadian genealogical information that is available on the Internet. Modelled on the USGenWeb project, this site has links to each of the main pages for the provinces/territories of Canada. The page for each territory has links to county/district pages, which provide further links to resources relevant to those areas. In addition, the CanadaGenWeb page has an historical timeline of Canada, information about famous Canadians and some facts and trivia about the country.

Canadian Archival Resources on the Internet

www.archivescanada.ca

Canadian Archival Resources on the Internet provides an index of the archives in Canada that have websites. In addition to some basic information about the different types of archives, this site has links to each of the archival resources that it identifies. The various archives are categorised as provincial, university, municipal, religious, medical and other, and are also cross-categorised by region (western, central, eastern and national).

Library and Archives Canada

www.archives.ca

This is the National Archives of Canada website, which aims to preserve the memories of the nation and government of Canada and to enhance a sense of national identity. The website provides information about researching on location and contains detailed descriptions of the types of records held by the Archives. Among the many resources are civil registrations of births, marriages and deaths dating from the 19th century; passenger manifests from 1865; immigration documents for people who arrived in Canada from the US; some naturalisation records from 1828 to 1850; and petitions for land. Of particular interest to those with ancestors who served in the military is an online index of about 620,000 personnel folders for the citizens who enlisted in the Canadian Expeditionary Force (CEF) during the First World War. The personnel folders contain various documents, including attestation and enlistment papers, medical records, discipline and pay records and discharge papers. You can search the index online; if your search is successful, you can order copies of the documents from the personnel folder. You can find information about how to do this on the website.

Caribbean

CaribbeanGenWeb Project

www.rootsweb.ancestry.com/~caribgw

CaribbeanGenWeb has websites set up or planned for each island of the Caribbean in order to provide information about and links to genealogical resources on the Internet relating to that particular island. In addition, the main CaribbeanGenWeb page provides links to some resources relevant to the Caribbean as a whole.

Europe

EuropeGenWeb Project

www.britishislesgenweb.org
www.rootsweb.ancestry.com/~ceneurgw
www.rootsweb.ancestry.com/~easeurgw
www.mediterraneangenweb.com

EuropeGenWeb is actually made up of four sites:

- BritishIslesGenWeb Project (www.britishislesgenweb.org)

- CenEuroGenWeb Project (www.rootsweb.ancestry.com/~ceneurgw)

- EastEuropeGenWeb (www.rootsweb.ancestry.com/~easeurgw)

- MediterraneanGenWeb (www.mediterraneangenweb.com)

Each section provides information about and links to the WorldGenWeb pages for countries that are located in that particular area. Each page relating to these countries then provides information and links to genealogical resources on the Internet to do with that particular country, as well as links to any state/county/province pages that fall under the heading of that country.

Middle East

Middle EastGenWeb Project

www.genealogynation.com/middle-east/

Middle EastGenWeb provides information about and links to the WorldGenWeb pages for countries that are located in the Middle East. Each page for these countries then provides information and links to genealogical resources on the Internet that relate to that country, as well as links to any state/county/province pages that fall within that particular country.

South America

South AmericanGenWeb Project

www.worldgenweb.
   org/%7Esouthamericangenweb/

The South AmericanGenWeb Project provides information about and links to the WorldGenWeb pages for countries in South America. Each WorldGenWeb page for these countries provides information and links to genealogical resources on the Internet relating to that particular country, as well as links to any state/county/province pages that fall within that country.

United States

Ancestry.com

www.ancestry.com

     £

Ancestry is the major genealogical resource site if you're researching US genealogy. This vast subscription database contains searchable images of the US census; birth, marriage and death records; an obituary collection; a learning centre; and a wealth of other resources besides.

Social Security Death Index

http://ssdi.rootsweb.ancestry.com/

The US government (through the Social Security Administration) assigns a unique nine-digit number to everyone who lives and works in the US. This number records who's eligible for Social Security benefits (similar to a supplementary retirement income) when they reach a certain age.

Whenever a claim for death benefits is filed with the Social Security Administration, the government adds the person's name and some other information to the Master Death Index. If your ancestors lived and worked in the US, the Social Security Death Index can be a useful tool in your genealogical pursuits. RootsWeb's online interface makes searching the index and seeing whether your ancestors are included easy.

To search the database of over 77 million names, go to the search site, enter your ancestor's name and click Search. (Only the last name is required, but knowing the first name can be helpful.) To narrow your search, complete any other fields on the form that you can. After you've completed the form and clicked Search, you get a list of people who match your search criteria. As well as the person's name, the list includes the Social Security number, date born, date died, residence, zip code to which the person's last Social Security benefit was sent, the state in which the person's Social Security card was issued and the date when the card was issued.

USGenWeb Project

www.usgenweb.org

The USGenWeb Project provides websites for each county in each state within the US. Each site aims to identify genealogical resources available on the Internet for its particular county. This main site provides links to all of the state pages, which, in turn, provide links to existing county pages. It also contains information about the USGenWeb's Archives project and explains how you can become involved in the USGenWeb.

World

The Federation of Family History Societies

www.ffhs.org.uk

Some overseas family history societies are members of this website. Check the list of family history societies to see if the place overseas that you're interested in has a family history society.

Parts of Europe have family history societies, too (for example, the Anglo-German Family History Society at www.AGFHS.org. uk).

World Factbook

www.cia.gov/library/publications/the-world-factbook/

The Central Intelligence Agency's (CIA) World Factbook site provides information about every country and ocean in the world. You can access the country pages from this main page via the drop-down menu at the top. Each country page includes a map and the geographical location of that country, as well as detailed information about the country's flag, geography, people, government, economy, transportation, communication and defence. The pages for the oceans

contain maps and geographical locations, as well as information about the
ocean's geography, economic relevance
and transportation. Although not directly
genealogically related, this site is great
for getting some background on places
to which your ancestors moved, or from
which they emigrated.

WorldGenWeb Project

www.worldgenweb.org

The goal of the WorldGenWeb Project is
to build a website for every country in
the world to contain information about
and links to genealogical resources on the
Internet. Although many of the countries
already have pages, more volunteers are
needed to complete the project.

Personal Websites, Family Associations and One-Name Study Sites

Distinguishing between personal websites,
family associations and one-name study
sites is difficult because their content's
fairly similar. Don't worry too much about
the differences: what you really want to
know is whether you can find a site that
contains useful info about the names
you're researching. Personal websites
usually provide information about the
specific research interests of an individual
or family and are the most common type
of surname-related site. Personal websites
usually have info about a particular branch

of a family. The format and presentation of
this information varies greatly. Some personal web pages simply list the surnames
that the site maintainer's researching;
others contain the GEDCOM file of the site
maintainer. Others still have narrative
histories about the family and the areas
where they lived.

Family associations tend to have an
underlying organisation, whereas one-
name study sites do not. Formal family
associations may focus upon a surname
as a whole, or upon a particular branch.
Projects that a family association is under-
taking (such as writing a book or putting
together a comprehensive database of
information from all members) may carry
over to the website. The most distinguish-
able characteristic of a family association
is that the website may require you to
become a member of the family association
before you can fully participate at the site
or access some of the information online.

Unlike personal web pages, which provide you with detailed information about
an individual's research and particular
branch of a family, one-name studies give
you a wide range of information about
one particular surname. Usually the
information presented at these sites isn't
constrained by geographic boundaries – in
other words, the site may have information about the surname in several different
areas or countries. One-name study sites
usually have information that includes
a history of the surname (including its
origins), variations in spelling, heraldry
associated with that name and databases
and queries submitted by researchers
worldwide.

Thousands and thousands of these three
types of sites exist, but we list just a few
examples here to give you a flavour of
what's out there. To assess the quality of
a site when you begin to search yourself,
look at the variety and usefulness of the
information provided and how clearly it's
arranged. Doing this gives you an idea

of how much the maintainer cares about genealogical research and sharing their information with others.

Entwistle Family History Association

www.entwistlefamily.org.uk/links.htm

This site provides all kinds of information and facilities to do with the Entwistle name, including a large amount of genealogical data, background information, a members' forum, maps, information about the origin of the name and a great deal more.

Harrington Family from Great Tey

www.philharrington.co.uk

This site relates to the branch of the Harrington family from Great Tey in Essex. On this site you find a family tree, a surname history, documents, photographs, family tales and stories and information about famous Harringtons and other Essex Harringtons. A links page is also present along with a forum in which those searching for Harrington ancestors can post their messages and queries.

Metcalfe Society

www.metcalfe.org.uk

Another organisation that asks for membership before information is shared, the Metcalfe Society has attracted over 1500 members interested in studying the name. This site contains a rich supply of genealogical information, and offers links, contact lists, a message board, a history of the Metcalfe Clan and much more.

Wells Family History

www.richardphillips.org.uk/fh/Wells.htm

A site dedicated to the surname 'Wells' from all over the country. As well as an indexed family history, it provides infor-

mation about the Wells Family Genealogy Forum and the Wells Family Research Association, and contains information about the Wells Family DNA Project.

Professional Researchers

During the course of your research, you may decide to hire a professional researcher to pursue a particular family line. Perhaps you'll find that you've exhausted all your leads on a family line, that you no longer have the time to devote to research or that the records you need are held abroad, and you have neither the time nor the money to travel there. A wide selection of research services is available – some from reputable companies, others from individuals who just want to help others.

The following are just a few professional research services available in different parts of the world. Chapter 9 provides more information about finding and choosing professional researchers.

Family Tree

www.familytree.hu

£

Family Tree is a genealogical and probate research bureau that was formed in Hungary in 1988. Its researchers work in Hungary, Slovakia, Austria (Burgenland), Transylvania (part of Romania), Croatia, Slovenia, the former Yugoslavia (Banat) and the Ukraine (Sub-Carpathia), and they communicate in English, Hungarian, French, German, Russian, Romanian, Polish, Czech, Slovak and Serbo-Croatian. The website explains how the bureau sets about its research in various places, and provides historical information about Hungary, as well as details about Jewish genealogy and probate searches in the area.

genealogyPro Services

genealogypro.com/directories

£

Here you can search for professional genealogical researchers worldwide. Simply click on the location that interests you, and you'll find a list of researchers who are registered in that area. Each link includes contact details, qualifications, services offered and costs.

National Archives' Independent Researchers List

www.nationalarchives.gov.uk/irlist

£

This site is a great place to find researchers who specialise in your particular area of interest. The site focuses mainly on researchers within the UK.

Sticks Research Agency

www.sra-uk.com

£

Sticks Research Agency (SRA) is an international research agency with branches in the UK (covering Scotland), Ireland and Australia. Founded in 2000 by Dr Nick Barratt, SRA is responsible for the genealogy research for the BBC's *Who Do You Think You Are?* television series. SRA also undertakes research for private clients and has an expert team on hand to help solve all your family history mysteries.

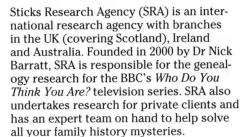

Surname-related websites help you search for info relating specifically to the name in which you're interested. We list a few of them below. If you don't find what you're after in any of these sites, try typing in the name you're interested in into a genealogically focused search engine, a comprehensive genealogical site or even a general search engine.

Guild of One-Name Studies

www.one-name.org

The Guild of One-Name Studies is a repository of information relating to particular surnames. You simply enter the name that you want and click Search. If the name's registered, you'll find the contact details for whoever holds the relevant information. The site also contains general information about the Guild and how you can join.

Yourfamily.com

www.yourfamily.com

Among other services, Yourfamily.com provides a free, searchable index of family home pages. By entering the surname you want to search and clicking the Search button, the search engine produces a list of links to pages that may meet your specified name. You can then look through the list and any accompanying comments about the sites and pick the home pages that you want to visit. You can register your own family home page if you wish.

Miscellany of Helpful Sites

Clooz

www.clooz.com

Clooz helps you to organise and store all of the various sources that you'll use during the course of your research.

DeedMapper

www.directlinesoftware.com

DeedMapper, which is produced by Direct Line Software, is a program that enables you to transfer information from land records to maps that you can see and use on your computer.

Families in Time

www.familiesintime.co.uk

Families in Time is a website dedicated specifically to finding ancestors that were adopted and to tracing birth relatives. You have to pay for the service. Contact the website for more details, as costs vary depending on your requirements.

GEDClean

www.raynorshyn.com/gedclean

GEDClean is shareware that helps to clean your GEDCOM file of information about living people, or of other types of information that you don't wish to disclose.

Gedpage

www.gedpage.com

Gedpage converts your GEDCOM files to HTML so that you're able to post them on the web. The software is available for Windows and Macintosh.

HELPERS (Higher Education Libraries in Your Personal History Research)

http://helpers.shl.lon.ac.uk

A key resource for genealogists and local historians in London, this site points you in the direction of library and archival resources held by London University. You'll find information about your research and how the site can help, as well as links to useful websites and collections of all kinds.

Pharos Teaching and Tutoring

www.pharostutors.com

£

This site offers a selection of online genealogy courses which take you through and beyond the basics of genealogical research. Pharos is a great place to find out about records and how they were created – in your own time, and without leaving the comfort of your home.

Sparrowhawk

www.bradandkathy.com/genealogy/
   sparrowhawk.html

Sparrowhawk is a GEDCOM to HTML converter for Macintosh computers.

Part IV
Share and Share Alike

'...and then there was Great Aunt Doris who
was related to Hereward the Wake while
Great Grandfather Entwhistle claims
descendancy from Madam Pompadour...
further more our cousin Ethel's nephew's
brother is the fourth great nephew nine times
removed of George Washington & do you know,
I am <u>Anastasia</u>, the last tsar's youngest
daughter...'

In this part . . .

Here you discover how to get the most out of your online research. We show you how to store and organise information in your computer, how to benefit from other people's research and how to share your findings with the online genealogical community.

Chapter 8

Storing and Organising Information on Your Computer

• •

In This Chapter

▶ Getting started with genealogical software

▶ Producing genealogical reports

▶ Selecting accessories for your computer

• •

*S*atisfying though it may be to compile boxes full of paper relating to your family history, and then to file them neatly with your photographs and other paraphernalia, a good idea is to enter all of your research and scan all of your documents into a computer. A computer may be your best friend when it comes to storing, organising and publishing your genealogical information.

With your computer, you can upload information to genealogy websites, use genealogical software to maintain information on thousands of individuals, access CD-ROMs containing indexes to and digital images of valuable genealogical records, scan images to preserve your family heritage and share information with researchers throughout the world via the Internet. This chapter examines genealogical database software and websites and what they can do for you, and looks at a few gadgets that may enhance the capabilities of your computer.

 A number of monthly family history magazines have a computer section and review new software. Some packages are more suitable for the American market, so do your homework before buying any software.

Finding and Running Genealogical Software

Several kinds of software program enable you to keep track of your ancestors without the risk of people disappearing into the depths of the system, or ending up apparently related to the wrong people. You can store facts and stories about your relatives, attach files containing scanned photographs of them with their biographical information and generate numerous reports at the click of a button. Certain programs even enable you to store audio and video recordings – a capability that is especially useful if you want to put together a multimedia presentation on your genealogy to present at a family reunion.

Most currently available genealogical software programs have many features and system requirements in common. To ensure that you make the most of your computer and software, look closely at the box or CD case to check the specific system requirements and the features on offer when deciding what to use.

Checking system requirements

To guide you in the decision-making process, we recommend the following features as the minimum requirements for your computer system to run most genealogical software adequately. However, bear in mind that if you want additional accessories for your computer, such as a scanner, digital camera and so forth, to assist in your genealogical project or if you want to store electronic images, you may need to have a higher-end system, with a faster microprocessor, more random-access memory (RAM) and more hard-drive space.

If you have a PC, you need a minimum of the following:

- A Pentium processor
- Windows 95, 98, 2000, ME or XP
- A CD-ROM drive
- 500 megabytes of free hard-drive space
- 64 megabytes of RAM
- VGA (video graphics array) display with at least 256 colours
- A Microsoft-compatible mouse

If you have a Macintosh computer, you need a minimum of the following:

- A PowerPC processor
- Mac OS 8.5 or later
- A CD-ROM drive
- 500 megabytes of free hard-drive space
- 64 megabytes of RAM

Looking at the features on offer

You may already have found the perfect research partner for your project – a patient and enthusiastic friend or relative who accompanies you to every library and archive and is willing to listen for hours on end as you untangle the intricacies of your family tree. But you also need another, more silent, partner. It comes on CD-ROMs or is downloadable from the Internet; you install it on your computer and then let it perform all sorts of amazing tasks for you.

Software programs can store and manipulate your genealogical information. They share a number of standard features; for instance, most serve as databases for family facts and stories, have reporting functions to generate pre-designed charts and forms and have export capabilities so that you can share your data with others. Each software program also includes a few unique features – for example, the capacity to take information out of the software and generate online reports at the click of a button – that make it stand out from the others.

An alternative silent partner actually resides on the Internet: subscription websites. Most subscription websites enable you to upload your findings directly, as you go along, without the need for software packages on your computer. Software packages are great for storing the information on your hard drive and for transferring the information in a recognisable format, but if you subscribe to one of the popular genealogy websites, direct upload may work out as a cheaper option. Many sites, such as www.family relatives.com and www.ancestry.co.uk, have specific sections with inbuilt software that enables you to enter information as you find it, to a pre-formatted family tree. You can create a specific homepage for each person on the tree, enter as much genealogical detail about each person as you like and save more than one tree at any one time. These sites also allow you to attach digital images, not only from their website but also from your own hard drive, to the trees.

A handy feature of these websites is that some, like www.ancestry.co.uk for example, check the details you enter on your tree to see if they match any of their records. Many sites are updating the facilities that they offer all the time, adding additional exciting features. However, keeping your own copy of your family tree file on your hard drive is still important, for safety and reference, just in case your preferred subscription website should ever have problems. This way, you always have your own record of your research.

Here's a list of the features that you may like to consider when evaluating different software packages:

✔ **How easy is the software/website to use?** Can you operate the graphics by common sense and intuition, or do you have to wade through pages of complicated detail to discover how and where to enter particular facts about an ancestor?

✔ **Does the software/website generate the reports that you need?** For example, if you're partial to family group sheets, does this software support them?

✔ **Does the software/website enable you to export and/or import a GEDCOM file?** *GEDCOM* is a file format that's widely used for genealogical research, and most current packages automatically convert your files to GEDCOM, saving lots of time and effort. For more info about GEDCOM, see the 'GEDCOM: The genealogist's standard' sidebar later in the chapter.

✔ **How many names can this software/website hold?** Make sure that the software/website can hold an adequate number of names and accompanying data to accommodate all the ancestors about whom you have information, and more whom you've not yet found.

Keep in mind that your genealogy continues to grow with time.

✔ **Can your current computer system support this software?** If the requirements of the software cause your computer to crash every time you use it, or if you have a slow, old computer that takes time to load the pages of a subscription website, you won't get far in your genealogical research.

✔ **Does this software/website provide fields for citing your sources and keeping notes?** Including information about all of your sources alongside the data that they have provided is sound genealogical practice. Take a look at Chapter 10 for more information about the importance of citing sources and how to do so.

GEDCOM: The genealogist's standard

As you've probably already discovered, genealogy is full of acronyms. One such acronym that you see and hear repeatedly is *GEDCOM (GEnealogical Data COMmunication)*. GEDCOM is the standard tool used by individuals and software manufacturers to export and import information to or from different genealogical databases. In simple terms, GEDCOM is a file format intended to make data transferable between different software programs so that people can share their family information more easily.

The Church of Jesus Christ of Latter-Day Saints (more commonly known as the Mormon Church) first developed and introduced GEDCOM in 1987. The first two versions of GEDCOM were released only for public discussion; they were not meant to serve as the standard tool. But with the introduction of Version 5.*x* and subsequently later versions, GEDCOM did indeed come to be accepted as the standard.

Having a standard for formatting files is beneficial to you as a researcher because you can share the information that you collect with others who are interested in some – or all – of your ancestors. It also enables you to import GEDCOM files from other researchers who have information about family lines and ancestors in whom you're interested. And you don't even have to use the same software as the other researchers! You can use Reunion for Macintosh and someone with whom you want to share information can use Family Tree Maker; having GEDCOM as the standard in both software programs enables each of you to create and exchange GEDCOM files.

To convert the data in your genealogical database to a GEDCOM file, follow the instructions provided in your software's manual or Help menu. You can create the GEDCOM file relatively easily; most software programs guide you through the process with a series of dialogue boxes.

In addition to creating GEDCOM files to exchange with individual researchers, you can generate GEDCOM files to submit to larger co-operatives that make the data from many GEDCOM files available to thousands of researchers worldwide via the World Wide Web and email. Here are three co-operatives you may wish to explore:

✔ `www.genserv.com`

✔ `www.ancestry.co.uk/trees/awt/getting_started.htm`

✔ `www.genesreunited.co.uk/help/default.aspx`

For a more international focus, try `http://wc.rootsweb.ancestry.com/`

You can also convert your GEDCOM file to HTML so that you can place the data directly on the World Wide Web for others to access. Simple software tools such as GED2HTML are available to convert your GEDCOM files to HTML. Although this facility may come as standard for many software packages, you can find a list of the most popular ones at `www.geocities.com/turkel.geo/GED2WWW/g2hcompare.htm`.

Sharing Your Genealogical Success With Others

After you've entered as much information as possible into your genealogical software, you're in a position to share it with others or to generate notes to take with you on research trips. (If you haven't organised your information yet, Chapter 2 can help you.)

Your genealogical software can help you by generating printed reports of the information that you've collected and entered. The advantage here is that you only have to enter the information once to produce a range of different charts, and you can share them more easily with others when stored in this single format.

Although you can download a variety of charts from the Internet, you can also produce them easily with your genealogical software. Most genealogical software packages have several standard reports or charts in common, including a pedigree chart (also called an ancestral chart), family group sheet, descendant chart, outline of descendants and kinship report. If you decide to purchase a software program, check its capacity for producing the charts you want before making your choice.

This section examines the different types of reports that you may find useful when it comes to presenting your research.

Pedigree charts (or ancestor trees)

The *pedigree chart* or *ancestral chart* flows horizontally across a page. It begins by listing the name and details of a primary individual and uses lines to show the relationship to that individual's father and mother, then to each of their parents and so on until the chart runs off the page. Each member of the family is denoted by name, date and place of birth, date and place of marriage and date and place of death. Figure 8-1 displays a pedigree or ancestral chart downloaded from Ancestry.com (www.ancestry.com/save/charts/ancchart.htm) and completed with the details of a certain Hannah Graham.

Family group sheets

A *family group sheet* or *family group record* is a summary of vital information about a particular family. At the top of the page, it shows the *husband* followed by the *wife* and then any children of the couple, as well as biographical information such as dates and places of birth, marriage and death. Figure 8-2 shows a family group sheet downloaded from Ancestry.com (www.ancestry.com/save/charts/familysheet.htm).

Descendant charts

A *descendant chart* contains information about an ancestor and spouse (or spouses if more than one exists), their children and their spouses, grandchildren and spouses and so on down the family line. A descendant chart usually flows vertically rather than horizontally like a pedigree or ancestral chart. Figure 8-3 shows a descendant tree generated by Family Tree Maker software.

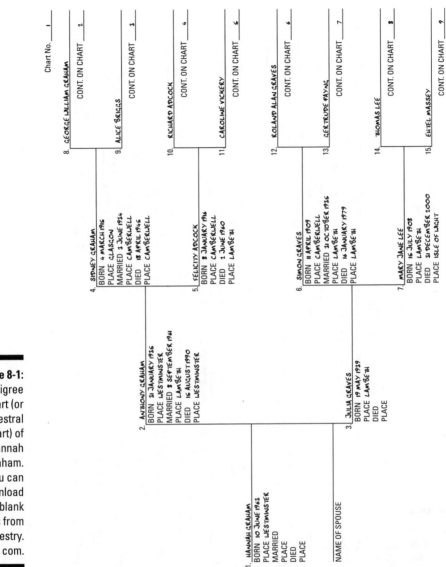

Figure 8-1:
A pedigree
chart (or
ancestral
chart) of
Hannah
Graham.
You can
download
blank
charts from
Ancestry.
com.

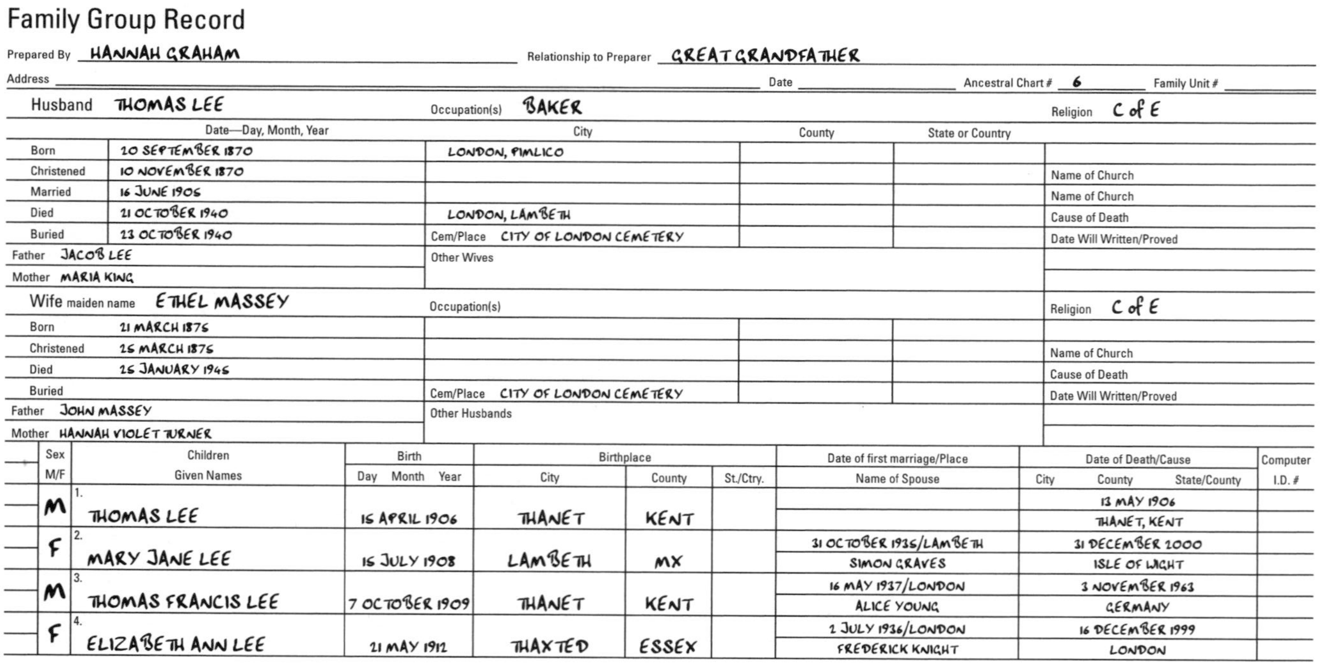

Family Group Record

Prepared By **HANNAH GRAHAM**
Relationship to Preparer **GREAT GRANDFATHER**

Address _____ Date _____ Ancestral Chart # **6** Family Unit # ___

Husband **THOMAS LEE**
Occupation(s) **BAKER**

	Date—Day, Month, Year	City	State or Country
Born	20 SEPTEMBER 1870	LONDON, PIMLICO	
Christened	10 NOVEMBER 1870		
Married	16 JUNE 1906		
Died	21 OCTOBER 1940	LONDON, LAMBETH	
Buried	13 OCTOBER 1940	Cem/Place CITY OF LONDON CEMETERY	

Religion **C of E**
Name of Church _____
Name of Church _____
Cause of Death _____
Date Will Written/Proved _____

Other Wives _____

Father **JACOB LEE**
Mother **MARIA KING**

Wife maiden name **ETHEL MASSEY**
Occupation(s) _____

	Date—Day, Month, Year	City	State or Country
Born	21 MARCH 1876		
Christened	26 MARCH 1876		
Died	16 JANUARY 1966		
Buried		Cem/Place CITY OF LONDON CEMETERY	

Religion **C of E**
Name of Church _____
Name of Church _____
Cause of Death _____
Date Will Written/Proved _____

Other Husbands _____

Father **JOHN MASSEY**
Mother **HANNAH VIOLET TURNER**

	Children Given Names	Sex M/F	Birth Day Month Year	Birthplace City	County	St./Crty.	Date of first marriage/Place Name of Spouse	Date of Death/Cause City County State/County	Computer I.D. #
1.	THOMAS LEE	M	16 APRIL 1906	THANET	KENT		31 OCTOBER 1936/LAMBETH SIMON GRAVES	13 MAY 1906 THANET, KENT	
2.	MARY JANE LEE	F	16 JULY 1908	LAMBETH	MX		16 MAY 1927/LONDON ALICE YOUNG	31 DECEMBER 2000 ISLE OF WIGHT	
3.	THOMAS FRANCIS LEE	M	7 OCTOBER 1909	THANET	KENT		2 JULY 1936/LONDON FREDERICK KNIGHT	3 NOVEMBER 1963 GERMANY	
4.	ELIZABETH ANN LEE	F	21 MAY 1912	THAXTED	ESSEX			16 DECEMBER 1999 LONDON	

Figure 8-2:
A family group sheet or family group record for the family of Thomas Lee.

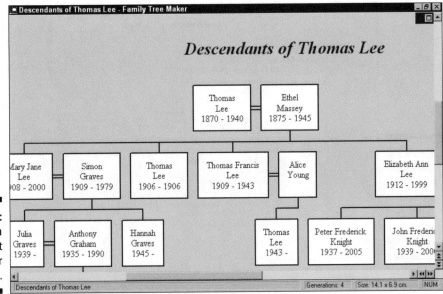

Figure 8-3:
Part of a
descendant
chart for
Thomas Lee.

Outline reports

A family *outline* is a list of the descendants of a particular ancestor. The first numbered line contains the name (and sometimes the years of birth and death) of a primary ancestor. The next line shows the name of the ancestor's spouse, followed by the next numbered line, which contains the name of the ancestor and spouse's first child. If that child is married and has children, the name of the child's spouse follows, as do names and information for each of that child and spouse's children. Figure 8-4 gives an example of an outline descendant tree generated using Family Tree Maker software, which calls the list an *outline descendant tree*.

Kinship reports

A *kinship report* is a list of family members together with details of how they relate directly to one particular person. The report includes the name of the family member, the person's relationship to the primary ancestor and the civil and canon codes reflecting the degree of relationship between the two people.

Figure 8-5 gives an example of a kinship report generated by Family Tree Maker software.

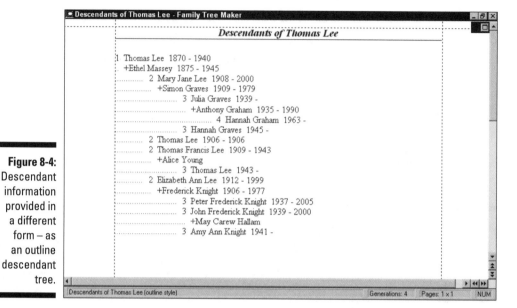

Figure 8-4: Descendant information provided in a different form – as an outline descendant tree.

Figure 8-5: A kinship report showing both civil and canon relationships.

Civil and *canon codes* clarify the bloodline relationship in legal terms – in other words, they identify how many steps or *degrees of separation* there are between two people who are related by blood. Civil law counts each step between two relatives as a degree, so that two people who are first cousins have a degree of separation equal to four, which is the total of two steps between one cousin and the common grandparent, and two steps between the *other* cousin and the common grandparent. Canon law counts only the number of steps from the nearest common ancestor of both relatives, so that the degree of separation between two first cousins is two. Two steps separate the grandparent from each of the cousins.

Talking Hardware: Is Your Computer Equipped?

As you grow more accustomed to using the information that you store in your computer, you may consider adding other hardware and peripheral equipment to your system to enhance the range and quality of the reports that you can generate. You might start including electronic images of the photographs and original documents that you have in your paper filing system. You may decide to incorporate audio recordings of your grandmother's reminiscences, or a video of your grandchild greeting people at the family reunion. So what kind of computer hardware or other equipment do you need in order to combine images and other enhancements with your genealogical information?

You need to consider several pieces of equipment as you prepare to enhance your genealogy with audio, video and electronic images. The equipment includes writable CD-ROM or DVD drives, sound cards, video-capture boards, scanners, digital cameras and extra hard drives.

Writable CD-ROM and DVD drives

A writable CD-ROM drive saves a great deal of memory space on your computer, as well as storing information in a light and easy format for you to carry about when visiting archives or attending a family reunion. With a writable CD-ROM drive, you can cut your own data CDs, filling them with family photos (which usually take up a lot of space on your computer) or family files. Writable CD-ROM drives are available in internal and external varieties. Similar to writable CD-ROM drives are writable DVD drives that can hold more data than a CD-ROM.

CD-Rs – the disks that you use with a writable CD-ROM drive – can hold about 650–700 megabytes. DVD-Rs – the disks that you use with writable DVD drives – can hold about 4.7 *gigabytes* (a gigabyte is 1,000 megabytes).

Sound cards

A *sound card* is a standard internal feature on most modern computers. It allows you to hear any audio accompaniments that come on software or audio files that you download from the Internet. In most cases, the card also enables you to record your own audio from your stereo, radio, video camera or microphone, but you need to have software that supports recordings. If your sound card is capable of recording and you have adequate software, you simply plug the sound source into the microphone jack (or the sound-in jack on the back of your computer) and set your software to record. After you've made the recording, you can import it into your genealogical software if your genealogical software supports audio.

Video-capture boards

Similar to a sound card, a *video-capture board* enables you to transfer images from your video camera or VCR. You can use moving images or still pictures, depending on the type of video-capture board and accompanying software that you install in your computer. Video-capture boards aren't usually a standard feature on computers. They have varying system requirements depending on the manufacturer and the software that's included, so be sure that your computer system can handle a particular video-capture board and software before you make your purchase.

Scanners

Scanners remain one of the most popular computer accessories for genealogists. Many people want to include family photos with their genealogy, or to preserve precious documents electronically. With the cost of scanners decreasing – and the availability of bundled software that allows you to use a scanner not only as a scanner, but also as a fax machine and copier – adding a scanner to your computer equipment makes good sense. It can render your genealogical research more colourful and efficient and you can purchase one at a reasonably modest price.

A variety of scanners is available. The most common types are snapshot, sheet-fed and flatbed, and you can choose between colour and black and white. The system requirements for scanners vary greatly, so make sure that you read the packaging of any scanner carefully before you decide to buy it. Also, each scanner requires software to make it work, so read the software's system requirements and capabilities as well. Here's a quick rundown of the major types of scanners:

- **Photo scanners:** These scanners are ideal for creating electronic images of photographs that measure 13×18 centimetres (5×7 inches) or smaller: they're designed to work primarily with that size of photograph. Photo scanners (also called snapshot scanners) are compact and easy to use. You feed the photograph into the scanner, and the scanner then captures an image before sending the photograph back out. A number of photo scanners have a removable top that you can use as a hand-held scanner when you want to capture images larger than 13×18 centimetres (5×7 inches).

One precaution to bear in mind with photo scanners: don't use them with old, fragile photographs because the scanner can damage the photograph as you feed it through.

- **Film scanners:** A film scanner is ideal if you want to produce your own photographs directly from negatives. These compact scanners can capture images in colour or black and white. You feed the negative manually into the scanner, although some film scanners have optional slide feeders.

- **Document scanners:** Document scanners are also called sheet-fed scanners – appropriately enough, because they're usually a little bit wider than an A4 sheet of paper. They're still rather compact as far as scanners go, but all are external. You feed the photograph or document into the scanner, which then captures an image as the document goes through. In common with many photograph scanners, some document scanners have a removable top that you can use as a hand-held scanner to capture images larger than an A4 width. Of course, you must take care when feeding fragile photographs into these scanners.

- **Flatbed scanners:** These scanners used to be large and bulky but are now incredibly light and compact. You lift the top of the scanner and place your document or photograph on the bed, close the lid and tell the scanner (through your software) to capture the image. Flatbed scanners are somewhat safer for photographs and old paper records than are other types because you lay the photos on the scanner's glass plate rather than feeding them through the device.

- **Hand-held scanners:** Although ideal for genealogy because of their flexibility and mobility, hand-held scanners are also more difficult to find these days. You can use them not only for scanning photographs and paper documents but also for books. Hand-held scanners are external and compact, and are also the perfect size to carry with you when you're out and about on a research project. You scan photographs and other objects by holding the scanner and slowly moving it over the object while holding down a button. The quality of the scanned image depends greatly on how steady your hand is, how good the lighting is where you're scanning and the size of the original document.

Coordinate your research via phone and GPS

Carrying your mobile phone with you on research trips enables you to call relatives in the town or county you're visiting and to ensure that a record exists in a particular location before you travel there. Another key reason to carry a certain type of mobile phone on your genealogical jaunts is that some phones have built-in global positioning system (GPS) receivers. GPS is a satellite system that enables the person controlling the receiver to determine his or her geographical coordinates. It can come in handy when you're recording the locations of family markers, such as gravestones and houses. After all, markers such as rocks, trees and buildings may move or disappear entirely with time, but the latitude and longitude of a location remains the same. For more info about using GPS for genealogical purposes, check out Chapter 4.

Digital cameras

Over the past few years, digital cameras have increasingly captured the interest of genealogists as well as the general public. The ability to take all of your photographs with a camera from which you can download the images directly to your computer is very appealing. And the fact that you can easily attach or import digital photos to your genealogical database is definitely exciting. Certain digital cameras include a document setting, so you don't need both a scanner and a digital camera. You'll find this feature extremely convenient when you're out and about researching – you can use your digital camera to capture images from church or graveyard visits, pictures of long-lost cousins at reunions, and some archives may even allow you to take pictures of some records. You store digital photographs within the camera on memory cards, from where you can download them to your computer with the aid of a USB cable.

As with every other computer accessory, if you're considering purchasing a digital camera, read carefully the software requirements to make sure that your computer system can support the equipment. For more information, read *Digital Photography For Dummies*, 6th Edition, by Julie Adair King and Serge Timacheff.

Travelling With Your Genealogical Tools

Whether you're going to a family reunion, travelling a hundred miles to research in a particular county or town or giving a presentation at a conference, the chances are that you want to transport your research from one place to another. You may consider getting a laptop or notebook computer instead of a desktop system. Portable computers give you the flexibility to take your genealogical database with you wherever you go, as well as offering presentation possibilities that desktop systems don't allow because of their size. They also enable you to take advantage of the fact that many archives and record offices now have free wi-fi access, meaning that you can access the Internet on the go. This can be a really useful bonus if you're uploading your tree directly to a genealogy website.

Portable databases

As you get more involved in genealogy and begin to take research trips, you may find it useful to have your database with you. Of course, you can always print out the contents of your database, but the further you get with your research, the more papers you'll be carrying. One alternative is to take a notebook computer with you. Notebooks are quite popular, especially as they've become more affordable and more powerful over the years. Most notebook computers have capabilities as good as their desktop counterparts, but in a more convenient package, and you can add your software to the notebook and update as you go along.

Personal digital assistants (PDAs), which are also often called *palmtops*, can be useful tools, too. PDAs are hand-sized computers that can contain some of the same programs as desktop computers. You can transfer information from a PDA to your desktop or laptop PC. You can even have a scaled-down version of your genealogical database on your PDA. For example, GedStar (`www.ghcssoftware.com/gedstar.htm`) enables you to view and edit GEDCOM files on a PDA running a Palm OS 3.1 or later operating system. The storage capacity for GedStar is limited only by the capabilities of your PDA.

Storage on the run

If you already own a desktop system and aren't in the market to buy a notebook or palmtop, don't worry! You have other means of transporting your data and reports without spending money on another computer.

CD-Rs, DVD-Rs and memory sticks hold a lot of data, can easily accommodate your genealogical database and buying a writable CD-ROM or DVD drive tends to be much cheaper than buying a laptop computer. Memory sticks are even cheaper. (Refer to the section 'Talking Hardware: Is Your Computer Equipped?' earlier in the chapter for more on writable CD-ROM and DVD drives.) Computer retailers sell a number of other external storage options as well as

CD-ROMs and DVDs. Of course, the drawback to using a disk or stick to transport your data is that you need a computer on the other end that can handle the disk and accommodate the information contained on it. So before you take all of your family information to a reunion at Aunty Doris's, make sure that Aunty Doris has a computer with a CD-ROM drive or a USB port (for memory sticks) and any necessary software to open the contents of your disk.

One other occasional problem that you may encounter is the need to transfer information from a computer source away from home to your own computer. Most public libraries and family history centres have genealogical information on computers. You can save this information in a few different ways. Popping a blank CD or memory stick into the computer at the library to download a few lines of information about an ancestor is much easier than writing out everything. Simply cutting and pasting information into a Word document for printing out can also be a time saver.

More and more archives are now providing wi-fi access, enabling you to access both the Internet and your documents from the comfort of your own laptop or PDA. Because of this, archives are now restricting the importing of external data onto their own computers so as to decrease the risk of passing computer viruses around. Viruses can wreak havoc on many of the programs on your computer, including your genealogical database, so investing in a laptop is the more convenient option, or you can simply wait until you get *home to write up all your findings.*

Chapter 9

Coordinating Your Attack: Getting Help from Other Researchers

*Y*ou can think of genealogical research as a long journey. You may begin the journey by yourself, but before long you discover that progress is much quicker when someone else is by your side. In your genealogical journey, these travel partners can take various forms – an individual researching the same family, a research group searching for several branches of a family in which you're interested or a genealogical society that coordinates the efforts of many people who are researching different families.

This chapter explores ways of finding (and keeping) research partners, as well as ways in which research groups and genealogical societies can help you to meet your research goals.

Putting All Your Eggs in One Basket: Relying Only on Your Research

Don't try to do all the research yourself. As you may already have discovered, an awful lot of people are energetically researching: what a shame for you not to take advantage of the work that they've already done – and vice versa.

The benefits of sharing genealogical data cannot be emphasised enough. Sharing is the foundation on which the genealogical community is built, and the various online communities that have grown up have made sharing information with other researchers easy. Message boards, forums and frequently-asked-questions (FAQ) sections of genealogy websites are not only a great source of information, especially if you're having difficulties or have hit a brick wall in your research; they can also be a great way to interact with other genealogists who may be researching the same lines as you. Many genealogy websites flag up any possible links between information already on the site, uploaded by other researchers, and your family tree. Genealogy is popular all over the world, and you never know – you might find a researcher far away in Australia who is connected to a branch of your family tree and can help you with your particular problem. In turn, you may be able to provide them with information and new leads to follow. Before long, you can find yourself working side-by-side with someone you never previously knew, sharing your finds and helping each other out.

But your contact doesn't have to come from the other side of the world. You can also join forces with one of your known relatives within the UK. Perhaps you live closer to an archive that holds records relating to your ancestor than does the cousin with whom you're communicating online – but your cousin lives near a family gravesite of which you'd like to have a photograph. Rather than duplicating efforts to collect the records and photographs, you can make arrangements for each of you to obtain the items that are closest to you and then exchange copies via the Internet or by post. By knowing the family lines that other researchers are pursuing, and the places in which they're pursuing them, you can coordinate your efforts with theirs, sharing the information you've already collected and working together towards a common goal.

Each new discovery brings extra satisfaction if you're aware that someone else will be as thrilled as you are with your findings. However, just be sure that your initial excitement doesn't make you get carried away! Obviously, you fastidiously check your own research to make sure your facts are correct, and you need to apply the same standards to any information provided by other researchers. Check all sources, and never assume that someone else has been as careful as you at verifying all the information in their tree. Linking to someone else's family tree, only to find that they've made a serious mistake in their research, would be devastating.

Aiming High: The Shotgun Approach

No doubt you're wondering how to find people with whom to share your information. Well, you can start by going through telephone books and calling everyone with the surname that you're researching. However, some people feel dubious, or even hostile, towards telemarketers and cold callers, and we don't recommend using this method as a strategy.

A similar but more effective technique is to send an email to anyone and everyone you can find with your surname. We refer to this mass email strategy as the *shotgun approach.* Basically, you send out a bunch of emails, hoping to hit one or two targets. Bear in mind that although you may find one or two people who answer you in a positive way, a lot of people find unsolicited email irritating. Instead of bearing their wrath, you can try visiting a site that focuses on genealogy (such as Rootsweb at `www.rootsweb.ancestry.com` or Genuki at `www.genuki.org.uk`) to find the names of researchers who are interested in your surname. Obviously, this strategy works better with less common surnames, but is still worth a go even if your name is Smith or Jones. You can also use the message boards on these sites to appeal for information. These are much kinder, better ways to find others with the same interests as you.

Making Friends (and Keeping Them) Online

The best place to begin your search for other people doing similar research is the Roots Surname List (`rsl.rootsweb.ancestry.com`) (see Figure 9-1), one of the oldest genealogy resources on the Internet. The Roots Surname List is a list of would-be genealogists, the surnames they're researching and where those surnames occur worldwide. (For more info on using the list, check out Chapter 3.) Other places to find fellow researchers include query pages on the Internet, newsgroups and mailing lists. (If you need a reminder on how to use these or other surname resources, you can find more information in Chapter 3.) After you've identified a few potential online friends, email them to introduce yourself and briefly give your reasons for getting in touch. Be sure to include a list of the ancestors that you're researching.

Figure 9-1: Example of the Roots Surname List for the surname Monk.

Surnames matching monk

New entries are marked by a +, modified entries by a *, and expiring entries by an x. Clicking on the highlighted code words will give the name and address of the researcher who submitted the surname. (If no names are listed below this line, then none were found.)

Alternate Surnames (Click for a detailed list of alternates)

See the monk resource page for more searches

You might have to scroll left or right to view all of the information

Surname	From	To	Migration	Submitter	Comment
Monk	1066	now	DEV>LND,ENG>MA,USA>NS>ON,CAN>MA,USA	bobmonk	
Monk	1066	1897	London England and Eire	pollitt	
Monk	1400	1650	"Potheridge, Devonshire,ENG"	kloesel	
Monk	1600	now	DBY,ENG	alex1976	
Monk	1600	1800	Kent,England	johnhh	Sandhurst/Hawkhurst

Before you begin to contact people, however, we want to give you a few pieces of advice:

- ✔ **Before you send a message to a website maintainer, explore the site to find out whether that contact is the appropriate person to approach.** More often than not, the person who maintains a website is indeed the one who is researching the surnames that you find on that website. However, some site maintainers host information on their sites for other people. If they do, they'll usually have separate contact addresses for those individuals and an explanation that they're not personally researching those surnames. Some even go so far as to post notices on their sites stating that they don't entertain research questions. Look around a little before you compose your message to ensure that you're addressing the most appropriate person.

- ✔ **Make your messages brief and to the point.** Email messages that run to five or six pages can overwhelm the recipient. If the person to whom you send the message is interested in your information and responds positively to you, you can send a more detailed message at a future date.

- ✔ **Ensure that your message includes enough detail for the recipient to decide whether your information relates to their research and to determine whether they can help you.** Include names, dates and places as appropriate.

- ✔ **Use net etiquette, or *netiquette*, when you create your messages.** Remember that email can be an impersonal medium. Although you may mean one thing, someone who doesn't know you may mistakenly misinterpret your message. (For more on netiquette, see the sidebar 'Netiquette: Communicating politely on the Internet' in this chapter.)

- ✔ **Don't disclose personal information that may violate a person's privacy.** Information such as addresses and birth dates of living people is private and you shouldn't share it freely with other researchers. Also, we don't recommend that you send out much personal information about yourself until you know the recipient a lot better – when first introducing yourself, your name and email address should suffice, along with the information about the deceased ancestors that you're researching.

- ✔ **Get permission before forwarding messages from other researchers.** Sometimes researchers provide information that they don't want made available to the general public. Asking permission before forwarding a message to a third party eliminates any potential problems and avoids violating the trust of your fellow researchers.

Netiquette: Communicating politely on the Internet

Part of being a fine, upstanding member of the online genealogy community is learning to communicate effectively and politely on the Internet. Online communication is often hampered by the fact that you can't see the people with whom you're corresponding, and you can't hear the intonation of their voices to determine the emotions that they're expressing. To avoid misunderstandings, follow a few simple guidelines – called *netiquette* – when writing messages:

- Don't send a message that you wouldn't want posted on a bulletin board at work. You should expect that every email you send is potentially public.

- Make sure that you don't violate any copyright laws by sending large portions of written works through email. (For more information on copyright, see Chapter 11.)

- If you receive a *flame* (a heated message usually sent to provoke a response), try to ignore it. Usually no good comes from responding to a flame.

- Be careful when you respond to messages. Instead of replying to an individual, you may be replying to an entire group of people. Checking the To: line before you press the Send button is always a good idea.

- Use mixed case when you write email messages. USING ALL UPPERCASE LETTERS INDICATES SHOUTING! The exception to this guideline is when you send a query and place your surnames in all-uppercase letters (for example, Charles MONK).

- If you participate in a mailing list or newsgroup, and you reply with a message that interests only one person, consider sending that person a message individually rather than emailing the list as a whole.

- If you're joking, use smileys or enter **<grins>** or **<g>**. A *smiley* is an emoticon that looks like this: :-). (Turn the book on its right side if you can't see the face.) *Emoticons* are graphics created by combinations of keys on the keyboard to express an emotion within an email. Here are a few emoticons that you may run into:

:-)	Happy, smiling
;-)	Wink, ironic
:->	Sarcastic
8-)	Wearing glasses
:-(	Sad, unhappy
:-<	Disappointed
:-o	Frightened, surprised
:-()	Moustache

Forming Research Groups

If your relatives are tired of hearing about your genealogy research trips or the information that you've found about Great-Uncle William, but you'd like to share your triumphs with someone, then you may be ready to join a research group.

Research groups consist of any number of people who coordinate their research and share resources to achieve success. Groups may start conducting research because they share a surname, family branch or geographical location. Research groups may consist of individuals who live close to one another, or the members of the group may never have met in person. Such groups may have a variety of goals and may have a formal or an informal structure. Their organisation is quite flexible and depends entirely on the membership of the group.

Typically, each member of the group contributes the results of his or her personal research and provides any information that they've found, which may be of use to other members of the group. Additionally, the group as a whole may choose to sponsor research by professional genealogists in other countries to discover more about their ancestors there. All findings can be shared and debated by the members of the group through email.

Not all surnames are catered for to the same degree, but thanks to the growing popularity of genealogy you'd be unlucky not to find someone else interested in your line of research. To find research groups, your best bet is to visit a comprehensive genealogical website or a site that specialises in surnames, such as the GeneaSearch Surname Registry at `www.geneasearch.com/surnameregister.htm` or SurnameWeb at `www.surnameweb.org`. You could also try a simple website search, for example with Google (`www.google.co.uk`) or Yahoo! (`www.yahoo.co.uk`), entering your surname and 'research group' to see if you can find a group this way.

The following steps show you how to find groups pertaining to a surname on the site:

1. **Launch your web browser and go to the SurnameWeb site at `www.surnameweb.org`.**

   As the page loads, a search field and the letters of the alphabet appear near the top centre of the page.

2. **Choose the first letter of the surname you're researching.**

   For example, when you click on 'P', you're confronted with a web page with the P index.

3. **Select the Po link near the top of the page.**

   This brings up a list of surname links that begin with the letters 'Po'.

4. **Scroll through the list and select a surname link.**

   To find sites relating to the surname *Polard*, click the link for the Polard surname, which takes you to a results page entitled 'Polard Surname Resource Center'.

5. Choose a site to visit.

Scroll down past all the links to search other commercial websites until you reach the links you're most interested in – in our case, those links that take us directly to personal and group web pages that contain information about people named Polard.

In addition to using comprehensive genealogy sites and specialised surname sites, you can use other strategies to identify possible research groups. One way to find research groups pertaining to surnames is to visit a one-name studies index. You can find a list of one-name study sites at the Guild of One-Name Studies page (www.one-name.org). You can also look to existing larger groups that may have specific research components, such as genealogical societies. The following section goes into more detail on genealogical societies.

If you can't find an established online group that fits your interests, why not start one yourself? If you're interested in researching a particular topic, chances are that others out there are interested as well. Perhaps the time has come to coordinate your efforts and start working with others towards your common research goals. Starting an online research group can be relatively easy – just post a message stating your interest in starting a group at certain key locations, such as message boards, newsgroups and mailing lists. Have a look at the Ancestry site at www.ancestry.co.uk/community and Cyndi's list at www.cyndislist.com/surnames.htm for ideas about how and where to launch your research group.

Becoming a Solid Member of a (Genealogical) Society

Genealogical societies can be great places to learn research methods and to coordinate your research. Several different types of societies exist. They range from the more traditional geographical or surname-based societies to newer *cyber-societies* (societies that exist only on the Internet) that are redefining the way that people view genealogical societies.

Geographical societies

Chapter 4 introduces geographically based genealogical societies as groups that can help you to discover resources in a particular area in which your ancestors lived, or as groups in your own town or county that can help you to discover how to research more effectively. However, local genealogical societies can provide another service to their members. These societies often coordinate members' local research efforts in the form of projects. To locate geographical societies, visit the Genuki website at www.genuki.org.uk/indexes/SurnamesLists.html (for more details on Genuki, have a read of Chapter 4). You may also like to visit the Federation of Family History Societies' website at www.ffhs.org.uk/members2/contacting.php.

If you go to the Northumberland and Durham Family History Society homepage (www.ndfhs.org.uk), for example, you'll see that they list current and ongoing projects, as well as information about how to join the society (see Figure 9-2). These societies are always glad of new members and willing volunteers to assist in their enterprises.

Figure 9-2: The Northumberland and Durham Family History Society homepage, with links to the various projects currently being undertaken by the society.

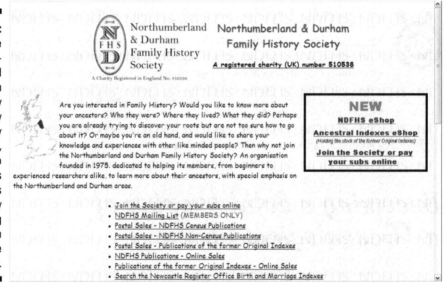

Smaller groups of members sometimes work on projects in addition to the Society's official projects. For example, you may belong to a county genealogical society and decide to join a few members to write a history of local mill-owners, local gentry or early migrants. If each member of the team shares the fruits of his or her research, you can cover three or four times the ground that you could by yourself.

Family and surname associations

In addition to geographically based associations, you can find groups tied to particular names or family groups. Usually they're referred to – as you've probably already guessed – as surname or family associations or research groups.

Family associations also frequently sponsor projects that coordinate the efforts of several researchers. Projects may focus on the family or surname in a specific geographical area or time, or they may attempt to collect information about every individual who possessed the surname at any time and then place the information in a shared database.

You can find family and surname associations through comprehensive genealogy sites (listed in the *Genealogy Online For Dummies* Internet Directory in this book), general Internet search engines (also listed in this book's directory section) or sites specialising in associations.

If a family or surname association isn't currently working on a project that interests you, by all means suggest a project that does interest you (as long as the project is relevant to the association as a whole).

Using Family Reunions as a Research Occasion

Interviewing relatives is a great way to glean information about your ancestors to use as clues in finding records and to enhance the scope of your research. We emphasise this point in Chapter 1, so now is a good time to read that chapter if you haven't already done so. Well, what better way to gather information from relatives than by attending a family reunion?

Family reunions can add a lot to your research because you find many relatives all in one place, often talking or reminiscing about the past – both within and beyond living memory. A reunion is an efficient way to collect stories, photographs, databases (if others in the family are also researching and keep their records in their computers) and even copies of records. You may even find people interested in researching the family along with you. And a family reunion can be great fun, too.

If you attend a family reunion, it may be wise to take along your notebook, together with a list of prepared interview questions (see Chapter 1 if you haven't developed your list yet) and a camera. You can also take a few printed charts from your genealogical database, too; you may be surprised at how many of your relatives are interested in seeing them.

Rent-a-Researcher

A time may come when you've exhausted all the research avenues directly available to you and you need help that family, friends and society members can't give you. Perhaps the records you need to get past a research 'brick wall' are in a distant place or you don't have enough time to devote to your research. Don't fret! Professional researchers are happy to help you.

Professional researchers charge a fee to dig around and find information for you. They retrieve specific records that you want, or they can prepare an entire report on a family line using all types of resources available. As can be expected, the amount you pay depends on the level of service that you need. Professional researchers are especially helpful when you need records from locations to which you can't travel conveniently.

Asking the right questions

When looking for a professional researcher, you need someone who's reputable and experienced in the area in which you need help. Here's a list of questions that you may want to ask when searching for a professional researcher:

- Are you certified or accredited and, if so, by which organisation?
- How many years' experience do you have in research?
- What is your educational background?
- What foreign languages do you speak fluently (if you think you need to search abroad)?
- What records and resources do you have access to?
- What is your experience in the area in which I need help? For example, have you conducted interviews in the past or do you have experience in researching records pertaining to a particular ethnic or religious group?
- How do you charge for your services – by the record, by the hour or by the project? How long will the research take to complete? What methods of payment do you accept? What is your policy on refunds or dissatisfaction with your services?

✔ How many other projects, and what kinds, are you currently working on? How much time will you devote to my research project? When will you send me the results?

✔ Can you give me any references or the names of some satisfied customers whom I can contact?

Uncovering a researcher

You can find professional researchers by looking for them on comprehensive genealogy sites or on regulated lists, such as the National Archives' list of professional researchers (www.nationalarchives.gov.uk/irlist).

For Scottish research, you may like to try the following:

✔ Association of Scottish Genealogists and Researchers in Archives: www.asgra.co.uk.

✔ Scottish Roots Ancestral Research Service at www.scottish-roots.co.uk.

For Irish research, try the following:

✔ Sticks Research Agency at www.sra-uk.com/ireland.

✔ Genealogy.ie. at www.genealogy.ie.

If you're seeking a professional researcher abroad, try searching www.genealogypro.com by the relevant country.

Many family history societies and local and national archives hold lists of professional researchers on their websites. Have a look at the National Archives website for an example:

1. Call up the National Archives website at www.nationalarchives.gov.uk/irlist/.

2. From the dropdown menu of categories for which researchers are available, select the appropriate category (for example, General Genealogy or Probate and Wills Records).

3. Click on Find Researchers to view a list of names and contact details for people offering their services in that area. Many of these professionals have their own websites, giving further info about the researcher, such as the services they offer and the prices they charge.

When you make initial contact with a professional researcher who looks promising, be as specific as possible about your needs. Specific information helps the researcher to pinpoint exactly what they need to do – and makes it easier to calculate how much it'll all cost. You can always ask for a little research at first and then commission more if you're happy with the results.

Chapter 10

Sharing Your Wealth Online

· ·

· ·

*I*nevitably a time comes in your research when you want to find ways in which to share the valuable information that you've discovered – after all, sharing information is one of the foundations of the genealogical community. When you share information, you often get a lot of information in return from other researchers. You may find others who are researching your name or have records about a branch of your family that you had no idea existed. You may even find relatives that you never knew before, who've already done some of the more tedious legwork in researching your family tree.

In this chapter, we focus on methods you can use to share information (except for placing your information on the Internet, which we cover in Chapter 11) and ways in which you can let other researchers know that you have information to share.

Finding Out Why Other People Are Interested in Your Research

You may experience a second of hesitation, when you ask yourself 'Why would anyone want my stuff?' It seems like a logical first question when you stop and decide whether to make the many titbits and treasures that you have collected available to others online. Who would want a copy of that old, tatty-looking photograph that you have of your great-great-grandma as a girl sitting on a wall outside a Lancashire cotton mill? You probably only ended up with it because nobody else wanted it in the first place. The picture has sentimental value only to you . . . Please don't let thoughts like these distract you. Your great-great-grandma may have other descendants who are looking for information about her. They, too, would love to see a picture of her when she was a little girl – even better, they'd love to have their own electronic copy of that picture.

As you develop more and more online contact with other genealogists, you may find a lot of people who are interested in exchanging information. Some may be interested in your findings because you share common ancestors, and others may be interested because they're researching in the geographical area where your ancestors lived. Aren't these the same reasons that you're interested in seeing other researchers' stuff? Sharing your information is likely to encourage others to share theirs with you. Exchanging information with others may enable you to fill in a few gaps in your own research reports or perhaps even to link into someone else's family tree online. Even if research findings received from others don't directly answer questions about your ancestors, they may give you clues as to where to find more information to fill in the blanks.

Research findings received from other researchers can often be extremely useful, but do be wary – you need to verify this information, and it can also lead to you taking out subscriptions to other areas of a website.

Also, you don't need to have traced your family history back to the Middle Ages for your information to be valuable. Although you need to be careful about sharing information on living people, you're free to share any facts that you have about deceased ancestors. Just as you may not be aware of your genealogy any further back than your great-grandfather, someone else may be in the same boat – and with the same person! Meeting that fellow researcher can lead to a mutual research relationship that can produce a lot more information in a shorter amount of time.

Spreading the Word on What You Have

So you're at the point where you recognise the value in sharing your genealogical information online. How do you begin to communicate the information that you have? Well, the first thing to do is to come up with a marketing plan for your information, much as a business does when it decides to sell a product.

Masterminding a surname marketing plan

A *surname marketing plan* is simply a checklist of places and people to contact so as to effectively inform the right individuals about the information you have to contribute to the genealogy community. As you devise your plan, ask yourself the following questions:

- ✔ **Which surname sites would be interested in my information?** To find surname sites, see Chapter 3.

- ✔ **Which geographical sites would be interested in my information?** For geographical sites, see Chapter 4.

- ✔ **Which association sites (family and geographical) would be interested in my information?** See Chapter 3 for association sites.

- ✔ **Which general sites (such as query sites and GEDCOM collections) would be interested in my information?** See Chapters 3 and 4 for examples of these sites.

You may want to use all available Internet resources to pass on your information, including mailing lists, newsgroups, online family trees and websites. For example, say you have information about the O'Connor family that you'd like to put online. You've discovered a branch of the family living in County Kerry, Ireland, and another living just outside Liverpool. To identify sites where you can post this information, you search for one-name study pages on the surname O'Connor, for personal pages that have connections to the O'Connor family and for geographically specific websites (see Chapters 3 and 5 for information on how to find all these kinds of sites). Through these sites, you may discover a mailing list dedicated to discussing the family, or find sites specific to County Kerry and Liverpool that contain information about past inhabitants. Finally, you search for a subscription website to which you can upload your family tree. You also search those websites for family trees with links to the O'Connor family to see if any of these trees link into your own.

Contacting your target audience

After you've located the names and addresses of sites that may attract an audience that you want to target, the next step is to notify them. To do so, create a brief but detailed email message to make your announcement. Before you compose your message, look at the format required by each resource that you're contacting. Certain genealogical sites have a specific format for subject lines. A number of *query sites* (places where you can post genealogical questions to get help from other researchers) also have specific formats, so you may need to modify your message for each of these sites. For more information about query sites and posting queries, refer to Chapter 3.

Here's a sample message to give you a few ideas:

```
O'CONNOR, 1840-1940, Co. Kerry, Ireland and Liverpool,
England

I have information on the family of Patrick O'Connor of
County Kerry and Liverpool. Patrick was born in 1840,
moved to Liverpool by 1851 and married Angela O'Neill
in June 1865. He had the following children: Patrick,
Angela Ann, Leonard, Francis, Fanny and Thomas.
```

Most people understand that you're willing to share information about the family if you post something on a site, so you probably don't need to say that in your message. Remember that people are most likely to read your message if you include a short but descriptive subject line, brief and to-the-point text and enough information for readers to determine whether your information can help them (or whether they have information that can assist you).

Sharing Your Information

After you've made contact with other researchers who are interested in your information, you need to consider the best way to share your information with them. Of course, you can simply type everything up, print it and send it to them. Or you can export a copy of your genealogy database file, which the recipients can then import into their databases and run as many reports as they want – and save a few trees in the process. Your software package should be able to do this quickly and easily for you. However, plenty of other ways in which you can share your information online are available to you.

GEDCOM files

Most genealogical databases subscribe to a common standard for exporting their information called *Genealogical Data Communication*, or GEDCOM. (Be aware that some genealogical databases deviate from the standard a little, making things a little confusing.)

A *GEDCOM file* is a text file that contains your genealogical information with a set of tags that tell the genealogical database importing the information where to place it within its structure. For a little history and more information about GEDCOM, see Chapter 8.

Most genealogical software has the ability to make GEDCOM files. The software should come with instructions on how to create and make sense of the files. Although GEDCOM files do look a bit confusing, you don't need to understand the format in which the information is presented in order to make use of the files. However, you may find it useful to examine Figure 10-1, which presents the same family details in the form of a simple descendents tree and then translates the data into the format of a GEDCOM file.

You may be asking 'Why is GEDCOM important?' Well, GEDCOM can save you time and energy in the process of sharing information. The next time someone asks you to send them data, export your genealogy data into a GEDCOM file and send the file instead of entering the relevant data or saving a copy of your entire database.

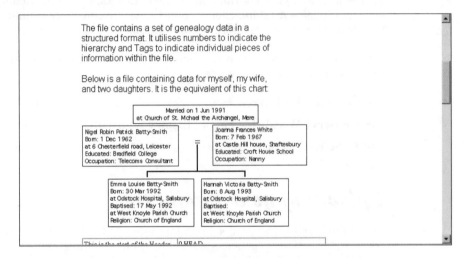

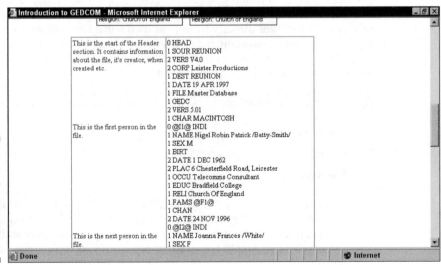

Figure 10-1:
The Batty-Smith family converted into a GEDCOM file.

Posting info on the web

Instead of sending information to several different individuals, consider placing your information on your own website where people can access it at their convenience (see Chapter 11 for more information). If, however, you're not ready to take the web-designing plunge, you do have other options to choose from.

One method is to find other researchers who are working on the same surnames or geographical areas as you and who already have web pages, and ask them to post your information on their sites. Don't be offended if they decline, though – most Internet accounts have specific storage limits and they may not have room for your information.

A second option is to submit your information to a general site that collects GEDCOM files. Examples include:

- ✔ **Ancestry World Tree:** www.ancestry.com/share/awt/main.htm
- ✔ **Genserve Worldwide Family History Information:** www.genserv.com
- ✔ **GenCircles Global Tree:** www.gencircles.com/globaltree

Uploading your family tree

One of the very best ways to share information on the Internet is through the community sections of genealogical subscription websites. One of the best and easiest sites to which you can directly upload information is www.family relatives.com. You have to register to begin your research, but you can export GEDCOM files directly from your own software to display on the site if you've already come some way with your research (see Figure 10-2). The benefit of Family Relatives is that it enables you to control who sees your tree, and you can choose to keep it private if you wish.

Other sites that contain sections to which you can upload your tree include:

- ✔ **Ancestry:** www.ancestry.co.uk
- ✔ **Genes Reunited:** www.genesreunited.co.uk
- ✔ **My Heritage:** www.myheritage.com

As well as being able to receive your GEDCOM files, a key benefit of using these websites is that they also enable you to upload information as you go along. This applies both when you're starting out from scratch with details about yourself or adding to the existing research you've uploaded to the website in your GEDCOM file. You just enter as much or as little detail as you want about your parents, grandparents and so on, along with photos, scans and documents to enliven your tree. This means that your tree can really grow as soon as you find any information. Some sites also alert you when the information in your tree may match other users' information, making it easy for you to identify possible research contacts and people who would be glad to hear from you.

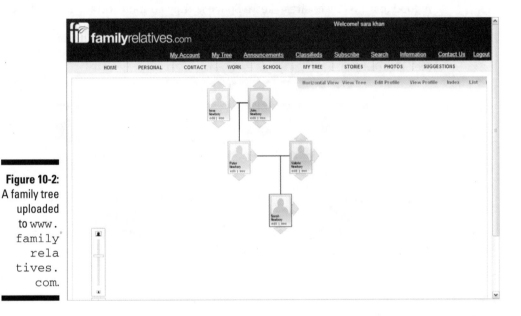

Figure 10-2:
A family tree uploaded to www.family rela tives. com.

Getting pally with social networking sites

Social networking sites aren't all about arranging your social life and sharing music. Sites like Facebook (www.facebook.com), Bebo (www.bebo.com) and YouTube (www.youtube.com) have grown in popularity over the past few years, and are getting bigger all the time, now having millions of users. These websites grow quickly as you can invite other people to view your pages and profiles, and they all work in basically the same way, so have a look around and see which site suits you best.

One of the best social networking sites for finding and sharing information is MySpace (www.myspace.com). With more than 180 million users worldwide, you can imagine the possibilities when looking for help with your family tree! Creating an account here is quick, free and easy, and you can easily start sharing information with family and your new-found research friends. All you need to do is create a homepage that includes things like photos, genealogy links and information about your surname or other related questions and invite people to view your information and photos. You can think of MySpace as basically a mini-website that you can play around with and customise to make it work for you and your research. Some people upload photos and documents for ancestors that are proving hard to find in the archives, as well as post blogs of useful hints and tips.

A good feature of websites like MySpace is they contain certain groups that you can join up to (see Figure 10-3). You can even create your own group that is specific to your family tree, and invite other members to join. Simply log into the site, go to the groups page and click on the Create a Group button (see Figure 10-4).

Figure 10-3:
A family history research group on MySpace.

Be careful what information you display on your profile page, particularly about putting names, addresses and contact details of living people on display, and always ask people if they are happy to have their photos on display. See 'Respecting People's Privacy' later in the chapter for info on why it pays to be careful with the details you reveal online.

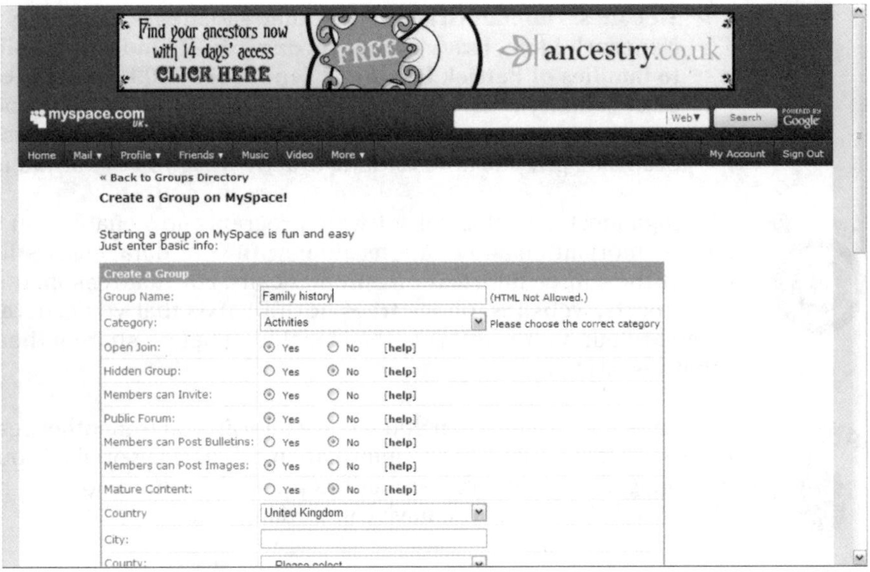

Figure 10-4:
Creating
a family
history
research
group on
MySpace.

Citing Your Sources

We can't stress enough the importance of citing your sources when sharing information, whether online or through traditional means. Be sure to include references that detail where you obtained your information; that's just as important when you share your information as it is when you research it. Not only does referencing provide the other person with leads to possible additional information, but it also gives you a place to return and double-check your facts if someone challenges them. Sometimes, after exchanging information with another researcher, you both realise that you have conflicting data about a particular ancestor. Knowing where to turn to double-check the facts (and, with any luck, find out who has the correct information) can save you time and embarrassment.

Here are a few examples of ways to cite online sources of information:

- ✔ **Email messages: Hannah Graham [hgraham@nosuchdomain.com or 18 Nonesuch Lane, Essex], <mhelm@tbox.com>.** 'Looking for Patrick Lee' Message to George Graham, 12 September 2009. [Message cites vital records in Graham's possession.]

- ✔ **Newsgroups: Hannah Graham [hgraham@nosuchdomain.com or 18 Nonesuch Lane, Essex] <mhelm@tbox.com>** 'Computing in Genealogy' in soc.genealogy.computing, 12 September 2009.

> ✓ **Websites: Hannah Graham [hgraham@nosuchdomain.com or 18 Nonesuch Lane, Essex]: Genuki.org.uk – found two possible links to families of Patrick Lee on 12 September 2009. <genealogy.tbox. com>** January 2009. (Of course, with a note like this, you expect your next two citations to be the two websites that looked promising. For each site, provide notes stating exactly what you did or did not find.)

Although most genealogical software programs now enable you to store source information and citations along with your data, many still don't export the source information automatically. For that reason, double-check any reports, websites, online trees or GEDCOMs that you generate to see whether your source information is included before sharing them with other researchers.

The same rules apply when you receive information from other researchers – make sure that you verify any information by checking original sources. Assuming that another researcher has put in the same amount of hard work checking their facts as you have can be dangerous.

Respecting People's Privacy

We couldn't sleep at night if we didn't give you the mandatory lecture on maintaining the privacy of living individuals when you share your genealogical information.

In the rush to get genealogical information posted on the Internet, people sometimes forget that portions of the information in their research are considered to be private by the people they relate to. Why worry about privacy? Check out a few of the reasons . . .

You may have heard horror stories about names, ages, addresses and family details of living individuals ending up on the Internet. For example, people have found out that their biological parents weren't married (to each other, anyway) through online databases. Private detectives and other people who search for information on living people frequently use genealogical databases to track people. For these reasons, sharing information about living people on the Internet without first getting each person's written permission to do so is illegal in certain countries, and very inadvisable in all others. To avoid an invasion of privacy and any legal problems that may arise from you sharing your information, always clean out (exclude) any information on living individuals from your tree before you give it to anyone, and be careful about the details you reveal on any websites.

More and more genealogists are now aware of the privacy implications of online research and sharing information. As a result, some have designed programs to clean out information on living individuals from GEDCOM files: visit `www.spub.co.uk/wpg/software.html` and follow the link to Privacy Software to find out more and obtain what you need. But be warned, even if you use software to clean a file, be sure to double-check the data in the file to ensure that the software catches everything and that you *don't* share any information on living people.

Chapter 11

Creating a Place to Call Home

. . . .

In This Chapter

▶ Finding a home for your home page

▶ Getting to grips with HTML

▶ Using genealogical software utilities

▶ Enhancing your web pages with photographs

. . . .

After you've filled your genealogical database with information about your relatives and ancestors, and you've shared your data with others by email, you may be ready to create and post your home page on a website. In this chapter, you discover how to post a simple site and where you can do so. Also, this chapter gives you the basics of creating a home on the Internet where your information can reside and accept visitors.

If you're after detailed information about creating a full-blown website or using advanced HTML programming, you'll need to go beyond this book. This chapter covers the basics to get you started, but for more info we recommend that you check out the following *For Dummies* books (all published by Wiley): *Creating Web Pages For Dummies*, 8th Edition, by Bud Smith; *The Internet For Dummies*, 11th Edition, by John R. Levine, Margaret Levine Young and Carol Baroudi; and *HTML 4 For Dummies*, 5th Edition, by Ed Tittel and Mary Burmeister.

Looking for Home, Sweet Home

Before you build your *home page* (the first page that opens when someone looks at your website), you need to find a *host* – that is, an Internet home – for the page. You can design a basic home page on your own computer using no more than a word processor, but other people won't be able to view the page until you put it on a web server on the Internet. A *web server* is a computer that's connected directly to the Internet and that displays web pages when you request them using your computer's web browser.

Commercial Internet service providers

If you subscribe to a commercial *Internet service provider* (ISP) such as BT, Tiscali, Yahoo! or Virgin, or if you subscribe to a local provider, you may already have a home for your web pages. Most commercial ISPs include a specific space allocation for user home pages in their memberships, as well as tools to help you build your site. Check your membership agreement to see whether you have space. Then you can follow the ISP's instructions for creating your website (using the service's page builder or editor), or for getting your independently created web pages from your computer to the ISP's server. (If you didn't keep a copy of your membership agreement, don't fret! Most ISPs have an information web page that you can get to from your ISP's main page; the information page reviews membership benefits.) You may as well take advantage of this service if you're already paying for it.

If your particular membership level doesn't include web space, but the ISP has other membership levels that do, pause for thought before upgrading your membership. You can take advantage of any free web-hosting services that may save you money (see the following 'Free web-hosting services' section).

Free web-hosting services

A number of websites give you free space for your home page provided you agree to their rules and restrictions. We can safely bet that you won't have any problems using one of these freebies, because the restrictions, such as no pornography, nudity or explicit language allowed, are genealogist-friendly.

If you decide to take advantage of web space, remember that the companies that provide the space must pay their bills. They often make space available free to individuals by charging advertisers for banners and other advertisements. In such cases, the web host reserves the right to require that you leave these advertisements on your home page. If you don't like the idea of an advertisement on your home page, or if you have strong objections against one of the companies that advertise with the site that gives you free space, you need to find a fee-based web space for your home page.

For a list of places where you can get a free web page, check out the Yahoo! Free Web Site Hosting Providers page at uk.dir.yahoo.com/business_ and_economy/business_to_business/communications_and_ networking/internet_and_world_wide_web/network_service_ providers/hosting/web_site_hosting/free_hosting/ or try the WebHostDirectory site at uk.webhostdir.com/default.asp?overide AutoSite=1. Again, we don't have enough room in this book to provide information about all the companies and services listed at these sites, so we focus on a couple of services that have been around for a while.

Tripod

`www.tripod.lycos.co.uk`

Tripod currently provides 1024 MB of free space for your web pages and access to tools to help you build your web pages.

Here's how to find out more about (and join) Tripod.

1. **Go to `www.tripod.lycos.co.uk`**
2. **Click the Join Tripod now! link in the middle of the page.**

   You're asked to read and accept the terms and conditions. You're also asked to fill in your details and to provide a password – and a reminder question in case you forget the password. After you've submitted the registration form, Tripod takes you to the Confirmation page, where you can click the Activate Your Account and Start Building link to begin to build your website using various tools. If you already need to update any registration information that you provided, you can click the Registration Information link to do so.

RootsWeb.com

`http://accounts.rootsweb.ancestry.com/`

RootsWeb.com is a genealogical site that offers homes to many projects, societies and individuals who want to post family history-related material on the web. The site is a division of MyFamily.com and sister site to Ancestry.com. RootsWeb.com has been around for several years and is quite well known in the genealogical community. Its reputation makes it a good place to post your website. Conveniently, it offers free space if you're posting acceptable material. To apply for free space, you need to read and agree to the RootsWeb agreement for a Freepages web space account. You then complete an online form that includes a justification as to what you plan to use the web space for, and then click the Submit button. One catch to getting free space at RootsWeb.com is that you must wait three to five days for your request for space to be processed.

Speaking HTML

HyperText Markup Language (or HTML) is the language of the World Wide Web. *HTML* is a code in which text documents are written so that web browsers can read and interpret those documents, converting them into graphical images and text that you can see through the browser. HTML is a relatively easy language to grasp, and many genealogists who post web pages are self-taught. If you prefer not to read about it but to find out by experimenting, look out for HTML classes and workshops at local colleges, community centres and genealogical societies. Chapter 13 suggests a few sites that you can use to find online courses and other tools to help you build your website.

For more information about the World Wide Web and web browsers, take a look at the Appendix at the back of this book.

Here are a couple of things to remember about HTML:

- ✔ You write HTML as a text document using a text editor, an HTML editor or a word processor, and you save it as a text document, with the file name extension of .htm or .html.

- ✔ You use a web browser to interpret HTML documents as graphics and text pages on the Internet.

Investigating HTML

To get an idea of what HTML looks like – both as the text document and as the converted graphical image – take a look at some extremely simple HTML tags created for a web page called The Smith Family. Figure 11-1 shows the web page that's created by the tags.

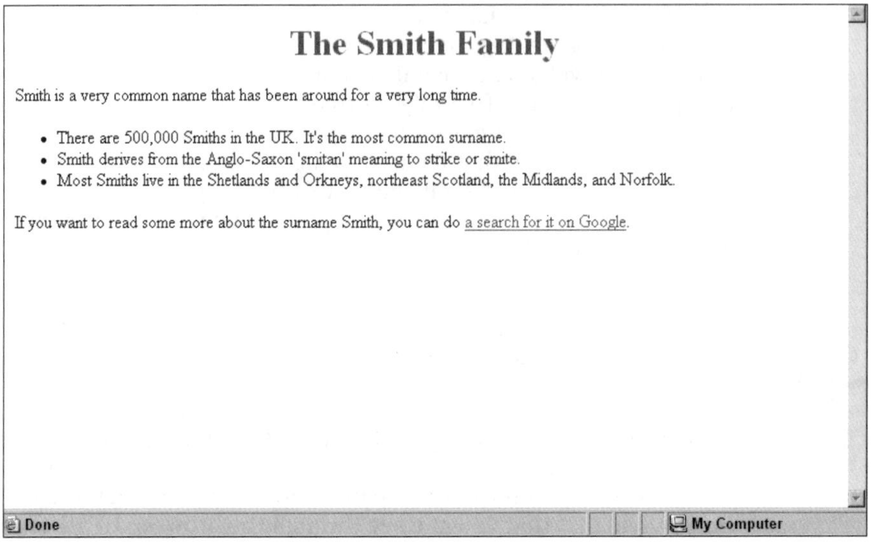

The Smith Family

Smith is a very common name that has been around for a very long time.

- There are 500,000 Smiths in the UK. It's the most common surname.
- Smith derives from the Anglo-Saxon 'smitan' meaning to strike or smite.
- Most Smiths live in the Shetlands and Orkneys, northeast Scotland, the Midlands, and Norfolk.

If you want to read some more about the surname Smith, you can do a search for it on Google.

Done — My Computer

Figure 11-1:
The Smith
family web
page.

Here's what the HTML codes (also called tags) look like:

```
<HTML>
<HEAD>
<TITLE>The Smith Family</TITLE>
</HEAD>
<BODY BGCOLOR = 'WHITE'>
<H1><FONT COLOR = 'GREEN'><CENTER>The Smith Family</
        CENTER></FONT></H1>
<P>Smith is a very common name that has been around for a
        very long time.</P>
<UL>
    <LI>There are 500,000 Smiths in the UK. It's the most
        common surname.</LI>
    <LI>Smith derives from the Anglo-Saxon 'smitan' meaning
        to strike or smite.</LI>
    <LI>Most Smiths live in the Shetlands and Orkneys,
        northeast Scotland, the Midlands, and
        Norfolk.</LI>
</UL>
<P>If you want to read some more about the surname Smith,
        you can do
<A HREF="http://www.google.co.uk/">a search for it on
        Google</A>.</P>
</BODY>
</HTML>
```

The tags are placed within angle brackets, for example: <BODY>. The tags tell the browser how to interpret the text that follows and whether to actually show that text on the web page. Just as you have to tell the browser when to begin interpreting text in a certain manner, you also have to tell it when to stop. The ending command consists of an open bracket, a forward or front slash, the tag word and a close bracket, like this: </BODY>.

For example:

```
<TITLE>The Smith Family</TITLE>
```

In this line, the <TITLE> tag tells the browser where to begin treating text as a title and </TITLE> tells it where to end that treatment. Treat HTML tags as on and off commands where < > indicates on and </ > indicates off.

Understanding basic HTML tags

The previous section 'Investigating HTML' contains an example of what HTML codes or tags look like. But what are these tags? HTML involves too many tags to do justice to them all here, but we cover a few to give the general idea.

If you're interested in more advanced HTML programming, Chapter 13 suggests a few websites to visit. For an even more detailed read, check out *HTML 4 For Dummies*, 5th Edition, by Ed Tittel and Mary Burmeister (Wiley). Or if you're looking for more information than we offer here, but not quite as much detail as you'll find in an HTML book, have a look at *Creating Web Pages For Dummies*, 8th Edition, by Bud Smith (Wiley) or *Building a Web Site For Dummies*, 3rd Edition, by David A. Crowder (Wiley).

Table 11-1 lists some basic HTML tags and their functions. For each of the listed tags, the off or ending command is the same word, preceded by a / (slash symbol), in brackets. (We explore a few exceptions to the off-command rule in Table 11-2.) You turn off tags in the reverse order in which you turned them on. For example, if you use the tags <HTML><HEAD>, you close them with </HEAD></HTML>.

Table 11-1		Tag, You're It!
Tag	*What It Means*	*What It Tells the Browser*
<HTML>	HTML	This text document is written in HTML and is to be interpreted as such.
<HEAD>	Head element	The following text is the document header, where you put the title and any descriptive information.
<TITLE>	Title	The following text is the web page title, which appears in the title bar at the top of your browser.
<BODY>	Body	This is the body or main part of the document, where you put all pertinent information that you want to appear on your web page.
<H1>	Heading	Denotes a heading for the page or section of text and the size that it should be. Headings come in six levels: <H1>, <H2>, <H3>, <H4>, <H5> and <H6>, where <H1> is the largest and <H6> the smallest.
<P>	Paragraph break	Skip a line and begin a new paragraph.
<CENTER>	Centre	Centre the following text on the page or within a table cell or column. (The tag is spelled in the American way.)

Tag	What It Means	What It Tells the Browser
<B>	Bold	Make the following text bold.
<I>	Italicise	Italicise the following text.
<U>	Underline	Underline the following text.
<A HREF= "URL">	Hypertext link	The following text is a link to another reference page or site and takes people there when they click on it. The *URL*, or uniform resource locator – that is, the address of the website – for the other site goes in the quotation marks. The off command for this code is simply </A>.
<FONT COLOR= "(colour)">	Font colour	The following text must be a particular colour. The colour, written in code or plain English, goes in the quotation marks. The off command is </FONT>. (The tag is spelled in the American way.)
<FONT SIZE= "(number)">	Font size	The following text must be a particular size. The size goes in the quotation marks. The off command is </FONT>.
<FONT FACE= "(font name)">	Font face	The following text must be printed in a particular font or typeface. The font or typeface name goes in the quotation marks. The off command is </FONT>.
<OL>	Ordered list	The following is a numbered list. Use this code with <LI>, which I explain in Table 11-2. The off command is </OL>.
<LI>	List item	Identify this new item on its own line in a list.
<UL>	Unordered list	The following is going to be a bulleted list. Use this code with <LI>. The off command is </UL>.

You don't necessarily have to close all HTML tags. Table 11-2 shows codes that are exceptions to the off-command rule. You don't have to use a </> code to tell the browser when to stop interpreting something.

Table 11-2	Closing-Tag Exceptions	
Tag	*What It Means*	*What It Tells the Browser*
 	Line break	End a line here, and then go to the next line to begin the next command or line of text.
<IMG SRC "image URL">	Image source	Picks up a graphics image from a URL to insert here. The URL or address of the graphics file goes between the quotation marks.
<HR>	Horizontal rule	Puts a horizontal line across the page here to divide up the page.
<BODY BGCOLOR= "(colour)">	Body background	The background colour of the document needs to be specified in a particular colour, such as green or blue. The colour, written in code or plain English, goes inside the quotation marks. (The tag is spelled in the American way.)

You've probably noticed that we use all uppercase letters in our coding, but that's just our own preference. You can use lowercase, uppercase or a combination of both when programming in HTML. We prefer all uppercase so that we can identify more easily where the codes are when we need to edit an HTML document. We also like to skip lines between commands so we can skim through the HTML document to see how we coded it.

Writing some HTML

You can use the basic codes that we provide in the preceding section to design and write a simple but functional website based on the example in the previous section. To make the process easier, you can use your word processor to copy the codes for the site as they appear in the previous section, simply substituting your own ancestor's information where the personal information appears in our example. You'll probably want to change the title of the web page to indicate that it contains information about one of your ancestors. After you finish, save the file in plain-text format with an HTML extension (.htm or .html). Save the file to your hard drive or a memory stick. (When you're ready to make your real home page, save the file to your hard drive and then upload it to the web server that hosts your site. Although you may be able to save your page directly to the web server, be sure to keep a backup copy of the file on your own machine or on a memory stick.)

Want to see what the page looks like through a browser's eyes? Try the following:

1. **Launch your web browser.**

   Usually you open the browser by double-clicking its icon or by using the Start menu to get to your programs. You don't necessarily have to be online to look at your web page, so don't worry about going through the steps for signing onto your Internet service provider account. Just open the browser.

2. **Use your browser's Open Page command to open the document.**

   Most browsers have an Open Page command in the File menu. When you click Open Page, a dialogue box appears, asking you which file you want to open. Enter the name of the file in which you saved your HTML document (or use the Browse feature to search for your document) and then press Enter or click the OK button.

Does anything look strange? For example, is everything past a certain point all in bold, all italicised or in a huge font? If so, go back and double-check your coding to make sure that you turned off all the codes at the appropriate points in the document. To find out more about turning off codes, see the section 'Investigating HTML' earlier in the chapter.

Using an HTML editor

An HTML editor is a program that walks you through HTML programming so that you don't have to memorise all the codes and remember to turn them on and off. Some editors use text that you've already written in your word processor, whereas others ask you to enter text directly into the editor. To tell the editor how particular text should appear on a web page (such as the format it must take – title, body of text, a list and so on), you click an icon or dropdown menu option and the editor applies the necessary codes.

Some sites that host web pages for free have online HTML editors and tutorials you can use (also for free) if you sign up for a website with them. Similarly, many commercial Internet service providers have HTML editors in the form of wizards or templates that help you to design your web pages. The tutorials and editors walk you through designing your web page, prompting you to select the items that you want on your page, and even reminding you to save your page at appropriate times. They then write the actual HTML tags for your page. Follow the instructions for using the editors provided by the free hosting service or Internet service provider.

Getting a Little Help from Genealogical Software Utilities

When you know how to write basic HTML – or use HTML editors to code documents for you – you're ready to design your home page. Before you do so, however, decide exactly what you want your home page to contain. In Chapter 10, we look at sharing GEDCOM data online without using the World Wide Web. You'd probably like to share your GEDCOM file on your own home page so this section explains how to prepare your GEDCOM file to share it on the web, and shows you how to format it without manually converting your GEDCOM to HTML. (For more about GEDCOM, check out Chapter 8.)

First and foremost, make sure that your GEDCOM file is ready to share with others. It needs to be free of any information that can land you in the dog-house with other people. (For more about ensuring that your GEDCOM file does not contain information about living individuals, head to Chapter 10. You can also take a look at the sidebars 'Privacy' and 'Copyright' later in this chapter.)

You can find genealogical software programs that enable you to indicate whether you want information about each relative included in reports and GEDCOMs. Other programs don't allow you to do this, however. Imagine what a hassle it is to work through a GEDCOM file line by line, deleting information on living relatives when you have several hundred or more individuals in your database. To alleviate the necessity of this task, a fellow genealogist developed a helpful little program called GEDClean.

GEDClean is a freeware utility that searches through your GEDCOM file and removes any information about living people. It then saves the cleaned GEDCOM for you to use with other genealogical utilities designed to help you put your information on the web. You can download a free copy at www.raynorshyn.com/gedclean/. Here's how to use it:

1. **Install and open the GEDClean program that you've downloaded from www.raynorshyn.com/gedclean/.**

   A yellow window pops up showing the three steps for GEDClean.

2. **Click Step 1: Select the Name of Your GEDCOM File.**

   A dialogue box asks you to specify the GEDCOM file on which you want to use GEDClean.

3. **Choose the GEDCOM file that you created in Chapter 10, or another GEDCOM that you have readily available. Click OK.**

   This brings you back to the yellow window. The name and directory path of your GEDCOM file appear under Step 1.

4. **Click Step 2: Select Individuals to Exclude from Your GEDCOM File.**

   A dialogue box asks you what you want to do in order to exclude living individuals from your GEDCOM. You can use an existing file that identifies all living people whose data you've included in your GEDCOM file. You can tell GEDClean to scan your GEDCOM file looking for anyone with a specific note that indicates that the person is still alive. Or you can get GEDClean to scan your entire GEDCOM file and look for anyone who may still be alive.

   Unless you have an existing file that states who needs to be excluded, or you've somehow marked your GEDCOM file to reflect living individuals, you should choose Option 3 and tell GEDClean to scan the whole GEDCOM looking for people who may be alive.

5. **Click Option 3: Analyse GEDCOM and then click OK.**

   For each person that GEDClean finds with no vital information (primarily birth date or death date), you get an Unknown Status window, asking what you want to do with that person's data.

6. **If GEDClean prompts you with an Unknown Status window, enter** living **(details to be excluded in the cleaned GEDCOM) or** not living **(details are included).**

   If you have a lot of people in your database, and thus in your GEDCOM file, the process of responding to each window for Unknown Status can be time-consuming. However, making sure that you exclude information on living relatives is well worth the effort.

7. **Click Step 3: Clean the GEDCOM File.**

   GEDClean scans the GEDCOM file and removes information on those people whom you indicated are still alive. It then saves your original GEDCOM file under a new name (with the extension .old) and saves the cleaned GEDCOM file under your original GEDCOM file name.

8. **Choose File⇨Exit to exit GEDClean.**

When you have a GEDCOM file that is free of information about all living people, you're ready to prepare your GEDCOM file for the web. You can choose from several programs to help you convert your GEDCOM to HTML. One such example is at `www.starkeffect.com/ged2html/`. Follow the instructions to use it with your cleaned GEDCOM file:

1. **Open the GED2HTML program that you downloaded from `www.starkeffect.com/ged2html`.**

   A dialogue box asks you to enter the location of your GEDCOM file. (You can browse if you can't remember the path name for the GEDCOM file.)

2. **Enter the path for your GEDCOM file and then click OK.**

   A typical path looks like this: `c:\my documents\helm.ged`

   GED2HTML runs a program using your GEDCOM file. You can watch it going through the file in a black window that appears.

3. **After the program is complete, press Enter to close the program window.**

   GED2HTML saves the output HTML files in a folder (appropriately called HTML) in the directory in which the GED2HTML program is saved.

4. **Open your web browser.**

   Usually you open the browser by double-clicking its icon or by using the Start menu (in Windows 95 or higher) to get to your programs.

5. **Use your browser's Open Page command to open any of the HTML output files.**

   Most browsers have an Open Page command in the File menu. When you choose Open Page, a dialogue box asks you which file you want to open. Browse to the directory where GED2HTML put your HTML output. Select an HTML document to look at.

   After checking what your output looks like and reviewing it to make sure that it doesn't contain any information that you don't want to be posted, you're ready to add it to your website or link to it as its own web page.

6. **Follow any instructions from your web host, and upload your GED2HTML files to your web server. Put any links to those files on your home page so that you can share your GEDCOM information online.**

   For example, suppose GED2HTML saved an HTML-coded index of all the people in your GEDCOM to a file called `persons.html`. After uploading or copying the file to your web host's server, you can use a link command such as `<A HREF = "[directory path]/persons.html">` from your main home page to the HTML-coded index of people to share it on the web.

Privacy

Sometimes, genealogists get so caught up with the records of dead people that they forget one basic fact: much of the information they've collected and put in their databases pertains to living people. In their haste to share information with others online, genealogists often create GEDCOM files and reports and send them off to recipients without thinking twice about whether they may offend or invade a person's privacy by including personal information. Be careful.

Well, okay, why shouldn't you include everything you know about your relatives?

✔ You may invade someone's right to privacy: Your relatives may not have given you permission to put their personal details online.

✔ Genealogists aren't the only people who visit genealogical Internet sites: Private detectives pay discreet visits, seeking information that may help in their investigations. Estranged spouses visit sites to track down their former partners. People with less-than-honourable intentions visit genealogical websites looking for potential scam or abuse victims. And information such as your mother's maiden name, may help unscrupulous visitors carry out fraud.

Your safest bet when sharing genealogical information is to include only the data that relate to people who have long been deceased – unless you've obtained written consent from living people to share information about them. By 'long been deceased', we mean deceased for more than ten years – although the time frame can be longer depending on the sensitivity of the information. Bear in mind that UK census details are kept confidential for 100 years before they're released online.

Deciding Which Treasures to Include

Genealogical web pages that contain lots of textual information about ancestors or geographical areas may be very helpful, but all-text pages won't attract the attention of your visitors. People inevitably get tired of reading endless narratives on websites. If you want to hold their attention, include other features such as graphics, icons and photographs that personalise a website and are fun to look at. A couple of nice-looking, strategically placed photos of ancestors make a site feel more like a home.

If you have photographs that you've scanned and saved as .jpg or .gif images, you can post them on your website. Just make sure that you upload a copy of the .jpg or .gif file to your web host's server in a directory that you can point to with HTML codes on your home page. By using the <IMG SRC = " "> code, you can tell browsers where to go to pick up that image or photograph. (Be sure to enter the filename for that image exactly as it appears on your hard drive or other resource.)

Just as you must be careful about posting factual information about living relatives, be careful about posting photos of them, too. If you want to use an image with living people in it, get their permission before doing so. People can be extremely sensitive about having their pictures posted on the web. Also, use common sense and taste in selecting pictures for your page. Although a photo of little Susie at age 3 wearing a lampshade and dancing around in a tutu may be cute, a photo of Uncle Ed at age 63 doing the same thing may not be so endearing. (And if Susie is now 33 she may not be that thrilled with the memory either.)

As well as using your own family photographs, many websites allow you to save images of their documents to your own PC, so you may like to include these on your website. However, do be careful – some of these images come with copyright restrictions, so make sure you check directly with the website that they're happy for you to include the images on your site. (See the 'Copyright' sidebar for more on this subject.)

Copyright

Copyright is the controlling right that a person or corporation owns over the duplication and distribution of a work created by that person or corporation. Although facts themselves can't be copyrighted, works in which facts are contained can be copyrighted. So, although the fact that your grandmother was born on 1 January 1900 can't be copyrighted by anyone, a report that contains this information and was created by Aunty Doris may be copyrighted. If you intend to include a significant portion of Aunty Doris's report in your own document, you need to secure permission from Aunty Doris before you use the information.

With regard to copyright and the Internet, remember that just because you found information on a website or other Internet resource doesn't mean that it's not copyrighted. If the website contains original material and facts, that material is copyrighted to the person who created it, regardless of whether the site contains a copyright notice on it.

Take the following measures to protect yourself from infringing someone's copyright and possibly ending up in a legal battle:

- Never copy another person's web page, email message or other Internet creation (such as graphics) without written consent.

- Never print out an article, story, report or other material to share with your family, friends, genealogical or historical society, class or anyone else without the creator's written consent.

- Always assume that a resource is copyrighted.

- Always cite sources of the information in your genealogy and on your web pages.

- Always link to other web pages rather than copying their content on your own website.

If you don't understand what copyright is, or you have questions about it, check out the UK Copyright Service at `www.copyrightservice.co.uk/copyright`. And remember: where copyright's concerned, always make sure.

Part V
The Part of Tens

'Just because you've got Viking ancestry is no
excuse for running off with the church silver
plate & the organist, Mr Johnson'

In this part . . .

The Part of Tens is a staple of *For Dummies* books. Use the chapters in this part for quick reference when you're seeking the following resources:

- ✔ Online databases.
- ✔ Ideas to ponder when you're designing your own genealogical web pages.
- ✔ Places to visit when you need a bit of help with your research.

Chapter 12

Ten (Or So) Handy Databases

In This Chapter

▶ Discovering online databases with useful data

▶ Finding databases that can provide research hints

*T*hroughout this book, we talk about online genealogy databases. You may find the following databases useful during the course of your research. This chapter gives you a brief description of some of the most useful databases and how to use them to further your research.

Access to Archives

www.nationalarchives.gov.uk/a2a/

Here you can discover the records and documents that are held in archives all over England and Wales. The database is searchable by keyword and/or location. The results of your search indicate whether the relevant records exist – and, if so, where they're held.

Archives Network Wales

www.archivesnetworkwales.info/

This database lists some of the most important documents held in repositories in Wales. The site isn't comprehensive: It focuses on collections of documents rather than individual documents, but it still gives you an idea of what's available. Equipped with information from Archives Network Wales, you can then contact the archives directly to find out more about their collections.

BBC British History

www.bbc.co.uk/history

Great for enabling you to put your ancestors into their historical context; this site counts English, Welsh, Scottish and Northern Irish history among its impressive collections. Links throughout the site give you access to ever-more-detailed information about the topics that interest you.

British History Online

www.british-history.ac.uk

British History Online is a digital library containing some of the core printed primary and secondary sources for the medieval and modern history of the British Isles. It can really help you to put all your family history findings into context, and is a great source for local history.

Family Relatives

www.familyrelatives.com

Family Relatives is a chargeable site, but contains lots of database material that you may not find on some of the other subscription sites. For example, the site has a growing collection of parish records, a wealth of military material and a new section devoted to Irish records (which provide access to Quaker records), wills and many more sources of information.

Moving Here

www.movinghere.org.uk

Moving Here is dedicated to migration to Britain during the past 200 years and is an aid to tracing your Caribbean, Irish, Jewish and South Asian ancestors. The site describes migration patterns and helps you establish a background picture of the life and times of your ancestors on the move. You can search for your ancestors by name, although this facility covers only certain record types. If the resources you want aren't online, the site tells you where to find the relevant records and what you can discover from them.

The National Archives

www.nationalarchives.gov.uk

A fantastic site that holds the UK census collection and a wealth of advice about creating your family tree. The site also contains numerous other invaluable resources, including wills, military records and hundreds of research and in-depth instruction guides covering a multitude of topics over a broad range of years. The online catalogue shows what's available in the offline collections at The National Archives, and you can use the site to make enquiries, hire researchers and browse the bookshop.

Origins Network

www.originsnetwork.com

Origins Network is a chargeable database containing resources relevant to the whole of the British Isles, including Boyd's Marriage Index (a collection of over 7 million English marriages between 1538 and 1840), a selection of pre-1858 wills and probate indexes (see Chapter 6 for more), over 350,000 apprenticeship records from all over Great Britain and a collection of militia, inheritance and burial records. You can choose from a number of options if you decide to join up to Origins Network, depending on the time frame that's best for you. At the time of writing, membership for 72 hours costs £7.50, monthly membership costs £10.50, quarterly membership costs £18.50 and annual membership costs £34.50.

The Public Record Office of Northern Ireland

www.proni.gov.uk

This site enables you to search the indexes for pre-1858 wills and to use the pilot online search facility for the 1911 Irish Census.

ScotsFind

www.scotsfind.org

ScotsFind is a site housing a large collection of genealogical databases relating to Scotland, including parish registers, apprentice records and monument inscriptions. Everything's indexed by location or name.

The Scottish Archive Network

www.scan.org.uk

SCAN is a Scottish database similar to Access to Archives. It enables you to search the holdings of over 50 archives in Scotland using their online catalogues and search engines. This site can also help you find archives' contact details, including links to their websites and opening times.

Chapter 13

Ten Things to Remember When Designing Your Genealogical Website

*Y*ou've probably seen hundreds of websites during the course of your research, and perhaps half of them look alike, as though the maintainers have simply plugged their surnames in specified spots and maybe changed the background colour of the page. Usually such pages don't contain much information of any value – just lists of surnames with no context and perhaps a few links to some of the better-known genealogical websites.

You don't want your genealogical website to look just like everyone else's. Neither do you want your website to contain almost exactly the same information. You want your site to be unique and useful to other genealogists so that a lot of people visit your site and recommend it to others. What can you do to avoid the genealogical web-ite rut that many genealogists find themselves in? Here we offer a few ideas and suggest places where you can find help.

Be Unique

Please, please tell us that you want to set your home page apart from all other genealogical websites. Of course, you don't really need to be told not to copy other sites, but when you design your site and the pressure's on, coming up with ideas for text and graphics can be rather daunting. We understand that pressure of this kind makes it awfully tempting for you to take ideas from other websites that you like. Although you can certainly look to other sites for ideas about formatting, design and content, don't copy them! Websites are copyrighted by the people who created them – even if they don't display a copyright notice – and you can get into trouble for copying them. (See Chapter 11 for more about copyright.)

The other reason not to copy other websites is that you want your page to attract as many visitors as possible, and in order to do so you need to offer something unique that encourages visitors to stop and explore. After all, if your site provides the same old information as another site, people have no particular need to visit your page. And because several comprehensive genealogical sites already exist, posting a website that merely consists of links to other genealogical pages doesn't make much sense. Similarly, if you're thinking about creating a one-name study site on a surname for which four or five one-name study sites already exist, you may want to focus your home page on a different surname that you're researching.

Be creative. Look around and find out what existing genealogical websites offer, and then seek to fill the void. Pick a unique topic, name or location that doesn't have much coverage. Better still, pick something that doesn't have any coverage at all. If you really want to post a surname site, you can perhaps develop a site for your surname in a particular country or county, or consider posting transcribed records from a particular place that would benefit genealogists who are researching ancestors from that area.

If you find coming up with enough unique and original content for your site too challenging, consider involving others in your efforts. You can turn to relatives or other researchers who are interested in the same family lines as you are. Perhaps you correspond with someone who doesn't have Internet access but offers some good ideas for your site or who has access but doesn't have the time or motivation to create his or her own site. You can bring all the ideas together.

Include Key Surnames and Contact Info on Your Website

If the purpose of your website is not only to share your collection of genealogical information but also to get information from others, be sure to include a list of the names that you're researching. And don't be stingy with information: A simple list of surnames isn't going to be much help to visitors to your site, particularly if any of the surnames on your list are common – Smith, Johnson, Jones, Martin and so forth. You need to provide enough information to enable other researchers to link their family trees into yours. An online version of the information contained in your GEDCOM (see Chapter 11 for more info on GEDCOM) does the job well because it includes an index of surnames that people can look through and also gives information about your ancestors with those surnames.

Be sure to include your name and email address on the site so that people are able to get in touch with you in order to share data. If you change your email address, don't forget to update your website, and let people know. That way you won't miss any vital information!

 If you're happy to do so, you can include your mailing address on your website so that people who don't have email access can contact you. Alternatively, if you're uncomfortable providing such personal information but you want other researchers to be able to contact you, consider getting a post-office box that you can post on your website and use for receiving genealogy-related mail.

Make It Attractive but Don't Be Too Flashy

Choose your colours and graphics wisely. Although using some colour and graphics (including photographs) helps your website stand out and makes it more personal and easier on the eye, be careful about using too much colour or too many graphics. By 'too much colour', we mean backgrounds so bright that they almost blind your visitors or make the rest of the site hard to look at, or backgrounds that drown out the colours of your links. Your site needs to appeal to other people as well as to you. Before using neon pink or lime green, stop and consider how others may react.

 The more graphics you use and the larger they are, the longer a computer takes to load them. Animated graphics are even worse: not only do they take a long time to load, but they can make your visitors dizzy and disoriented if you have several graphics moving in different directions at the same time. Graphics files aren't the only things that affect how quickly computers load files: the amount of bandwidth of your Internet connection and the amount of space available on your hard drive also affect the download time, and you can't assume all genealogists are going to have cutting-edge home computers.

Waiting for a page to load that contains more graphics than useful text is frustrating – you can guarantee that people lose interest at the smallest provocation, so concentrate on making your page as user-friendly as possible from the beginning. Use graphics tastefully and sparingly.

If you have a large number of family photos that you'd like to share, put each picture on its own page and then provide links to the photo pages from your home page. This way, visitors who aren't interested in seeing any of the photos don't have to wait for the images to load on their computers just to view the other contents of your site, and visitors who are only interested in a particular image don't have to wait for all the other photos to load.

The section 'Ask for Help' later in the chapter identifies some online resources that lead you to sites with web-safe colours and graphics that you can download and use on your website.

To shrink the size of the graphics on your website, try using a *graphics optimiser* – a tool that formats your graphics to make them load faster. A good graphics optimiser is NetMechanic GIFBot, at `www.netmechanic.com/accelerate.htm`.

Take Care with What You Post

Remember to be careful and thoughtful when designing your website and posting information contributed by others. Don't post any information that may hurt or offend someone. Respect the privacy of others and post information only about people who've been dead for many years. (Twenty-five years is a good, conservative figure to use when in doubt.) Even then, be cautious about telling old family stories that may affect people who are still alive. (For more information about privacy, see Chapters 10 and 11.)

Cite Your Sources

We can't stress this enough! Always cite your sources when you put genealogical narrative on your website or when you post information from records that you've collected or people you've interviewed. If you cite your sources rigorously, people who visit your page and take data from it can see exactly where you obtained the information and can follow it up if they want to. (Also, by citing your sources, you keep yourself out of trouble because others may have provided the information for you, and they deserve the credit for the research.)

Remember That Not All Web Browsers Are Created Equal

Different web browsers interpret HTML documents differently depending on who created the software. Also, some web browsers have HTML tags specific to the browser. So, although you may create a website that looks professional and exciting using Microsoft Internet Explorer, it may look off-centre or somewhat different when using Netscape Navigator or Opera. Because of the centring problem, try not to use tags specific to any one browser when you create your website. Whenever possible, test your page in several browsers before posting it for public access. Better still, use a testing service that allows the experts to look at your page and give you feedback. You can look for testing services using online search engines. A popular HTML validation checker is http://validator.w3.org/.

Another consideration is to make your web pages readable by screen-reading browsers – browsers that enable visually impaired researchers to access information on the Internet. To check whether your content is accessible, use the free page scan on the IBM website at www-01.ibm.com/software/rational/offerings/websecurity/.

Check and Recheck Your Links

If you include links on your site to other websites that you've designed or sites maintained by someone else, double-check the links when you post your pages. Make sure that the links work properly so that visitors have no trouble navigating around sites that you recommend or that support your home page. A lot of genealogical websites tend to be transient – the maintainers move them or take them down entirely for one reason or another – so we advise you to run a check once a month or so to make sure that the links still work.

If you have a lot of links on your website and you don't have the time to check each one yourself, you can use the validation checker at http://validator.w3.org/. The site links to a list of programs that check your website and notify you about any broken links. You can also try:

- ✔ **Linkscan:** www.elsop.com
- ✔ **The Rel Software Web Link Validator:** www.relsoftware.com/wlv

Market Your Website

After you've put together your website and posted it on your provider's server, you need to let people know it exists so that they can pay it a visit. To do this, we recommend that you follow the same tips in Chapter 3 for marketing the research that you've done on your surnames; for example using mailing lists if the site deals with particular surnames or geographical areas. In particular, one of the best ways to promote your website is to register it with several comprehensive genealogical websites that receive a lot of traffic from people looking for genealogy-related pages.

Also, most of the major search engines have links to registration or submission pages within their sites that enable you to submit your URL. Or to save time, visit Add Me at www.addme.com/submission.htm, which forwards your website information to up to 14 search engines for free. You can also try:

- ✔ **Submit Express:** www.submitexpress.com/submit.html
- ✔ **Evrsoft FastSubmit:** www.evrsoft.com/fastsubmit
- ✔ **Search Engine Submission and Optimization:** www.addpro.com

Help Others: Doing So Is Its Own Reward

After you've designed your website, don't go overboard promoting your home page simply to receive awards from other sites, magazines and societies. Post your genealogical home page with the intent of helping other genealogists and encouraging a sharing genealogical community. If you use the majority of your page to advertise your awards and beg people to vote for your site in popularity contests, you'll lose a lot of valuable space where you can post information that's useful to genealogists. You'll also lose credibility with your visitors, who may then boycott your site, which defeats the purpose of self-promotion in the first place.

We're not saying that you shouldn't acknowledge awards that your site receives if it contains good and sound genealogical content. We recognise that it's good business to give a little traffic back to the sites, magazines, societies and other sources that send visitors your way by awarding your page some honour. We're simply saying that you can acknowledge the honours you receive in a tasteful and humble manner. You don't have to plaster the graphics for every single award across the top of your page. Instead, set up a separate web page for awards and provide a link from your home page so that those who are interested in seeing your honours can go there.

Ask for Help

Chapter 11 describes how to create a simple website and discusses some HTML editors that are available from web hosts. But these resources may not even begin to cover all the wonderful things that you intend to do with your website. If you'd like to find out more about how to do fancier things with your website, check out colleges in your area and workshops offered by local libraries or genealogical societies. Colleges and workshops often offer classes or sessions on how to make a website, walking you through the basics of HTML and posting a website.

If the thought of attending a structured class sends a shiver up your spine, you can discover more about HTML and web design in other ways. Many books and online sites are available to help you. You might consider: *HTML 4 For Dummies*, 5th Edition, by Ed Tittel and Mary Burmeister; *Creating Web Pages For Dummies*, 8th Edition, by Bud Smith; *Web Design For Dummies*, 2nd Edition, by Lisa Lopuck; and *Creating Family Web Sites For Dummies*, by Janine C. Warner (all Wiley).

The following online sites have links to many resources for designing and programming web pages and resources that have colours, backgrounds, graphics and other website enhancements available to download:

- ✔ **Yahoo! World Wide Web Beginner's Guides:** `dir.yahoo.com/ Computers_and_Internet/Internet/World_Wide_Web/ Beginner_s_Guides`
- ✔ **Web Building Tutorial:** `www.w3schools.com/site/default.asp`

Chapter 14

Ten (Or So) Sites That Offer Help

• •

In This Chapter

▶ Finding how-to genealogy sites

▶ Locating Scottish, Irish and Welsh sources

• •

Do census records leave you dazed and confused? Are you panicking at the idea of using complicated computer systems to locate a surname? Or have you read so much information that you've simply no idea where to start? Visiting the following websites may take away a little of that anxiety.

The National Archives: Getting Started in Family History

www.nationalarchives.gov.uk/familyhistory/films/default.htm

The National Archives website guides you through the opening stages of your genealogical research. With the help of text and visual clips, the site introduces you to the world of genealogy, with advice on how to extract your first clues from your family and your home. On this site you find films about building your family tree, data about birth, marriage and death certificates, the national census, getting your research together and moving your project forwards, all presented by Dr Nick Barratt.

The BBC Family History Site

www.bbc.co.uk/history/familyhistory

Here you can find an excellent video introduction on how to get started in your family history. The site includes sections on birth, marriage and death records, immigration, oral history, census returns and more.

ScotlandsPeople: Getting Started

`www.scotlandspeople.gov.uk/content/help/index.aspx?r=551&1`

This website offers the key information you need to get your Scottish research under way. Read about planning and conducting your research, understanding and recording your findings and making the most of the resources available on the site. The site also provides links to discussion groups.

Gareth's Help Page for Welsh Genealogy

`http://home.clara.net/tirbach/hicks.html`

Gareth's Help Page site provides everything you need to know about researching your ancestors in Wales, including a basic beginner's guide to genealogy, lists of resources, mailing lists, maps, Welsh language sites and an explanation of technical terms.

Tracing Your Irish Roots

`www.irishfamilyresearch.co.uk`

This website contains links to searchable databases for wills and headstones. You can also find useful links to other websites, and make use of a members' area.

Irish Family History Foundation: Guide to Genealogical Research

`www.irish-roots.net/genealogical-research-guide.asp`

Here you find a detailed account of the resources available to genealogists seeking their Irish roots. Follow the links to discover the records you can use, their background and where to find them. For even more info, check out the National Archives of Ireland at `www.nationalarchives.ie/genealogy/beginning.html`. Here you can search elements of the Irish 1911 census online.

Ancestry.co.uk

www.ancestry.co.uk/learn/library/archive.aspx

Ancestry is well known for its collection of databases and digitised images, but it also contains a valuable collection of articles, regular columns and other online resources to assist you in your research. These resources are produced by genealogists all over the world. Browse at your leisure by selecting from a list of topic headings, including *How-to*, *Preserving Family History*, *Religion* and *Technology*.

The Good Web Guide: Choosing Family History Software

www.thegoodwebguide.co.uk/genealogy

The Good Web Guide site helps you choose the family history software that's best for you. It's full of tips, basic and advanced features to consider when choosing your software and lists of genealogy software. Links to other websites give you the chance to find even more detailed info.

British Genealogy Forums

www.british-genealogy.com/forums

Whatever your query, whatever your problem, you're bound to find a forum on the British Genealogy website that can help you. Discussion forums are available relating to all sorts of genealogy-related topics, from general genealogy, through researching specific places and specific periods in history, to genealogy software, historical events and more. Forums save you hours of trawling through the Internet to find the information you want: just ask someone who already has the information, or who can point you in the right direction. Registration is free, but you have to enter a user name and your email address, and select a password in order to be able to use the site.

Getting Started in Genealogy and Family History

www.genuki.org.uk/gs/

The Genuki website provides a list of helpful hints to get you started in your genealogical research. The extensive list covers more than a dozen topics, including deciding the aim of your research, using family history centres, joining a genealogical society, tracing migrants and writing up your results. The site includes a list of reference material in case you want to read more about the topics discussed on the site.

Genetic Genealogy

www.dnaancestryproject.com

This website offers helpful advice, information and articles about DNA testing and genetic genealogy. You can even buy your own DNA testing kit here.

Appendix

A Glossary of Terms

Abstract: A brief overview of the contents of a document or *website*.

Ahnentafel: A well-known genealogical numbering system that provides a mathematical relationship between parents and children. The word means 'ancestor table' in German. Also referred to as the Sosa–Stradonitz system.

Albumen print: A type of photograph produced on a thin piece of paper coated with albumen and silver nitrate and usually mounted on cardboard. Typically taken between 1858 and 1910.

Ambrotype: A type of photograph printed on thin glass and usually with a black backing. Typically taken between 1858 and 1866.

Ancestor: A person from whom you're descended.

Ancestral chart: A chart running horizontally across a page and identifying a primary person (including that person's name, date and place of birth, date and place of marriage and date and place of death), his or her parents, each of their parents, and so on until the chart runs off the page. Also called a *pedigree chart*.

Ancestral file: A database created and maintained by the Church of Jesus Christ of Latter-day Saints, with millions of names available in family group sheets and pedigree charts. Many ancestral files are available online, and others are accessible at family history centres.

Archive: A building or location in which historical documents and records are stored.

Automoderator: A computer program that determines whether a message to be posted to a *newsgroup* is appropriate and, if so, posts it to the newsgroup.

Backbones: High-speed data lines that form the basis of the *Internet*.

Bandwidth: The capacity of a phone line or other network cable carrying traffic to and from the *Internet* or computer network.

Banns: See *marriage banns*.

Baptismal certificate: A certificate issued by a church at the time of baptism. Often used to estimate a birth date in the absence of a *birth certificate*.

Bibliography: A list of books or other materials used in a piece of research, or a list of books or other materials available on a particular topic.

Biographical sketch: A brief written account of a person's life.

Biography: A detailed written account of a person's life.

Birth certificate: A legal record stating when and where a person was born, who his or her parents were, and other relevant details.

Bookmark: A method of saving links to your favourite *websites* within your *World Wide Web browser* so you can return to the sites easily.

Bouncing: The returning of an *email* message to the sender because it hasn't reached the recipient.

Browser: See *World Wide Web browser*.

Cable connection: A means of direct access to the *Internet* using cable lines.

Cache: A directory on your computer in which your *World Wide Web browser* stores information about web pages and images it has downloaded. Using the cache, the browser loads the page faster if you visit it again within a certain period.

Canon code: A code that explains the bloodline relationship in legal terms by identifying how many degrees of separation (or steps) exist between two blood relations. It is based on Canon law, which counts only the number of steps from the nearest common ancestor of both relatives.

Carte-de-visite: A type of photograph that was a small paper print mounted on a card. Collections were usually bound together in photo albums. Typically taken between 1858 and 1891.

CD-ROM: Acronym for compact disk read-only memory. Used in your computer's compact disk drive. A CD-ROM stores large amounts of information that can be retrieved by your computer.

Census: The counting or snapshot of a population undertaken by a government.

Census index: A list of people included in particular *census* records, along with links to images of actual census records.

Census return: The record or form on which *census* information is collected. Also called a census schedule.

Channel: An area within *Internet relay chat* with discussions on particular topics, including genealogy.

Charter: A formal or informal document that defines the scope of a *newsgroup*.

Chat room: An *Internet* site where you log in and participate in real-time conversations.

Church of Jesus Christ of Latter-day Saints: Otherwise known as the Mormon Church, this organisation has compiled a vast collection of parish records into the *International Genealogical Index*. It has also established family history centres in many parts of the world.

Cite: To name the source of some information and provide reference to the original source.

Civil code: A code that explains the bloodline relationship in legal terms by identifying how many degrees of separation (or kinship steps) exist between two blood relatives. It is based on Civil law, which counts each step between two relatives as a degree.

Civil registration: The recording of births, marriages and deaths by officials of the state. These records are also known as *vital records*.

Commercial Internet service provider: An organisation that supplies access to the *Internet* for a fee.

Community network: A locally based *Internet service provider* offering *Internet* access to people in the community, usually free of charge. Also called freenet.

Comprehensive genealogical site: A *website* that identifies a large number of other genealogical sites, which in turn contain information on a number of families, locations or other genealogy-related subjects.

Cookies: Pieces of information sent to your computer by other computers when you visit certain web pages. Cookies are usually used for navigation purposes or by commercial sites that want to rotate advertisements for their visitors.

Copyright: The exclusive right of a creator to reproduce, distribute, perform, display, deride, sell, lend or rent his or her creations.

Cyberspace: A popular term for the *Internet*.

Daguerreotype: A type of photograph that required a long exposure time and was taken on silver-plated copper. Typically taken between 1839 and 1860.

Database: A collection of information that is entered, organised, stored and used on a computer.

Death certificate: A legal record stating when and where a person died, along with other relevant information, which may include some or all of the following: age, occupation, cause of death, time of death, date and place of birth, informant of the death and occasionally the names and ages of children and the place of burial.

Deed: A document that records the transfer of ownership of a piece of property or land.

Denization: The process by which an individual born outside a particular country becomes a subject of that country but does not enjoy full citizenship rights.

Denization record: The legal document proving that *denization* has been granted to an individual.

Descendant: A person descended from a particular *ancestor*.

Descendant chart: A chart that contains information about an *ancestor* and spouse or spouses, their children and their spouses, their grandchildren and their spouses and so on down the family line. Usually formatted vertically on a page.

Dial-up connection: A method of connecting to the Internet that uses a telephone line to call in to an *Internet service provider*.

Digest mode: An option for receiving postings to some mailing lists in which several messages are batched together and sent to you instead of each message being sent separately.

Digital camera: A camera that captures images to computer memory instead of to film and then downloads the images on to your computer.

Digital subscriber line (DSL): A means of accessing the Internet directly using a special phone line. This service is faster than a *dial-up connection*, which uses a traditional phone line.

Digitised record: An electronic copy of an image or record.

Direct connection: A means of direct access to the *Internet* from your home. You can have a direct Internet connection in four ways: through an Internet line that comes directly into the building and is plugged into your computer, through a *cable connection*, through a *digital subscriber line* (DSL) or through a *satellite connection*.

Directory: A collection of information about individuals who live in a particular place.

DNA: Our genetic makeup, which can be used in *genetic genealogy*.

Download: A means of getting a file (information or a program) to your computer from another computer.

DVD: This stands for Digital Versatile Disk, and is a means of storing vast amounts of data (much more than a CD-ROM), that can be retrieved by your computer.

Electronic mail: Messages that are sent from one person to another electronically over the *Internet*. Also called *email*.

Email: Short for *electronic mail*.

Emigrant: A person who leaves or moves away from one area or country to settle in another.

Enumeration district: The area assigned to a particular enumerator of a *census*.

Enumerator: A person who collects details of individuals during a *census*.

Estate: The assets and liabilities of a dead person.

Family association: An organised group of individuals researching the same family.

Family association site: A *website* designed and posted by an organisation devoted to researching a particular family.

Family group sheet: A summary of a particular family, including biographical information about a couple and their children.

Family history: The written account of a family's existence over time.

Family history centre: A building or archive that specialises in records and services relevant to genealogists.

Family outline report: A list of the descendants of a particular ancestor.

FamilySearch: A collection of information compiled by the Church of Jesus Christ of Latter-day Saints including the Ancestral File, Family History Library Catalogue, International Genealogical Index and Scottish Church Records.

FAQ: Acronym for *frequently asked questions*.

FHC: Abbreviation for *family history centre*.

File transfer protocol: A means of transferring files from your computer to another, or vice versa, over the Internet. Abbreviated to FTP.

Flame: A personal attack via the Internet on another user.

Forum: A subject-specific area on the *Internet* in which members post messages and files.

Freenet: A locally based *Internet service provider* offering *Internet* access to people in the community, free of charge. Also called a *community network*.

Freeware: Software that you obtain and use for free by downloading it from the *Internet*.

Frequently asked questions: A web page or message posted to a *mailing list*, *newsgroup* or *website* that provides answers to the questions most commonly addressed to that site. A good starting point for new visitors to a site or resource.

FTP: Abbreviation of *file transfer protocol*.

Gateway: Computer(s) that forward messages and route data between networks.

Gatewaying: Relaying of traffic from a newsgroup to a related mailing list, and vice versa.

Gazetteer: Geographical dictionary providing information about places.

GEDCOM: Acronym for *genealogical data communication*.

Genealogical database: Software in which you enter, store and use information about ancestors, descendants and other people relevant to your genealogy.

Genealogical data communication: The standard file format used for exporting and importing information between genealogical databases. Intended to make data translatable between different genealogical software programs so you can share your family information easily. Abbreviated to GEDCOM.

Genealogical society: An organised group that attempts to preserve documents and history for the area in which the society is located and helps its members research their ancestors.

Genealogically focused search engine: A program that indexes the full text of websites of interest to genealogists and allows you to search the index for particular keywords.

GENDEX: An index of online genealogical databases that comply with the GEDCOM converted to *HTML* indexing format.

Genealogy: The study of *ancestors*, *descendants* and family origins.

Genetic genealogy: Using *DNA* to prove genetic connectivity.

Geographically specific website: A *website* with information pertaining to a particular town, county, country or other area.

Glass-plate negative: A type of photograph made by immersing light-sensitive silver bromide in gelatine. Typically taken between 1848 and 1930.

Gopher: A computer protocol that provides a means of categorising data on the Internet by using a series of text-based hierarchical menus through which you browse and click.

Henry system: A widely used and accepted genealogical numbering system that assigns a particular sequence of numbers to the children of a family's progenitor and to subsequent generations.

Hierarchy: The major grouping to which a *newsgroup* belongs; for example, `soc.genealogy.computing` belongs to the `soc` hierarchy.

Historical society: An organised group that attempts to preserve documents and promote the history of the area in which the society is located.

Home page: The entry point for a World Wide Web site.

HTML: Acronym for *HyperText Markup Language*.

HyperText Markup Language: The programming language of the World Wide Web. HTML is a code translated into graphics pages by software called a *World Wide Web browser*.

IGI: Acronym for *International Genealogical Index*.

Immigrant: A person who moves into or settles in a country or area.

Index: A list of contents or resources. An index can be a list of *websites*, types of records and so on.

Interface: An online form or page.

Interlibrary loan: A system in which one library loans a book or other material to another library for a reader to borrow or use.

International Genealogical Index: A list of baptisms, christenings, marriages, burials and other records of deceased individuals collected by the Church of Jesus Christ of Latter-day Saints. The International Genealogical Index (abbreviated to IGI) is part of the FamilySearch collection.

Internet: A system of computer networks joined together by high-speed data lines called *backbones*.

Internet relay chat: A network providing channels or areas in which you find real-time discussions about genealogy and participate in them, using chat software. Abbreviated to IRC.

Internet service provider: An organisation that provides access to the Internet through a direct or dial-up connection. Abbreviated to ISP.

Intestate: The estate status of a person who has died without leaving a valid will.

IRC: Abbreviation for *Internet relay chat*.

ISP: Abbreviation for *Internet service provider*.

Kinship report: A list of family members and how they relate directly to one particular individual in your *database*. Usually kinship reports include the *civil code* and *canon code* for the relationship to the individual.

Listowner: A person who oversees a mailing list.

Listserv: A software program for managing electronic mailing lists.

Lurking: Reading messages that others post to a mailing list or newsgroup without posting your own messages.

Maiden name: The surname with which a woman is born. Sometimes indicated by the word *née* (French for 'born') on records and documents.

Mailing list: An *email* exchange forum consisting of a group of people who share common interests. Email messages posted to the list come directly to your computer in full-format (*mail mode*) or *digest mode*. The list contains the name of everyone who joins the group. To send a message to the group, you post it to a single email address that subsequently delivers the message to everyone on the list.

Mail mode: The format by which a mailing list sends each message to you as soon as it's posted.

Marriage banns: A proclamation made in front of a church congregation expressing one's intent to marry.

Marriage bond: A financial contract guaranteeing that a marriage was going to take place. The bond was usually posted by the groom and another person (often the father or brother of the bride).

Marriage certificate: A legal document certifying the union of two individuals.

Marriage licence: A document issued by a civil or ecclesiastical authority granting a couple permission to marry.

Maternal: Relating to the mother's side of the family.

Microfiche: A clear sheet that contains tiny images of documents, records, books and other resources. You read a microfiche using a microfiche reader or other magnifying equipment.

Microfilm: A roll of clear film that contains tiny images of documents, records, books and other resources. You read a microfilm using a microfilm reader.

Modem: A piece of equipment that allows your computer to talk to other computers through a telephone or cable line. Modems can be internal (inside your computer) or external (plugged into one of your computer's serial ports or card).

Moderator: A person who determines whether a post to a newsgroup or mailing list is appropriate and, if so, posts it.

Mortgage: A legal agreement to repay money borrowed with property as collateral.

Muster record: A type of military pay record stating who was present with a military unit at a particular time and place.

Naturalisation: The official process by which an individual born outside a particular country becomes a citizen or subject of that country.

Naturalisation record: The legal document proving that a person is a naturalised citizen.

Netiquette: Simple guidelines for communicating effectively and politely on the Internet.

Newbie: A person new to the Internet.

Newsgroup: A place on the Internet in which to post messages on a particular topic so that groups of people at large can read them online. Messages are posted to a *news server*, which in turn copies the messages to other news servers.

News reader: Software needed for reading messages posted to a newsgroup.

News server: One or more computers that replicate newsgroups over the Internet.

Notebook computer: A compact portable computer.

Obituary: An account of a person's death in a newspaper or other type of medium.

One-name study: A piece of research focusing on one particular surname regardless of the geographical location in which it appears. You can find websites dedicated to one-name studies.

Online: Being connected to the *Internet*.

Orphan: An infant or child whose parents are both deceased. In some earlier times and places, a child was considered to be an orphan if his or her father had died even if the mother was still alive.

Palmtop: A portable hand-sized computer.

Parish records: Lists of christenings, baptisms, marriages and burials recorded at parish level. A major resource for genealogists before civil registration.

Passenger list: A list of the names of passengers who travelled from one country to another on a particular ship.

Paternal: Relating to the father's side of the family.

Pedigree chart: See *ancestral chart*.

Pension record: A type of military record stating the pension that the government paid to an individual who served in the military. Pension records also record the pension paid to the widow or orphans of such an individual.

Personal web page: A page on the World Wide Web designed and posted by an individual or family.

Platinum print: A type of photograph with a matte surface that appeared to be embedded in the paper. Images were often highlighted with artistic chalk, giving the photo a hand-drawn quality. Typically taken between 1880 and 1930.

Primary source: A document, oral account, photograph or any other item created when a certain event occurred. Information for the record was supplied by a witness to the event.

Probate: Settlement of a person's estate after death.

Probate records: Court records that deal with the settling of a person's estate after his or her death. Probate records include contested wills and will readings. The file may contain testimonies and the ruling in the case of contested wills.

PROCAT: The online catalogue of *The National Archives*.

Professional researcher: A person who researches your genealogy and obtains copies of documents for a fee.

Progenitor: The farthest-back ancestor that you know about in a particular family line.

Query: A research question posted to a *website*, *mailing list* or *newsgroup* so that other researchers can help solve your genealogical research problems.

Repository: A place in which documents are deposited and stored.

Research group: Group of people who coordinate their research and share resources to achieve success.

Robot: A program that travels throughout the *Internet* and collects information about sites and resources that it comes across. Also called a *spider*.

Roots Surname List: A list of surnames and the dates and locations for which these names have been researched, accompanied by the contact information for people researching those surnames. Maintained by RootsWeb.com. Abbreviated to *RSL*.

RSL: Abbreviation for *Roots Surname List*.

Satellite connection: A means of accessing the Internet directly using a satellite dish and signals.

Scanner: A device that captures digital images of photographs and documents and stores them in a computer.

Search engine: A program that searches a particular website or a large index of information generated by robots.

Secondary source: A document, oral account or any other record created after an event took place or for which information was supplied by someone who wasn't an eyewitness to the event.

Server: A computer that makes information accessible to other computers.

Service record: A military record that chronicles the military career of an individual.

Shareware: Software that you can try before you pay to license and use it permanently. Usually you *download* shareware from the *Internet*.

Shotgun approach: The process of sending mass *emails* to anyone you find with your surname, asking for information about your ancestors.

Signature file: A file attached to the bottom of your *email* messages that gives your name, contact information, the surnames you're researching or anything else you want to convey to others.

Site: One or more World Wide Web pages. Also called a *website*.

Snail mail: Mail delivered by the postal service rather than by *email*.

Sosa–Stradonitz system: See *Ahnentafel*.

Sound card: An internal computer device that allows you to hear the audio features of software or audio files that you *download* from the *Internet*.

Soundex: A system of indexing a census. A Soundex search produces names similar to the one you want as well as the name that you enter in the search box. Soundex therefore allows for inaccuracies in the recording of your ancestors' names on a census.

Source: A person, book, document, record, periodical and so on that provides information relevant to your research.

Spam: Unsolicited junk *email* that tries to sell you something or offers a service.

Spider: See *robot*.

Stereographic card: A type of double photograph that appeared as a single three-dimensional picture when used with a viewer. Developed in the 1850s.

Surname: A last name or family name.

Tax record: A record of tax paid, including property, inheritance and church taxes. Historically, many taxes were collected at the local level, but some of the records have now been turned over to county or national archives.

The National Archives: The major repository for historical documents in the UK. Collections include military and merchant navy records, naturalisation, denization and divorce records. A large collection of research guides and documents online is available at The National Archives' website at www. nationalarchives.gov.uk.

Thread: A group of messages on a *newsgroup* with a common subject.

Tintype: A type of photograph made on a metal sheet. The image was often coated with a varnish. Typically taken between 1858 and 1910.

Toggling: The process of flipping back and forth between open programs on your computer by using the Alt and Tab keys in Windows or the Application Switcher in Macintosh.

Transcribed record: A copy of a record that has been duplicated word-for-word.

Uniform resource locator: A standard online address provided for resources on the World Wide Web. Abbreviated to *URL*.

URL: Abbreviation for *uniform resource locator*.

Vital record: The primary record of a birth, death or marriage. Often called *civil registration*.

Webmaster: A person responsible for creating and maintaining a particular *website*.

Website: One or more World Wide Web pages created by an individual or organisation. Also called a *site*.

Will: A legal document explaining how a person wishes his or her estate to be settled or distributed after death.

Witness: A person who attests that he or she saw an event.

World Wide Web: A system for viewing and using multimedia documents on the Internet. Web documents are created in *HyperText Markup Language* (HTML) and are read by *World Wide Web browsers*.

World Wide Web browser: Software that enables you to view *HTML* documents on the Internet.

World Wide Web page: A multimedia document created in *HTML* and viewable on the Internet through a *World Wide Web browser*.

XML: A special computer code similar to *HTML* that uses tags to describe information. The broader purpose of XML is not only to display information but also to describe the information.

Index

• G •

• *H* •

Notes

Notes

FOR DUMMIES®

Making Everything Easier! ™

UK editions

BUSINESS

978-0-470-51806-9

978-0-470-74381-2

978-0-470-71382-2

FINANCE

978-0-470-99280-7

978-0-470-71432-4

978-0-470-69515-9

HOBBIES

978-0-470-69960-7

978-0-470-74535-9

978-0-470-75857-1

British Sign Language For Dummies
978-0-470-69477-0

Business NLP For Dummies
978-0-470-69757-3

Competitive Strategy For Dummies
978-0-470-77930-9

Cricket For Dummies
978-0-470-03454-5

CVs For Dummies, 2nd Edition
978-0-470-74491-8

Digital Marketing For Dummies
978-0-470-05793-3

Divorce For Dummies, 2nd Edition
978-0-470-74128-3

eBay.co.uk Business All-in-One For Dummies
978-0-470-72125-4

Emotional Freedom Technique For Dummies
978-0-470-75876-2

English Grammar For Dummies
978-0-470-05752-0

Flirting For Dummies
978-0-470-74259-4

Golf For Dummies
978-0-470-01811-8

Green Living For Dummies
978-0-470-06038-4

Hypnotherapy For Dummies
978-0-470-01930-6

IBS For Dummies
978-0-470-51737-6

Lean Six Sigma For Dummies
978-0-470-75626-3

8041_p1

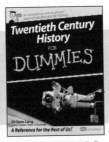
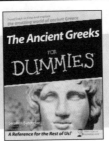

FOR
DUMMIES®

The easy way to get more done and have more fun

LANGUAGES

978-0-7645-5194-9

978-0-7645-5193-2

978-0-471-77270-5

MUSIC

978-0-470-48133-2

978-0-470-03275-6
UK Edition

978-0-470-49644-2

SCIENCE & MATHS

978-0-7645-5326-4

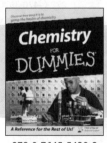

978-0-7645-5430-8

978-0-7645-5325-7

Art For Dummies
978-0-7645-5104-8

Bass Guitar For Dummies
978-0-7645-2487-5

Brain Games For Dummies
978-0-470-37378-1

Christianity For Dummies
978-0-7645-4482-8

Criminology For Dummies
978-0-470-39696-4

Forensics For Dummies
978-0-7645-5580-0

German For Dummies
978-0-7645-5195-6

Hobby Farming For Dummies
978-0-470-28172-7

Index Investing For Dummies
978-0-470-29406-2

Jewelry Making & Beading
For Dummies
978-0-7645-2571-1

Knitting For Dummies, 2nd Edition
978-0-470-28747-7

Music Composition For Dummies
978-0-470-22421-2

Physics For Dummies
978-0-7645-5433-9

Schizophrenia For Dummies
978-0-470-25927-6

Sex For Dummies, 3rd Edition
978-0-470-04523-7

Solar Power Your Home For Dummies
978-0-470-17569-9

Tennis For Dummies
978-0-7645-5087-4

The Koran For Dummies
978-0-7645-5581-7

Wine All-in-One For Dummies
978-0-470-47626-0

FOR DUMMIES®

Helping you expand your horizons and achieve your potential

COMPUTER BASICS

978-0-470-27759-1

978-0-470-13728-4

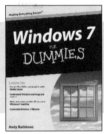
978-0-470-49743-2

DIGITAL PHOTOGRAPHY

978-0-470-25074-7

978-0-470-46606-3

978-0-470-45772-6

MAC BASICS

978-0-470-27817-8

978-0-470-46661-2

978-0-470-43543-4

Access 2007 For Dummies
978-0-470-04612-8

Adobe Creative Suite 4 Design
Premium All-in-One Desk Reference
For Dummies
978-0-470-33186-6

AutoCAD 2010 For Dummies
978-0-470-43345-4

C++ For Dummies, 6th Edition
978-0-470-31726-6

Computers For Seniors For Dummies,
2nd Edition
978-0-470-53483-0

Dreamweaver CS4 For Dummies
978-0-470-34502-3

Excel 2007 All-In-One Desk Reference
For Dummies
978-0-470-03738-6

Green IT For Dummies
978-0-470-38688-0

Networking All-in-One Desk Reference
For Dummies, 3rd Edition
978-0-470-17915-4

Office 2007 All-in-One Desk Reference
For Dummies
978-0-471-78279-7

Photoshop CS4 For Dummies
978-0-470-32725-8

Photoshop Elements 7 For Dummies
978-0-470-39700-8

Search Engine Optimization
For Dummies, 3rd Edition
978-0-470-26270-2

The Internet For Dummies,
11th Edition
978-0-470-12174-0

Visual Studio 2008 All-In-One Desk
Reference For Dummies
978-0-470-19108-8

Web Analytics For Dummies
978-0-470-09824-0

Windows Vista For Dummies
978-0-471-75421-3

08049_p4